Security Interdependence in the Asia Pacific Region

Studies of the East Asian Institute—Columbia University

The East Asian Institute of Columbia University

The East Asian Institute is Columbia University's center for research, publication, and teaching on modern East Asia. The Studies of the East Asian Institute were inaugurated in 1962 to bring to a wider public the results of significant new research on the countries of the region.

Security
Interdependence in the
Asia Pacific Region

Edited by
James W. Morley
East Asian Institute
Columbia University

Lexington Books
D.C. Heath and Company/Lexington, Massachusetts/Toronto

Library of Congress Cataloging in Publication Data

Security interdependence in the Asia Pacific region.

   Includes index.
   1. East Asia—National security.   2. Asia,
Southeastern—National security.   3. East Asia—
Politics and government.   4. Asia, Southeastern—
Politics and government.   I. Morley, James William,
1921–
DS518.1.S33   1986   3420.95   86–45053
ISBN 0–669–13090–7

Chapter 2 reprinted from ORBIS with permission of the Foreign Policy Research Institute, Philadelphia, PA, from "Southeast Asia and U.S. Global Strategy, Continuing Interests and Shifting Priorities" (Summer 1985).

Published simultaneously in Canada
Printed in the United States of America
International Standard Book Number: 0–669–13090–7
Library of Congress Catalog Card Number: 86–45053

The paper used in this publication meets the minimum requirements of American National Standard for Information Sciences—Permanence of Paper for Printed Library Materials, ANSI Z39.48–1984.
⊗™

86 86 88 89 90 8 7 6 5 4 3 2 1

Contents

Foreword

This volume is a result of a research project conducted by Columbia University's East Asian Institute and International Economic Research Center. Entitled "The United States, Japan, and Southeast Asia: The Issues of Interdependence," the project, which was begun in 1981, had as its focus the economic, political, and strategic interactions of the non-Communist countries and entities of the Asia Pacific region and their market economies, particularly the United States, Japan, South Korea, Taiwan, Hong Kong, and the members of the Association of Southeast Asian Nations (ASEAN): Indonesia, Malaysia, the Philippines, Singapore, Thailand, and now Brunei.

The project had three broad and interwoven objectives: to analyze the economic development strategies, particularly the export-oriented growth strategies, of the market economies in the Western Pacific; to examine the evolution of American and Japanese political, economic, and security relationships with these regimes; and to consider the impact of these factors on the bilateral United States–Japan relationship. This constituted an extremely complex and ambitious research agenda. To be pursued successfully, it required, first, cooperation between economists and political scientists and, second, recruitment of the necessary expertise from many different institutions in several countries.

To accomplish these goals, the East Asian Institute, of which I was director at the time, invited the then newly established International Economic Research Center, headed by Jagdish Bhagwati, to join with it in sponsoring a multiyear international research project. The collaboration that followed turned out to be a happy and fruitful one. James Morley of the East Asian Institute and Ronald Findlay of the International Economic Research Center joined the project in the critical roles of project directors for, respectively, international security affairs and international economic affairs. A steering committee consisting of the four of us and two additional Columbia faculty members, William R. Roff and Howard W. Wriggins, was established and exercised overall direction of the project.

Under the leadership of Findlay and Morley, the project sponsored a number of seminars, informal discussion meetings, a "mini-course," and lectures at Columbia University. The project also helped make it possible for the project organizers to visit the region and consult with specialists there. All of these activities were preparatory to an international conference held in Maui, Hawaii, in December 1983, at which fourteen distinguished scholars from Great Britain, Japan, Malaysia, Singapore, South Korea, Thailand, and the United States presented papers.

In addition, twenty-one other scholars, government officials, business leaders, and foundation executives from various parts of the world were invited to Maui to review the papers, exchange views on the issues involved, and consider a research agenda for the future. It was our thought from the inception of this project that it represented only a first step in a long-term program of research and teaching. The Maui conference therefore was both the culmination of several years' work and the starting point for a new phase in Columbia University's involvement in research on the Asia Pacific region.

In the course of the Maui discussions on strategic matters and the subsequent exchanges among the paper authors and critics, it became increasingly apparent that a solid conceptual base for this kind of regional strategic analysis was lacking. The premise of the conference—that the non-Communist countries of the Asia Pacific region were becoming more dependent on each other for their security—seemed demonstrable. But in what sense did these countries form a "region"? How were local security problems—such as those of South Korea, for instance—related to subregional security problems—such as those engaging the states of ASEAN? How were these, in turn, related to the regionwide concerns of China, the United States, and the Soviet Union and, indeed, to those of the world at large? And how did such external security concerns impinge on the domestic security concerns that had such priority in the thinking of the small and middle-sized powers?

A second conceptual problem also emerged. As paper authors set out to explain the security policies of their respective countries, it became clear that there was little common vocabulary. The words were not novel, but the content and emotion with which they were endowed obviously varied from country to country. The Americans, for example, characteristically explained their security policies in terms of "deterrence," the Japanese in terms of "stability," and the Southeast Asians in terms of "resilience." What exactly did each mean?

It was decided, therefore, to revise the security-related papers to confront these issues more directly—and this book is the result. It attempts (1) to set out a concept of regional security, suggesting how to think about the relationship between global, regional, subregional, and local strategic issues; (2) to explain the concepts that are guiding the security policies of some of the major non-Communist actors in the Asia Pacific region; and finally, (3) to reflect on the sensitive relationships between such external factors and political stability at home.

All of the participants at the conference—paper authors, discussants, and other commentators—made important contributions in the discussions, many of which have been incorporated in the revised versions of the papers that are presented here. Unfortunately, we were not able to publish all of the papers offered at the conference. On behalf of the conference organizers, I want to express our deepest appreciation to each of the people who traveled to Maui to take part in this conference:

Byung-joon Ahn, Yonsei University, Seoul

Narongchai Akransanee, The Industrial Management Co. Ltd., Bangkok

Paul Balaran, The Ford Foundation, New York

Robert Baldwin, University of Wisconsin—Madison

Romeo M. Bautista, International Food Policy Research Institute, Washington, D.C.

Richard Betts, Brookings Institution, Washington, D.C.

Jagdish Bhagwati, Columbia University, New York

John Bresnan, Columbia University, New York

Chan Heng Chee, National University of Singapore

Siow Yue Chia, National University of Singapore

W.M. Corden, Australian National University, Canberra

Ronald E. Findlay, Columbia University, New York

Haruo Hasegawa, Nissho Iwai Corporation, Tokyo

Wontack Hong, Seoul University

Yutaka Kawashima, Ministry of Foreign Affairs, Tokyo

Chongwhi Kim, National Defense University, Seoul

Shoichi Kobayashi, Asia Pacific Association of Japan, Tokyo

Ryutaro Komiya, formerly University of Tokyo, Tokyo

Chung-hoon Lee, University of Hawaii at Manoa, Honolulu

Michael Leifer, London School of Economics

James W. Morley, Columbia University, New York

Hla Myint, London School of Economics

Masashi Nishihara, National Defense Academy, Yokosuka

Toshio Obi-Nakamura, Bunkyo University, Tokyo

Robert O'Neill, International Institute for Strategic Studies, London

Hugh Patrick, Columbia University, New York

Kerniel Sandhu, Institute of Southeast Asian Studies, Singapore

M. Hadi Soesastro, Centre for Strategic and International Studies, Jakarta

Richard Solomon, The Rand Corporation, Santa Monica

Noordin Sopiee, Institute of Strategic and International Studies, Kuala Lumpur

Hiroshi Takeda, Sanwa Bank, Tokyo

Sarasin Viraphol, Ministry of Foreign Affairs, Bangkok

Takashi Yamakawa, Nissho Iwai Corporation, Tokyo

Yasukichi Yasuba, Kyoto University

In addition, I want to thank Ms. Deborah Bell, associate director of the East Asian Institute, who handled all the complicated administrative matters involved in this conference and in the overall project with extraordinary efficiency and unfailing good humor, and Jeff Kingston, who served as rapporteur and provided the discussion summaries that proved so useful in revising the papers.

Like all collaborative research projects, particularly those that draw on expertise from around the globe, this one entailed considerable expense and could not have been realized were it not for the generous financial assistance of a number of institutions in Japan and the United States. The support of two Japanese corporations was crucial for funding the Maui conference: the Nissho Iwai Corporation, one of Japan's major trading companies, and the Sanwa Bank, one of that country's largest banks. We are deeply appreciative of their support. In the United States, the project was given generous support by the Ford Foundation and the Henry Luce Foundation. We also want to express our deepest gratitude to both of these organizations. The project was also supported financially by the East Asian Institute, particulary by the Institute's Toyota Research Program, to which we also wish to express our heartfelt thanks.

The Asia Pacific region has an importance that is only now, and only slowly, beginning to be realized in academic circles and among government policymakers. Our knowledge of this region is still quite rudimentary in many important respects, a situation that is clearly incompatible with the region's economic and political importance. This volume does not presume to do more than provide an overview of some of the major intellectual and policy issues raised by developments in and among the countries in the region. But we believe that it has been successful in this objective and that, in doing so, it both fills an important gap in the current literature and sets the stage for further research activities.

Gerald L. Curtis
Executive Director,
Project on the United States,
Japan, and Southeast Asia

I
Introduction

1
The Structure of Regional Security

James W. Morley

In the fifteenth and sixteenth centuries, when Russian fur traders began pushing into the wilderness east of the Urals and European sea captains began penetrating the unexplored oceans beyond the Atlantic, the West was overwhelmingly impressed by the "otherness" of the Asian and Pacific peoples it met. The distances that separated the centers of their civilizations from those of the West seemed vast and the gulf of language and culture unbridgeable. Moreover, these peoples were so weak that the West felt little need to try seriously to understand or accommodate them. Instead, it fell into the easy habit of referring to these heterogeneous peoples simply as "Orientals" and the varied lands they inhabited as constituting a single region, the "Far East." Except for Thailand, China, and Japan, their states were not admitted to the comity of nations but were absorbed into the empires of Europe, Russia, and the United States, among whom the vital issues of war and peace were largely decided for hundreds of years.

The New Asia Pacific Security Region

How different the security map of the Far East looks today! China remains, with far greater authority than before; so does Japan, converted now into a peaceful giant; and so does Thailand. But the great Western empires have been replaced almost entirely by a host of small and middle-sized powers. On the one hand are the new Communist states on the Chinese and Soviet borders: Mongolia, North Korea, Vietnam, Laos, and Cambodia. On the other are the new non-Communist states that rim the Pacific: South Korea in the north; Taiwan in the central area; the Philippines, Brunei, Malaysia, Indonesia, Singapore, and Burma in the southeast; and the emerging island communities in the western and southern Pacific.[1]

Equally important as this transformation and proliferation of Asian states has been the change in the definition of the region and the relationship of various Western states to it. Although the European powers have largely withdrawn in the wake of their imperial collapse, the United States and the Soviet Union—joined more vigorously than before by Canada, Australia, and New Zealand—have moved in exactly the opposite direction. They have become more deeply conscious than before of the vitality of their Pacific interests and have strengthened their involvement. Today they look on themselves—and indeed have come to be looked on by Asians as well—not as visitors in a distant "East," but as indigenous residents of an even larger new realm, commonly referred to as the Pacific Basin or the Asia Pacific region, which links them permanently with the "Far Eastern" peoples in a thickening network of interdependent relationships.

The Soviet Union, for example, now locates the center of its population east of the Urals, not west. Since the 1970s, the United States has placed the bulk of its merchandise trade with markets in Asia, not in Europe. Australia, once an appendage of Britain, now looks to Japan as its most important trading partner. Canada, too, now searches the Pacific as the region of its greatest economic opportunity. Hahn-Been Lee goes so far as to call the market economies of the Asia-Pacific region a "de-facto trade bloc."[2] Bloc or not, they form one of the most dynamic centers of the world economy today.

They also form one of the most vital and at the same time least understood centers of international security concern. Unlike the European states at the end of World War II, which sought to end the era of intraregional wars by inviting Germany to join them in an exploration of the path to integration, the Asian victims of the Pacific war pursued no such course with Japan. Nor, in the face of the American-Soviet confrontation and the Cold War that followed, did they give way to the pressures to divide their patrimony into two camps in the style of Eastern and Western Europe.

The possibility of such a division seemed very real in the early postwar years, and indeed, the two superpowers worked energetically to bring it about. The competition began in the late 1940s and early 1950s in China, Korea, and Japan. It was intensified by the Korean War and spread quickly to embrace Taiwan and the struggling, still empire-ridden lands of southeast Asia.

The Soviet Union came closest to success. In 1950, it concluded a 30-year alliance with the new People's Republic of China. In 1965, it signed a treaty of friendship, cooperation, and mutual assistance with the Democratic People's Republic of Korea and, in 1966, another with the Mongolian People's Republic. In 1978, it signed a treaty of friendship and cooperation with the Socialist Republic of Vietnam, which has provided the framework for extending the political, diplomatic, economic, and military support required for Vietnam's war in Cambodia. Now, years later, the Mongolians remain loyal and the Vietnamese too dependent to test any other course; but the North Koreans have never been tractable, and the Chinese have finally left the camp altogether.

The United States has been only partially more successful. Its first idea was that pursued by John Foster Dulles—to form a regional collective security system on the model of the North Atlantic Treaty Organization (NATO). A Pacific Treaty Organization (PATO), however, attracted little support among the non-Communist countries in Asia. Most did not feel comfortable having their security linked to that of Japan so soon after the war. Nor did most see the advantage of such links to other Asian states, which were too weak to help them and might in fact involve them in conflicts they would wish to avoid. In 1954, following the collapse of the French at Dien Bien Phu, Dulles did succeed in persuading a number of states to sign the Treaty of Manila, on the basis of which the Southeast Asia Treaty Organization (SEATO) was established; but SEATO required far less commitment than NATO and did not have the participation of such important regional states as Japan, South Korea, the Republic of China, and Indonesia. It was, in fact, soon abandoned by several of its nonregional partners, and in 1977 it was abolished. The treaty remains, but only in a vestigial form as a formal link between the United States and Thailand.

Various multilateral security proposals by President Chiang of the Republic of China, President Quirino of the Philippines, and President Park of South Korea received even less attention; and efforts of Taiwan and Korea to give a regional security coloring to the Asia-Pacific Council (ASPAC)—organized in 1965 and joined by other non-Communist states in Asia for cultural and economic purposes—were quickly scotched.

Instead, the states of the region have preferred to seek security assistance through less inclusive and often less formal arrangements. For example, in addition to the aforementioned Manila Treaty, the United States has forged mutual security treaties separately with Japan, South Korea, and the Philippines, and jointly with Australia and New Zealand (the so-called ANZUS alliance). It has also offered weapons transfers and training assistance to selected partners, including Taiwan, and has extended a nuclear umbrella over all friendly, nonnuclear powers in the region. In addition, the Five Power Defense Arrangement draws together Malaysia and Singapore with Britain, Australia, and New Zealand; the ASEAN states have established an entente among themselves; and certain pairs of ASEAN states have concluded bilateral cooperative arrangements for training their forces and securing parts of their common international borders. But when one compares these provisions with the multilateral collective security ties binding the Soviet Union and the Eastern European states in the Warsaw Pact or those linking the United States and the Western European states in NATO, one cannot help but be impressed by the apparent "diffuseness" and "fluidity" of the overall structure in the Pacific.[3]

This impression has led many observers to seek explanations in the extraordinary diversity of the states in the region. After all, the non-Communist states alone vary in size—from mini-states like Singapore and Brunei to vast maritime archipelagoes like Indonesia and the Philippines to a continental power like the United States. In standards of living, for all the high average rate of growth, there are states like Indonesia that are comparatively poor, as well as states like the United States and Japan that are comparatively rich. There is no common religious culture in the region. Hinduism, Islam, Buddhism, Confucianism, Shamanism, and Christianity—each has its enclaves and influences. Polities in the region range all the way from relatively stable regimes of traditional monarchy and seasoned democracy to relatively unstable systems of ad hoc authoritarianism.

Moreover, these states have had no historic experience of having worked together as an integrated security community. No Roman Empire has ever imposed a sense of unity upon them. Even those located in closest proximity in Asia and the western Pacific have never been brought under sustained, coordinated direction. The power of the Chinese, even in the days of their greatest imperial expansions, was too land-based to reach coercively much beyond their immediate border states and territories. The European empires served more to divide than to unite. The Japanese conquest was too brief and distorted by the exigencies of war to have made the "co-prosperity sphere" more than a slogan. It is small wonder that as these states have emerged in the post-Pacific War period, they have looked at each other with caution.

But that is not to say that the dynamics of state behavior in the Asia Pacific region are generically different from those in the Europe Atlantic region. In fact, the imperatives of the balance of power are as compelling in one region as in the other. Nor is it to say that, in the event, no regional security structure has emerged. In fact, one has. It takes the form of what might be called three competing security nets, rather than tight, multilateral, adversarial alliances as in Europe; and although the states in one or another of these Asia Pacific nets take less explicitly coordinated action, they do show a high degree of sensitivity to each other and move in ways that, whether consciously taken for that purpose or not, serve the purpose of maintaining and using the net as their international security anchor.

One reason this structure has not hitherto been obvious is that the concepts commonly used to explicate such matters have been fuzzy. We begin, therefore, by trying to identify and define clearly—in some cases partly to redefine—the concepts that may be most useful for answering the following questions: What are the security imperatives under which these states operate? Why do they relate to the states to which they do relate? What is the tie that binds? We shall then review briefly the behavior of the Asia Pacific states since the late 1960s to demonstrate the vitality of one of these nets— that of the non-Communist states—in action.

The Balance of Power

It is important at the outset to realize that although the concept of the balance of power was derived from the behavior of European states, differences in geography, history, and culture have not made the states in the Asia Pacific region immune to its imperatives. Its explanatory power is as great there as anywhere else.

The concept is based on the widely held perception that the world is an anarchy in which each state must look out for its own survival. Each state must therefore be vitally concerned about the level and effectiveness of its power vis-à-vis its adversaries; it is under imperatives to increase, decrease, maintain, use or abandon that power, depending, first, on whether it sees itself as a status quo or anti-status quo power—that is, whether it does or doesn't have the international values it desires—and second, on whether it views the trend in the international balance of power—that is, in its own strength vis-à-vis its adversaries—as favorable or unfavorable. These imperatives are simple ones, not essentially different from those felt by schoolboys on their first day in the schoolyard; but they are powerful ones, felt by all states in every region of the globe.

Such bald statements make things seem simpler than they are. Power, after all, takes many forms, and action to increase or decrease it can be varied indeed. (See table 1–1.) To increase its power, a state may choose from a wide range of alternatives—for example, intensifying domestic controls to get more out of its people, enlarging its armed forces, strengthening its alliance relations, or seeking new ones and trying to deter or pacify its adversaries. Conversely, were it to decide that it is safe to relax its power-building or power-asserting efforts, it may liberalize its political controls at home, allow its own military power to decline, permit its relations with friends and allies to atrophy, or seek to expand normal relations with states formerly perceived to be adversaries.[4] Beyond these options, it is also true that states make choices among the realms in which they will act.

In recent years, it has become customary in most discussions of international security policy, after considerable attention has been devoted to military questions, for someone to remind the group that security is more than a military matter—that, to use the phrase popular in the Nixon-Kissinger era, economics, too, has become a matter of high politics, and the security of the nation is as dependent on the health of the economy as it is on the protection given by the armed forces; and so it is. But confusion has

Table 1–1
A Paradigm of the Balance of Power Imperatives

Perception of Balance of Power Trend	Imperatives for Status Quo Power	Imperatives for Anti-Status Quo Power
Radically favorable	Decrease power	Make or threaten war
Trending favorably	Decrease power	Increase power
In equilibrium	Maintain power	Increase power
Trending unfavorably	Increase power	Increase power
Radically unfavorable	Surrender or make war	Surrender or make war

crept into the analysis with the blurring of useful distinctions among the various realms in which threats are perceived and countermeasures taken.

In its generic sense, security is a concept meaning freedom from care. In the more limited sense in which nation-states speak of international security as a policy objective, it refers to the protection of values the nation-state holds vital. As such, it is indeed an overall concept, with economic, military, political, and even cultural aspects. But rather than stir these various aspects into a mish-mash, for analysis as well as for foreign policy planning it is useful to think of them as relating to separate and distinct realms of state activity. Of course, the responses a state makes to given threats depend in substantial part on the nature of the threats; but it is also true that for some period of time now, each state has displayed a certain strategic signature, a characteristic emphasis that it gives the various realms in devising its overall strategy to meet such threats.

Some states, for example, are far more inclined to emphasize military preparedness and military responses than others are. The data in table 1–2 are suggestive. However, one cannot rely on these figures for exactitude.[5] These countries vary in the degree to which their armed personnel are military professionals. In some, the uniformed forces have multiple uses—as, for example, in Indonesia, where they serve in influential political and economic capacities. Defense budgets, therefore, may not refer uniformly to expenditures for military defense only. In addition, all military-related expenditures are not necessarily in defense budgets, which most governments keep secret, making the gathering of reliable information difficult. Nevertheless, assuming that the general direction, if not the exact size, of these figures is correct, one may draw two very general conclusions. One is that

Table 1–2
Defense Expenditures of Selected Asia Pacific States as a Percentage of GDP/GNP, 1975–82

Country	1975	1979	1982
Indonesia	3.8	3.2	3.3
Japan	0.9	0.9	1.0
South Korea	5.1	5.2	5.6
Malaysia	4.0	5.7	8.2
Philippines	2.6	2.3	2.3
Singapore	5.3	5.7	
Taiwan	6.9	7.9	7.8
Thailand	3.7	5.7	5.0
United States	5.8	5.1	6.5
Average	4.2	4.7	5.1

Source: Data for 1975 are from International Institute for Strategic Studies, *The Military Balance: 1982–83* (London: IISS, 1982), p. 125; for 1979 and 1982, from *The Military Balance: 1984–85* (London: IISS, 1984), pp. 140–41. Data for Singapore, 1982, were not available.

for the entire region the average share of GDP/GNP going to military defense over the last 10 years has been increasing. The other is that although all states participated in this increase, some participated more than others. Those with a greater propensity to increase military preparedness included Taiwan, South Korea, the United States, Malaysia, Singapore, and Thailand. Those with a lesser propensity to do so included Indonesia, Japan, and the Philippines.

These budgetary propensities are reflected also in the international security policies of the various states—or perhaps I should say that the characteristic response each state has been making to international threats is reflected in these budgetary propensities—not always, but often enough to make one sensitive to the likelihood.

Consider, for example, the first oil crisis and Japan's response to it.[6] In the fall and winter of 1973, Japan's oil supply was threatened, first by shortfalls in the deliveries of the majors, occasioned by OPEC's action in banning all oil exports to the United States and reducing its own production by 5 percent, and then by a warning that Japan might be termed an "enemy" and placed on the ban list unless it changed its Israeli policy to favor the Arabs. With the bulk of Japan's economy dependent on oil for its energy and with the bulk of that oil coming from the Middle East, Japan was extraordinarily vulnerable to the Middle Eastern states. At the same time, Japan was extraordinarily vulnerable to the United States, depending on it for even more vital economic, political, and military necessities; and the United States opposed Japan's making any political concessions. What was to be done?

Japan might have thought of military reprisals to force a change in the Arab position. Of course, it did not; it had neither the capacity nor the inclination to do so. It might have made its primary effort in the political realm; but except for trying to persuade the Arab states of its sincerity in sympathizing with their cause, without actually changing its formal position, it did not. Perhaps its dependence on the United States was judged to be too great to consider more. At any rate, what it did do was to respond economically. It rationed domestic use, scrambled to find other sources of oil, and sent its ministers to the Middle Eastern capitals to buy relief with promises of economic aid.

It was perfectly reasonable, one may suppose, for Japan to respond with economic countermeasures when the threat was economic. But consider other instances in the years that followed, when the threats were more political and military: the movement of Soviet troops into the southern Kurils, the Vietnamese invasion of Cambodia, or the kidnapping of Kim Dae Jung. In each case, although Japan's economy was not directly threatened by the action, Japan's characteristic response was not to move troops or rupture diplomatic relations, but to restrict trade, discourage investment, suspend aid in progress, or break off talks for projected economic cooperation.

The fact is that Japan has been inclined to emphasize the economic realm ever since it recovered independence in 1952. In contrast, the United States has characteristically placed a higher priority on the military realm, whereas several of the Southeast Asian countries have turned more readily to politics.

It is important to realize, also, that whatever security policies states may adopt, they do not respond simply to the universal threat that is inherent in the international condition; rather, they respond primarily to their perceptions of specific threats by specific states at specific times in specific places. In short, they respond in certain theaters—a concept that needs to be redefined and rescued from the murky waters of regionalism.

Security Theaters

There has been a long-standing and widely accepted assumption that geographic proximity, especially if reinforced by traditional ethnic ties or cultural affinities, inevitably draws certain states into relatively permanent regional or subregional groupings, in each of which a common history has been and, to a certain degree, will continue to be played out.[7] From this viewpoint, it has become customary in the period since World War II to think of the diverse Asian states we are here identifying as the new Asia Pacific region as living their lives within one of three groupings or subregions: the East Asia of China, Japan, Mongolia, Korea and Taiwan; a Southeast Asia embracing the ethnically non-Western states from the Philippines around to Burma; and a Southwest Pacific of Australia, New Zealand, and the newly emerging island states of the Pacific Forum. In this common conception, the United States, the Soviet Union, and Canada are simply intruders.

There is some utility in this conception, as we shall see, but there is also dangerous distortion if one thinks of such regions too restrictively. The fact is that social and technological advances have fundamentally altered relationships on the globe. Geographic propinquity is no longer essential to intimacy; ethnic homogeneity is even less requisite for political community; and the ties of history are being loosened by the irresistible tugs of modernity. As a result, each state in the Asia Pacific region—and indeed in the world—is engaged not just in one regional relationship but in a number of different sets or systems of international relationships, some of which are confined to one group of states, some to another.

If this is so, what are the systems we need to identify to understand the security relationships in the Asia Pacific area? I suggest we begin with the concept of *theater*. Generically, *theater* refers to a place or region in which significant events take place. The military use the term in a more restricted sense; a "theater of operations" usually designates a region in which a given country deploys its forces under a single commander.[8] This is at bottom a unilateral conception and, as such is too narrow for our purposes. I suggest we broaden it a bit, internationalize it, and use the term *security theater* to indicate a region in which the security of each of a group of nations is vitally affected by the interactions among all. This implies, in turn, that at the core of each theater is an adversarial relationship; on one side is the power or powers in possession of the disputed value—the so-called "have" or "status quo" powers—and on the other is the power or powers that want to obtain it—the so-called "have-not" or "anti-status quo" powers.

Our requirement, then, is to identify where in the Asia Pacific region these adversarial relationships obtain and which states are involved in each of them. In doing so, we come to recognize that the traditional regional concepts are simply inappropriate for security analysis. It is immediately apparent that the Soviet Union and selected states of the "West" must be thought of as permanent or indigenous participants in many of these theaters. Moreover, an individual state's international security problems are not confined to dealing with adversaries in the single region with which it has customarily been identified, whether it be East Asia, Southeast Asia or the Southwest Pacific. In fact, most states find themselves participating in a multiplicity of theaters whether they like it or not: local, in which two or more countries are involved in particular controversies; subregional, in which the adversarial relations in several local theaters affect one another; regional, in which all countries in the Asia Pacific area are involved; and even global, in which the United States and the Soviet Union have the greatest reach.

As one might expect in a region with so many states, the number of local theaters is large. A selected list of some of the more persistent would include the Taiwan Strait, where China and Taiwan jockey for control of Taiwan; the Sea of Okhotsk, where Japan, supported by the United States, and the Soviet Union are in dispute over the ownership of the islands to the north of Hokkaido; the Korean peninsula, where North Korea, with its Soviet and Chinese supporters, and South Korea, backed by the United States, are locked in a struggle at least for survival and at most for peninsular control; and the Sino-Soviet border, where China, Mongolia, and the Soviet Union have forces arrayed in a confrontational posture.

In addition, there are four local theaters in the south. One is the South China border, where Chinese forces eye those of Burma, Laos, and Vietnam—the latter two backed by the Soviet Union—in varying degrees of hostility. Another is Cambodia, where Vietnam, backed by the Soviet Union and with the cooperation of Laos, is seeking to impose the Heng Samrin regime on the country against the opposition of the guerrilla forces of the Coalition Government, backed to varying degrees by China, the ASEAN states, the United States, and Japan; the spillovers from this controversy generate additional conflict along the Thai frontiers with Laos and Cambodia. A third is the intra-ASEAN theater, where a number of controversies have pitted the

ASEAN states against each other in recent times; these have now been shelved or diminished by the entente that drives the ASEAN process.[9] Finally, there is the South China Sea, where ownership of the Spratley and the Paracel Islands is hotly disputed by China, Taiwan, Vietnam, the Philippines, and Malaysia. This is a long list, but it probably is not complete and certainly is not unchanging.

The situation is complicated by the fact that, as the foregoing list shows, any one state or any one state's adversaries or supporters may be and frequently are involved in more than one local theater. This means that events in one theater may seriously influence the will and capability of a state to act in another. In such circumstances, the affected states must recognize that they are participants in a larger subregional theater, which embraces antagonisms to which they may not otherwise be a party.

At this level, the commonly accepted identity of subregions—with the addition of certain crucial powers—seems generally applicable. The Taiwan Strait, Sea of Okhotsk, Korean Peninsula, and Sino-Soviet border local theaters, for example, are linked together or overlap in what may be termed a larger Northeast Asian—or, if one prefers, East Asian—subregional theater, in which the balance among the subregionally available power of the United States, the Soviet Union, and the People's Republic of China, together with the more locally limited power of Japan, the two Koreas, Mongolia, and Taiwan, make up a system that affects the outcomes throughout. Similarly, one may identify a Southeast Asian subregional theater, in which the balance among the locally limited power of the ASEAN and Indochinese states and the locally available power of China, the Soviet Union, and the United States—and to a lesser extent, Australia, New Zealand, and Japan—constitutes a subregional security system that affects the outcomes in each of the South China border, Cambodia, intra-ASEAN, and South China Sea local theaters.

But even this does not end the complexity; it is evident that three of the participating powers—the United States, the Soviet Union, and China—are key players in most local and in both subregional theaters, as is Japan, though only in the realm of economics. Many small and middle-sized powers object to the big powers' "intervention" in "their" affairs, but the capability and intent of the big three is such that their participation is inevitable. For this reason, the small and middle-sized powers (including Japan militarily) in each of the local and subregional systems must be vitally concerned with the balance of power among the big three—to which each net is linked as the ultimate guarantor of the participating states' security. They must also be concerned, therefore, with the balance of power in local and subregional theaters other than their own, for the condition of the balances in these other theaters is a major determinant of the power each of the big three guarantors will be inclined to exert more broadly.

For example, when the American Seventh Fleet is called to Southeast

Asia and beyond, friends and allies in Northeast Asia have reason to be concerned about its availability on their behalf in the theaters in the north. When a crisis on the Sino–Soviet border calls for Chinese troop concentrations there, the Sino–Vietnamese border must ultimately, if not immediately, receive less Chinese attention. When the Soviet Union feels more threatened along its Chinese border, it may have to reduce its commitment to the South China Sea. We must recognize, therefore, that all states in this vast Asia Pacific region are drawn not only into various local and subregional theaters but also into a single Asia-Pacific-wide regional theater, in which the security of each state is vitally affected by the balance among all.

Beyond this region, of course, are other regions in which some Asia Pacific states are engaged—for example, China in the Himalayan theater and the United States and the Soviet Union in Europe. Most important for all states is the overarching global theater engaged in only by those nations that are interested in and capable of countering threats wherever on the globe they may occur—namely, the United States and the Soviet Union. Obviously, the Asia Pacific region is only a part of that vast theater, but it is an important part. Given the weight of the United States and the Soviet Union in the various balances in that region, no country there is exempt from the influence of their rivalry, and no state is immune from the desire to help determine its outcome. In that sense, all Asia Pacific states are part of the global system.

Thus, although the security map of the Asia Pacific region may seem more complex than that of most other regions of the world—especially the Europe Atlantic region—the complexity does not arise because of irrationality or because it is constructed from generically different material. Security theaters are building blocks the world over. What distinguishes the Asia Pacific region in this regard is the multiplicity of its theaters and the diversity of emphasis given them by participating states.

Diagrammatically, the adversarial structure of the Asia-Pacific security region might be represented by two overlapping circles—one representing the Northeast Asian theater, the other representing the Southeast Asian theater. Within each of these circles are other smaller overlapping circles representing the local theaters. We have identified four in each subregion, although others might be identified.

Within this configuration, there is a tendency for each state to emphasize one theater more than another. At one extreme, for example, are the United States and the Soviet Union, whose leaders, for all the myriad security systems in which they are involved around the world, are unique in being most deeply concerned with the global theater—that is, with any changes that might upset the bilateral balance between them, particularly between their nuclear forces. China, as befits its geographic position and relative power, places primary weight on the region. Most of the middle-sized and small states give greatest emphasis to the threats in their own local systems. Mongolia, for example, is primarily concerned with the Chinese border. The attention of the two Korea's is riveted on the rivalry in the peninsula. Japan worries most about the potential threats to its own home islands and territorial seas from the Soviet sector. Taiwan fears China's ambition. Vietnam has been galvanized by the hostile forces of China and the Coalition Government of Kampuchea. The ASEAN states give priority attention to the threats they, insurgents on their borders, or discontented ethnic and religious minorities acting transnationally might pose to each other if the ASEAN entente were to become unraveled; secondarily, they attend to the threats posed by the great powers or Vietnam, which each member-state perceives differently. Australia and New Zealand also have primarily local concerns; secondarily, however, they are being drawn increasingly into the broader Southeast Asian subregion as well as that of the Southwest Pacific.

Although one cannot say with absolute certainty to which theater a state will give priority attention at any one time, perhaps it is not wrong to assume that in any threatening situation, Asia Pacific states—like states the world over—are inclined to give greatest attention to the theater in which their leaders perceive the most severe threat to their own power and position.

Nevertheless, even though a state may be inclined to emphasize one theater more than another, the multiplicity of theaters and the overlapping of participation in them inevitably means that as a threat intensifies or subsides in one, the effect radiates to all the others. We therefore must ask our third question: What are the mechanisms that transmit these pulses? That is, what are the ties that bind—alliances? understandings? coalitions? ententes? These are the terms in common usage, but each is far too specific to indicate the core of the dynamic relationship that binds states together on the same side in one or many security theaters. If we are to understand the Asia Pacific region—and perhaps other regions as well—we need to apply a new and more generic concept to these relationships: interdependence.

Interdependence

Although *interdependence* is an old word—generally understood to signify mutual dependence—it has come into more precise scholarly usage in recent years, especially since the publication of Richard N. Cooper's *The Economics of Interdependence: Economic Policy in the Atlantic Community*[10] in 1968 and Robert O. Keohane and Joseph S. Nye's *Power and Interdependence: World Politics in Transition*[11] in 1977. In the course of the polemics that have followed, two distinct usages have been clarified.[12] One refers to a relationship of sensitivity, in which there is simply a covariance in the behavior of two or more states—for example, when price changes in one lead to sourcing changes in the other and when the opportunity costs are nil or easily borne, such as when other sources are available at reasonable prices or the commodity is simply not needed. The second usage refers to a relationship of vulnerability, in which one state depends on another for the satisfaction of a commodity or other value need and cannot move to another supplier without incurring high costs. The estimate of these costs is, of course, the measure of the state's vulnerability and, therefore, of the degree of its dependence. It is this concept of interdependence in the sense of vulnerability that seems particularly helpful in analyzing the dynamic relationships that bind states together on one or another side of a security controversy.

Drawing on the behavior of European states in the late nineteenth and early twentieth centuries, Glenn Snyder has recently shown how this works out in the case of alliances.[13] Each state in an alliance depends on the other to supply certain goods or services requird for its security. The relationship, therefore, is one of interdependence, in which each state is vulnerable to the other for this supply and consequently is driven by the same imperative: to concede what it must so that its ally will not abandon it, but to concede no more than it must lest it be trapped in a situation it would not wish to enter.

Consider, for example, one of the strongest and most intimate of Asia Pacific security relationships, the alliance between South Korea and the United States. South Korea, facing the threat of invasion from North Korea, which is backed by the Soviet Union and China, judges itself to be unable to deter such an attack—or, if it comes, to defend itself successfully—without extensive external support. It therefore turns to potential suppliers, of which only one is capable of doing the job: the United States. But is the United States willing? That would seem to depend on whether South Korea has something to offer in return. Fortunately, it does; it can offer diplomatic support, base facilities, and supplementary forces, which the United States, for all its size and power, finds necessary to hold the global line against the Soviet Union. Of course, South Korea is not the only potential supplier of these resources. If South Korea were unavailable, the United States might conceivably depend more heavily on Japan or beef up its own forces in the surrounding Northeast Asian subregion, but the cost of an alternative would be high. To that extent, the United States is likewise dependent on and vulnerable to South Korea. It is this condition of reciprocal dependency or interdependence that explains the alliance that has been constructed and the dynamics of the exchange that takes place within it.

Now let us turn to a much looser security relationship, that which obtains between two states that are not allied but are nevertheless associated in two other local theaters: Thailand and Indonesia in the subregion of Southeast Asia. We must recall at the outset that each of these countries perceives its most pressing international security need to be protection within its local environs from the threats that might come from disorder in the intra-ASEAN theater—that is, from invasions or revolutionary influences moving across national borders. Ideal in the perception of each would be establishment of a zone in Southeast Asia in which all the subregional states would agree to respect one another's independence, give up the use of force to settle disputes with one another, and persuade all external powers not to intervene. ZOPFAN ("zone of peace, freedom, and neutrality") is the code word for this conception.

But the ideal has not been attainable. Thailand, Indonesia, and other like-minded states have had to settle for something less: ASEAN, an association of states that the three Indochinese states have refused to join, and one in which various member states, including Thailand, insist on retaining their alliances with external powers. In spite of these disappointments, ASEAN has proved to be highly valuable to Indonesia, Thailand, and the other members. It has enabled them to resolve or shelve the contentions that plagued member-states in the preceding years. It has raised the weight of each in world councils and thereby the prestige of the leaders in their own countries. The effect has been to enable each of the member-states to devote substantially more energy than before to the problems each considers most pressing—nation-building or, as the leaders like to put it, increasing its "resilience." Obviously, the relationship between Indonesia and Thailand is one that may reasonably be termed security interdependence, taking the form not of an alliance but of an entente, arising out of a perceived mutual vulnerability.

That relationship has been complicated, however, since 1978, when Vietnamese forces, backed by the Soviet Union, entered Cambodia, drove out the internationally recognized government, and set up a regime favorable to themselves. With the forces of Vietnam—the most powerful military state in Southeast Asia—now on their border, the Thais have naturally felt under threat. It is a threat that the Thais, like the South Koreans in their peninsula, do not themselves have the strength to counter. Since Indonesia also is pledged to support the independence of states and to oppose foreign intervention, the question naturally arises of what kind of assistance Indonesia can be called on to offer Thailand.

So far, the answer seems to be limited to strong diplomatic support outside the subregion: maintaining solidarity with the ASEAN states in their demand for continued recognition of the former Cambodian government, withdrawal of the Vietnamese forces, and restoration of a neutral, independent regime in Cambodia. But within the subregion, Indonesia has not offered military assistance and indeed has pressed for a less confrontational stance against Vietnam. It argues that Vietnam must somehow be accommodated so as to persuade it to enter ASEAN and lend its weight to subregionwide efforts that Indonesia believes will be needed eventually to counter the greater threat of China.

Does the concept of interdependence throw a useful light on this response? I believe it does. Indonesia feels little if any immediate security threat from Vietnam as a result of Vietnam's invasion of Cambodia. But that is not to say that it has no concern. It does have a concern. If its ASEAN neighbors are to trust it to live up to its own pledge to settle disputes peacefully and not to intervene in the affairs of member-states, it can hardly condone such action on the part of Vietnam. Moreover, if it were to show no support for the position of Thailand at a time when Thailand feels endangered, in spite of the fact that it is under no obligation to do so, it might well lead the Thais to downgrade the importance of their relations with Indonesia, thereby seriously weakening if not destroying the ASEAN process. Indonesia may thus be said to be sufficiently dependent on Thailand for the maintenance of ASEAN that it feels it must at least give diplomatic support to the Thai position against Vietnam. Reciprocally, Thailand feels itself sufficiently dependent on Indonesia, likewise for the maintenance of ASEAN, that it must refrain from pressing Indonesia any harder. Thus, although the South Korea–United States tie may be a tight military alliance and that between Thailand and Indonesia a loose entente, the essence of the relationship in both cases is the same: interdependence. The relationships differ only in the specific nature of the vulnerabilities involved and in the dynamic balance between the partners.

Finally, as the Thai–Indonesian case exemplifies, the relationship of interdependence is not limited to co-adversarial states within one specific theater but extends to relations among all such states in the overlapping theaters that make up the subregional and the regional theaters. It is in this sense that we can speak of the non-Communist states, the Soviet-related states, and the China-related states as each being caught up in one of three complex webs of interdependence, which for convenience we have called regional security nets.

We are now in a position to demonstrate the vitality of these nets in action by reviewing briefly how the states in the non-Communist net, for example, have responded to shifts in the global and regional balance of power since the late 1960s.

The Non-Communist Regional Security Net in Action

It is now generally recognized that the post-World War II era of American global hegemony came to an end sometime in the mid-1960s with the Soviet acquisition of rough nuclear parity. It was hastened as well by a broad, national weariness in the United States with global confrontation, brought to a head particularly by the war in Vietnam, where the sacrifices seemed meaningless to an increasing number of the American people. In 1968, President Lyndon Johnson withdrew from the national scene in frustration over his inability to persuade the enemy to negotiate. In the domestic electoral competition, his Republican opponent, Richard Nixon, was elected by voters who were persuaded that he had a better way to end the war. In the end, he was forced to withdraw the troops. Defeat followed.

Nixon's policy was more complex than that, of course. He did not believe that America's position had so deteriorated that the United States had to withdraw its forces from around the world and abandon its global role. He did recognize, however, that America's relative power position had shifted and that the American people were not willing to rebuild the nation's military forces to their former preeminence. Moreover, he seems to have become persuaded that new economic powers had arisen in the international power struggle—namely, Europe and Japan—and that economic strength had become as important as military strength.

In these circumstances, he tried to mobilize the capabilities he could—as we would expect of a status quo power facing an adverse trend—but with limited ability to respond. While admitting in the Guam Doctrine in 1969 that the United States could no longer provide ground forces for endangered friends and allies on the front line in Asia, he tried to reassure them by reaffirming alliance commitments, pledging to give the supplementary support their own forces might require, and promising to continue to hold before them a deterrent nuclear shield. At the same time, he sought to relieve the global threat by bringing more powers into the central balance. He welcomed the organization of the European Community in 1965. He returned Okinawa to Japan in 1972 and grasped the hand of China in 1973, thereby seeking to give life to his vision of replacing the global bipolar structure with a triangular one: the USSR, China, and the "West," which now included Japan with the United States and the European Community.

The rest of the world was intrigued with this conception. But it is doubtful that many countries shared Nixon's anticipation that Europe, China, or Japan would or could play a significant role in maintaining the global balance of power in the future; nor were most countries prepared to entrust their military security to economic instruments. Most, in fact, seemed to interpret the American policy as an elaborate distraction to hide its global withdrawal. This was a misperception. A global withdrawal did not then and has not now taken place; in determining policy, however, it is the strength of the perception that counts, not the degree of its accuracy.

Apparently sharing the view of American weakness, the Soviet Union, an anti-status quo power, seems to have believed that its own position was improving. It must have been further heartened by the chaotic situation that the Cultural Revolution was producing in its second great adversary, the People's Republic of China. Accordingly, the Soviet Union moved vigorously to improve its position by intensifying its mobilization, as one would expect an anti-status quo power to do in a favorable environment. It sustained its military budget at an annual growth rate of about 4 percent a year until the mid-1970s. It moved heavy ground forces to the northern Chinese border. It augmented its eastern missile deployments and strengthened its Pacific fleet. It persisted, even against Chinese obstacles, to supply the Vietnamese. At the same time, it sought to quiet its American adversary by responding to the U.S. détente thrust. It negotiated the SALT I and ABM treaties. It also tried to expand its political power in the Asia Pacific region, proposing that the states there join it in a new but vaguely defined collective security arrangement.

Meanwhile, the third member of the Asian big three, the People's Republic of China, found its relative position to be weakening most of all. The Cultural Revolution was compounding the difficulties caused by ineffective economic policies. Its alliance relations with the Soviet Union had deteriorated to the point of outright hostilities on the northern border. A radical solution appeared to be required, and the leadership moved quickly to accomplish one. It brought the Cultural Revolution to an end at home. It also sought new friends and allies abroad, offering to normalize relations with the United States, Japan, and the other market economies, including those in the Asia Pacific region.

Weakened though China might be, what impressed the other Asian states more was the independence China was proclaiming from the Soviet Union. Although most of the leaders in these states considered the American conception of China as a great power a bit overblown, they were deeply conscious of China's size, historical role, and traditional conception of itself as the Middle Kingdom. They were therefore inclined to view it, if not as a global power, at least as a regional power, emerging to rival the Soviet Union and the United States in a tripolar Asian security balance. Of course, China could not deploy its strength effectively to offshore parts of the region, as the Soviet Union and the United States could; nor did it have so strong a supporting network of friends and allies (regionally then limited to North Korea and the Socialist Republic of Vietnam, both of which it had to share with its adversary, the Soviet Union). This suggests that it might be more realistic to say that the emerging structure was seen by most Asian states as a two-and-a-half-power rather than a three-power balance.

The effect on the non-Communist states in the region was dramatic. Through the multiple links of the security net binding them together, each felt that the power balance was trending adversely.

Responses varied, but each state—depending on the degree of interdependence it felt in its own relationships with the other non-Communist states, especially the United States—moved in the same direction: to reduce its adversarial relations and increase its power. Most of the non-Communist states followed the United States in exploring détente with China. Japan acted quickly; the Southeast Asian states followed more cautiously; and South Korea considered the matter positively, though without result. Obviously, they took these actions not because they looked on China as an alternative supplier of security—China was still seen as an anti-status quo power—but because they felt the need and the opportunity to reduce the adversarial quality of the relationship. Nor did these states shift their alignment to any other great power. In fact, none was available. The French had effectively withdrawn from SEATO; in 1971, the British had evacuated Singapore; and the Japanese, contrary to the Nixon conception, were seen as not having the military capability or, if they were to acquire it, a sufficiently benevolent interest to make them an acceptable alternative.

As a consequence, the characteristic response to the fear of American abandonment was for each of the non-Communist medium-sized and small powers to look more to itself and, in some instances, to one another. South Korea, for example, did its best to keep the United States engaged by maintaining its own troops in Vietnam to the end. It pursued a parallel détente policy toward North Korea, with which negotiations were undertaken, and toward the Soviet Union and China. It also pressed the United States to reaffirm its commitment and increase its military aid. At the same time, Seoul felt driven to strengthen itself against the day when it might be forced to go it alone. It examined the nuclear option, increased its military budget, and imposed more autocratic controls on its people with the Yushin Constitution.

The non-Communist states in Southeast Asia—perhaps too militarily weak to aspire to going it alone and certainly too overwhelmed by internal problems to place highest priority on external security—responded more moderately and more politically. Nevertheless, they did move in the same self-strengthening direction. In 1967, for example, they came together to try to shelve the disputes that had divided them by forming the Association of Southeast Asian Nations (ASEAN).

Least responsive were the Japanese. Their attention at this time was riveted on the challenge to their economy then posed by the first oil crisis and the textile, steel, and other disputes with the United States. Like the others, however, they did try to ease their security problem by exploring détente with the Soviet Union and normalization with the People's Republic of China (PRC).

It might be supposed that the end of the American effort in Vietnam would have been interpreted as a still more fundamental weakening of U.S. power, thereby revealing an even more drastic shift in the global and regional balances and calling for more drastic changes in the security policies of the non-Communist states in the Asia Pacific region, as in all states around the

world. In fact, it did not. It would appear to have been universally anticipated, and therefore most states in the early post-Vietnam years simply moved
more vigorously in the directions they had adopted in the late 1960s, when
the worsening of the security environment had first been perceived.

In the early Carter years, the United States did increase its defense out-
lays, but only slightly. Its major effort to improve its power position was to
try to reduce the level of antagonism between itself and the Soviet Union by
pursuing the SALT II negotiations with vigor. In addition, it pushed ahead
with the opening to China. In 1979, formal diplomatic recognition was
switched from Taipei to Beijing. Trade with China was encouraged. A strong
China was proclaimed to be in the American interest, and possibilities for
making China a partner in the competition with the Soviet Union were ex-
plored. Efforts also were intensified to persuade Japan to liberalize its economy and take a greater responsibility for the global economic system. It was
also urged to increase its defense budget and contribute to regional security
by taking a greater measure of responsibility for its own defense, thereby
lightening the burdens the United States had assumed in the past.

The Soviet Union, for its part, seems not have changed its views either.
It continued its previous course. So did the Chinese, who now offered the
doctrine of the "three worlds" as a theoretical basis for their new policy of
reaching beyond the Communist world for support. China cut off its aid to
Vietnam and sent high-level missions to the ASEAN states in an effort to
open relations. It completed normalization with the United States and Japan
and began a campaign to enlist both in a "united front" against "hegemony"
in Asia, by which it meant the Soviet Union.

Most other Asia Pacific states welcomed the continued easing of tensions
between the United States and the big Communist powers, but most also
continued to interpret the American policy as evidence of weakness. Moreover, President Carter's announcement of his intent to take the last U.S.
division out of Korea intensified the fear of many that America's overall
withdrawal from the region was clearly in progress—a fear that was compounded by the administration's advocacy of human rights, often jeopard-
izing what various states in the region felt were America's and their own
vital security interests.

South Korea felt that way almost to the point of desperation. At home,
the controls of the autocracy were tightened; in Washington, a frantic effort
was launched to bribe the U.S. Congress to reverse what the Park regime
feared was a policy that would expose its country to destruction. The ASEAN
states, not feeling under so great a threat, persisted in their thinking that if
they could strengthen their association sufficiently, perhaps they could withdraw from the subregional and regional systems. Thailand asked the Americans to remove their military base. The heads of all ASEAN states began
an intense round of bilateral conversations, followed in 1976 by a summit

meeting in Bali, where fundamental accords were reached to set aside the conflicts that had divided them so long and to work together to build in their area the aforementioned zone of peace, freedom, and neutrality.

Japan continued to feel the need to improve its situation but still felt less threat in the environment than its Asian neighbors did. It responded cautiously to U.S. pressure to strengthen its military posture, adopting in 1976 a new National Defense Outline, which called for a modest, scheduled increase in firepower. It did register uneasiness when the United States announced its decision to withdraw ground forces from Korea; but when that decision was reversed, Japan reaffirmed its essentially détentist policy, apparently less convinced than its neighbors that the United States was weakening or at least, if it was, that Japan would be victimized. It continued to base its security planning on an assumed Soviet–American nuclear parity. It normalized relations with China, but it strenuously resisted being drawn into the Chinese anti-Soviet web. Instead, it offered large investments to China and at the same time turned its attention southward, promising in 1976 to double its economic aid in the next five years and announcing in 1977, through Prime Minister Fukuda, its intent to seek a new relationship—not military—with the ASEAN states and the Indochinese states.

But the international mood of détente was severely jolted beginning in 1977–79 when the Soviet Union, apparently increasingly heartened by the trend in the balance of power, went on the offensive. Deployment of the ominous SS-20 ballistic missiles was begun against Western Europe; ground forces were moved into the Northern Territories against Japan; friendship treaties were negotiated with Afghanistan, India, and Vietnam; and Afghanistan was invaded. Moreover, backed by the Soviet Union, a number of Soviet friends and allies also sprang into action at this time and in the years that followed: the Sandinistas in Nicaragua, SWAPO against South Africa in Namibia, the Somalis against Ethiopia, and the Vietnamese against the rival Communist regime in Cambodia.

At the same time, Khomeini unleashed his attack on the government of the Shah of Iran, destroying this pillar of the non-Communist southwest security system and subjecting the United States to a new ignominy by holding its embassy staff hostage. Related radical Muslim groups challenged other established regimes throughout the Middle East, and war broke out between Iran and Iraq. The anti-status quo forces began to move in nearly every theater in the world. Suddenly, the status quo powers were jolted out of their wishful thinking and back to the realities of power and its imperatives.

The American people finally cut through the Vietnam syndrome; and in the years that have followed, under President Carter and particularly under President Reagan, the U.S. government has been taking a number of steps to mobilize strength against what finally has come to be perceived as a dangerously adverse trend in the global and regional balances. SALT II was withdrawn from the Senate. Arms control negotiations with the Soviet were temporarily deferred while major emphasis was placed on the r ation of the military budget and the deployment of countervailing .____ in Europe.

Although the Middle Eastern, Central American, and European theaters have been the objects of greatest concern, causing U.S. forces to be "swung" out of the Asia Pacific theater on occasion, increasing attention has been focused on that theater as well. For example, the announced troop withdrawal from South Korea was halted. Thereafter, the human rights campaign was quieted; military assistance to Korea was stepped up, including the promise of delivery of the advanced F-16 fighter planes; and that stern leader, President Chun, was given a warm embrace. Similarly, in the early years of this new policy line, dissatisfaction in the Philippines with President Marcos's regime was overlooked as the 1983 renegotiation of the base agreement was given priority attention. Recently, the reformist pressure on the Philippine government has been revived and intensified—this time not because of reduced concern for the strategic relationship but rather to counter the threat that growing instability in that country poses to the U.S. position.

The Japanese have been pressed to arm faster and to take on new "roles and missions," including the extension of surveillance over part of the sea-lanes extending south and east of the home islands. Toward the People's Republic of China, after a brief period of coolness, the Reagan administration has returned even more strongly to a supportive line. Attempting to convert China's "parallel" strategic posture into a cooperative one, it has offered to transfer certain gray-area technology and defensive weapons. In the local Taiwan theater, the United States has even sought to accommodate Beijing by agreeing to certain limits on its military supply to the island. In the Southeast Asian subtheater, the United States raised no objection to the Chinese incursion into Vietnam in 1979. In addition, it has strengthened its support for ASEAN and its member-states, in particular reaffirming its commitment to Thailand under the Manila Treaty, speeding up military deliveries to that country, offering extensive assistance to refugees, and backing the ASEAN policy toward the new war in Indochina. Most recently, the Congress has enacted legislation authorizing modest aid to the non-Communist forces under the Coalition Government of Kampuchea.

The Chinese, having decided long before that the trends were adverse, were heartened by the American response and at first took an extremely strong stand against the Soviet Union. They increased Chinese forces on the northern border and insisted that political relations with the USSR could not improve until the Soviets withdrew from that border, gave up their invasion of Afghanistan, and ended their support for the Vietnamese invasion of Kampuchea. In the south, a "punishment" of Vietnam was launched in 1979, and a second has been threatened. Major assistance has been given the Coalition Government of Kampuchea, and support for Thai defense has been pledged. In the first flush of enthusiasm for the new era, the PRC renewed its call for a "united front" against the "hegemonial" ambitions of both the Soviet Union and Vietnam.

Over time, the PRC has softened a bit. There may well be conflicting pressures at home, but it seems more likely that it has come to feel that the new activism of the United States makes the international situation less threatening. At any rate, it has given up its military preconditions for an improvement in relations with the Soviet Union, at least in the economic and cultural fields. While continuing its strong stance against Vietnam and the Heng Samrin regime in Cambodia, and while reaffirming its interest in securing technology from the United States, it made clear in 1982 that its fundamental policy, as most Asian observers had always believed, was not to allow itself to be co-opted into the non-Communist security net in the region any more than into that linked to the Soviet Union, from which it had earlier broken away. Rather, it was to assert and defend China's "independence," by which, I believe we can understand, it means to try to establish, to the extent it may require, its own autonomous, regional security net.

The impact of these shifts in the global and regional balances has been least noticeable in South Korea and Taiwan. These states were already living at a high level of military readiness. But the impact on the other non-Communist powers in Asia has been greatly to intensify their sense of threat, reminding them of the futility of trying to escape from the global and regional security nets that envelop them or denying the imperatives these systems generate.

The Japanese people, for their part, have now come to the view that the world in fact *is* a dangerous place. The majority have now decided that the Self-Defense Forces *are* necessary and that steps must be taken to make sure that the alliance with the United States holds. In 1978, a new structure was set up to facilitate planning for cooperation between Japanese and American forces. Joint—in fact, multinational—training exercises have been expanded. A concept of "comprehensive security" has been introduced, under which the relative priority given to defense appropriations in the national budget has been increased and a "strategic" aid program has been created. Japan has, in fact, gone so far as to proclaim itself to be a "member of the West," expressing a serious concern for the security of Europe and strategic nuclear deployments. It has thereby taken the first, at least verbal step toward acknowledging its participation in the global and regional balances.

For the ASEAN states, the Vietnamese invasion of Cambodia, supported by the Soviet Union and opposed by China, was primarily responsible for creating an awareness of the new imperatives for survival. Each state has continued to react somewhat differently from its neighbors. The Philippines and Indonesia, being offshore, have been least alarmed. Indonesia, with its large Chinese ethnic minority and its memory of the uprising of 1965, has continued to feel, as already suggested, that it is China, not Vietnam that represents the most serious danger. For its part, Malaysia, likewise with a large Chinese ethnic minority, has found it difficult to abandon the concept of neutralism, which it had fathered in the ZOPFAN idea. Nevertheless, the burden of the refugees has been too heavy, the violation of ASEAN principles too flagrant, and the threat to Thailand too real for ASEAN to survive without taking a stand. Over the years a common position vis-à-vis Vietnam has been formed, military budgets have been stepped up, Chinese and American military assistance has been welcomed, the United Nations has been appealed to, and international political support for the Coalition Government of Kampuchea has been sustained.

These events indicate that the perception of increased external threat has come to be widely shared among the non-Communist states in the Asia Pacific region. Responding to a common perception that the global and regional balance of power has been trending adversely to their interests, they generally have tended to increase their military capabilities and to work more closely together. They have thus been acting in general accord with the imperatives of the balance of power hypothesis.

The non-Communist states have also revealed a fine sensitivity to the interdependencies that bind them together. In so doing, they have demonstrated the vitality of the regionwide, non-Communist security net—a net that, in rivalry with those tied to the Soviet Union and China, structures the security relationships in the Asia Pacific region.

Notes

1. Although certain Pacific littoral states in Central and South America also have recently expressed the desire to be included in any discussions of possible new Pacific-wide arrangements, their security relationships with the countries in this sector are not sufficient to merit inclusion in the analysis that follows.

2. Hahn-Been Lee, "Generating Momentum Toward a Pacific Community," *East Asia Program Occasional Paper,* No. 12 (Washington: Woodrow Wilson International Center for Scholars, 1983), p. 4.

3. For a recent statement of this view, see Peter Polomka, "The Security of the Western Pacific: The Price of Burden Sharing," *Survival,* 26 (January/February 1984): 4–15.

4. For a perceptive analysis of the actions a small state may take vis-à-vis a big state, see Charles Morrison and Astrid Suhrke, *Strategies for Survival* (New York: St. Martin Press, 1979).

5. The difficulties in obtaining comparable figures for military expenditures are set forth well in Edward T. Fei, "Understanding Arms Transfers and Military

Expenditures: Data Problems," in Stephanie G. Neumann and Robert Hasbary, eds., *Arms Transfers in the Modern World* (New York: Praeger, 1979).

6. Michael M. Yoshitsu, *Caught in the Middle East: Japan's Diplomacy in Transition* (Lexington, Mass.: Lexington Books, D.C. Heath, 1984), pp. 1–12.

7. For an influential academic example, see "Introduction," in *The International Politics of Regions: A Comparative Approach*, ed. Louis J. Cantori and Steven L. Spiegel (Englewood Cliffs, N.J.: Prentice-Hall, 1970), which, while conceding the political and ideological factors make regional or "subordinate system" boundaries somewhat fluid, proceed to identify the regions of the world as relatively fixed entities within which member states conduct their primary international relationships.

8. Woodford Agee Heflin, ed., *The United States Air Force Dictionary*. Research Studies Institute, Air University (Maxwell Air Force Base, Alabama: Air University Press, 1956), pp. 522–523. For sale by the Superintendent of Documents, U.S. Government Printing Office.

9. For a persuasive argument that the ASEAN process is driven more by the desire to restrain its members from hurting each other than by the desire to defend them against threats external to the association or to advance their economic cooperation, see Michael Antolik, "The Anatomy of ASEAN" (PhD dissertation, Columbia University, Department of Political Science, 1985).

10. Richard N. Cooper, *The Economics of Interdependence: Economic Policy in the Atlantic Community* (New York: McGraw-Hill, 1968; reprinted New York: Columbia University Press for the Council on Foreign Relations, 1980).

11. Robert O. Keohane and Joseph S. Nye, *Power and Interdependence: World Politics in Transition* (Boston: Little Brown, 1977).

12. For a critique of the various usages, see David A. Baldwin, "Interdependence and Power: A Conceptual Analysis," *International Organization* 34 (Autumn 1980): 471–506.

13. Glenn H. Snyder and Paul Diesing, *Conflict Among Nations* (Princeton: Princeton University Press, 1977), p. 34 and pp. 476–77; and Glenn H. Snyder, "The Security Dilemma in Alliance Politics, *World Politics*, Vol. xxxvi, no. 4, July 1984, pp. 461–95.

II
The Mosaic of Non-Communist Strategies

2
The United States: Global Deterrence

Richard K. Betts

A sia has been a permanent arena of strategic concern to the United States throughout the twentieth century. Since 1939, the importance of Europe has usually ranked ahead of the Pacific in the thinking of American leaders; but since 1945, Asia has presented more frequent crises and violent challenges—most obviously, two frustrating wars in Korea and Vietnam. Europe has been more central but more stable; Asia has been secondary but more volatile and less susceptible to external controls by the superpowers.

Within the vast expanse of Asia, the northeast has been a more dominant concern than other regions. The two great nations of Japan and China are intrinsically vital elements in U.S. security. Japan is the largest liberal capitalist democracy outside the United States; it is both a fraternal and a competitive force, with unrealized military potential. China is poor but populous—and ideologically uncongenial—but it is a check on Soviet global ambitions. In Korea, the large U.S. military presence on the ground has institutionalized the peninsula as a significant factor in Pentagon planning. In contrast to Vietnam, the war there marked the beginning rather than the end of a continuous commitment.

The importance of stakes in Northeast Asia is matched by moderation in the means appropriate to pursuing stable security, which makes it easier for strategists to embrace the enterprise than if it threatened to involve a fiasco like the Vietnam War. Buffered by water, Japan is easier to defend militarily than the area of comparable importance—Western Europe. Maintaining a security relationship with China is a delicate and uncertain task, but it is a problem more of diplomatic management than of direct commitment of U.S. military power. Having to defend South Korea against another attack from Pyongyang would be an unfortunate eventuality, but it could be accomplished with more efficiency and confidence than the defense of the Saigon regime was in the 1960s.

Southeast Asia's position in U.S. strategy today presents a different, murkier picture. Military strategists or political leaders at the highest level who are not Asian specialists recognize the importance of China, Japan, and Korea, but they do not usually recognize a direct or vital linkage between the dominant concerns related to that part of Asia and the region to the south.

In this context, American military and political initiatives toward Southeast Asia are overwhelmingly conditioned by two facts. First, as a superpower, the United States frames these issues in global terms, and Southeast Asia competes for attention not only with Northeast Asia but also with the rest of the regions of the world. Second, U.S. strategy and military policy still labor under the painful hangover of the Vietnam War. This creates a potential tension between trends in objective interests and subjective recognition of these trends. Although the Reagan administration busily reasserted U.S. power and proudly cited the overcoming of the Vietnam syndrome in such actions as the invasion of Grenada, not even the most strident hawks were willing to focus much attention on the vulnerability of Thailand.

The first fact abets the second. With a plate full of trouble spots and commitments around the world, there is no compulsion for strategists to fasten on current problems in Southeast Asia, when none but Kampuchea has yet burst into flame, and when attempts at preventive activism (such as in Central America) would more clearly raise the specter of the experience of the 1960s in Vietnam. Yet the West has a substantial and growing interest in Southeast Asia:

> ASEAN is a counter to a Russian-backed expansionist Vietnam; it is an important trading partner . . . ; it is a moderate and generally friendly grouping within the more radical Third World; its strategic waterways control the access from the Pacific to the Indian Ocean; it will be . . . the most rapidly growing region of the world in the 1980s; it provides to the Third World an example of rapid growth via a free market economic system; it is the first successful regional grouping in the postwar history of Southeast Asia. . . . A great deal more needs to be done to acquaint the American people with the strategic importance of this region in the post-Vietnam war era.[1]

This is recognized, and when asked whether U.S. interests are important, those involved with security policy say yes. In bureaucratic jargon, however, this is a throwaway line. The practical issue is the *relative* ranking of these interests compared to other areas of concern. In these terms, Southeast Asia usually lies near the bottom of the in-box of high-level policymakers. They are concerned in principle about the region, but they are far more concerned in practice about others. Most of the time, Southeast Asia ranks about fifth among geographically defined priorities—after Western Europe, the Middle East, Central America, and Northeast Asia. It probably competes for fifth place with South Asia and South America (the latter ranks higher in political terms but lower in military terms, because external Communist military threats are so limited by geography). The only region that probably ranks lower, strategically, is Africa.

In part, this relative inattention reflects the apparent international stability that characterizes the region, apart from Indochina. Kampuchea is a source of anxiety, but it has become a nagging problem rather than a crisis. But even if that picture of stability changes, unless the other priorities fade in significance—through improbable events such as dramatic new détente with the Soviet Union and Cuba or settlement of the Arab–Israeli conflict— an intent focus on Southeast Asia is likely to remain restricted for some time to middle and lower levels of the policymaking apparatus, and that focus will be primarily on *internal* instabilities that could also metastasize into broader problems. The major example in this respect is the Philippines. The 1984 appointment of the U.S. ambassador in Manila, Michael Armacost, as under secretary of state for political affairs might symbolzie the potential for more sensitivity to local problems at high echelons. But personnel actions do not change the fact that high officials only have so many hours in a day, and other priorities remain until events force changes in the priorities. In Washington today, no revision of strategy toward Southeast Asia is waiting to happen. Danger lies in whatever possibility there is that a regional crisis is waiting to happen, which would compel belated adaptation under stress.

The Strategic Landscape

American stakes in Northeast Asia are well recognized, and commitments to Japan and South Korea are clearly established. There are critical ambiguities in regard to China—over the quality and intensity of economic and military cooperation and over Taiwan. But these ambiguities are recognized as necessary ones, to be managed delicately rather than resolved decisively, because they cover the pursuit of contradictory interests. Relations with Japan and China are matters of high policy, and the maintenance of deterrence in Korea is a well-institutionalized process. None of this can be said confidently about Southeast Asia.

If U.S. strategic interests in Southeast Asia were simple, clear, prominent, immediately compelling, and mutually consistent, the characterization in the previous section of security planners' attitudes would not be valid. It is valid because of the diversity of the interests, the diversity of the region, and the lack of perception of near-term threats. To winnow prospects for change from the confusion or indifference of nonspecialist policymakers, let us consider the interaction between global, regional, and subregional interests and between political aims and military conditions. Much of this can be subsumed under two considerations. First, apart from Japan, the strategic significance of Asia as a whole is still seen as largely derivative—that is, how events there affect the worldwide balance of power between the West and the Soviet Union. Interests intrinsic to Southeast Asia are primarily economic, and the linkage of economic and military concerns does not appear as clear as it does in Europe, Japan, or the Persian Gulf. Second, long-term political or ideological goals and short-term strategic requirements are not fully compatible in some cases. But the relative stability of most of the area, and the diverse character of the interrelationships between political and strategic aims, creates an inertia unconducive to decisive redefinition of priorities.

Derivative Interests

In the 1950s and 1960s, Asia was a theater of high strategic interest in its own right. Containment of China was the second U.S. global priority, after containment of Soviet power. For this period, these two priorities overlapped, given the characterization of the "Sino–Soviet bloc" as a unified global threat. (Consider one example of the operational consequences of this assumption. Until 1961, the U.S. nuclear war plan provided only for a comprehensive strike against all of the Warsaw Pact and China; no programmed option existed for sparing the PRC in the unanticipated event that it was not involved in the Soviet aggression that would provoke the U.S. nuclear retaliation.[2]) To the extent that Soviet and Chinese threats were differentiated, in the East it was the PRC rather than the USSR that was the primary concern. Moscow had negligible capacity to project its armed forces into the region, and Maoism appeared a greater political challenge. Except for minor cases, such as the Soviet airlift of food and fuel to Laos in 1960–61,[3] China was seen as the principal external threat in Korea and Southeast Asia. During the Eisenhower administration, Beijing was even elevated to near-parity with Moscow in terms of global strategy, as "Asia-firsters" in the Republican party challenged the traditional priority of Europe in U.S. policy. Throughout the Cold War in Asia, the Soviet Union was an indirect military threat (providing supplies to North Korea and guerrilla movements), whereas China was the direct threat (by virtue of its perceived potential for invading neighboring countries). American military involvement in Indochina in the 1960s was spurred by the derivative interest of worldwide containment and the Munich analogy, but even more by the regional interest of preventing Chinese expansion.

All that changed by the early 1970s. Exploitation of the Sino–Soviet rift became the centerpiece of the Nixon administration's global strategy. Courting Beijing in order to construct a triangular diplomatic balance, while the bulk of Soviet military power remained at some remove from most of the region, meant that the strategic warrant for allocating a large portion of U.S. military forces to the area was canceled. When Nixon withdrew one American army division from Korea, his secretary of defense, Melvin Laird, even pressed for further removal of the one remaining division.

For friendly Southeast Asian countries, the shift in orientation of U.S.

global policy, coinciding with the end of the Vietnam War, complicated the strategic calculus. Both China and a newly united Vietnam represented potential threats of attack or subversion, but the United States was not about to offer to deal with either one as it had in the previous era. The bitter legacy of the war precluded direct action against Vietnam, except possibly in the event of attack on Thailand, and even then Washington might well rely on Beijing to provide the principal counterpower.

Today, the United States has four main strategic interests in Asia, all of which continue to reflect the reduced military priority of the whole area and the even smaller priority of Southeast Asia. First is the cautious encouragement of Chinese military modernization as a prop to global containment of Moscow. The motive of tying down close to fifty Russian divisions in the Far East outweighs the concern with the Soviet threat in East Asia itself. The Soviet forces opposite China were created *de novo*, not diverted from Europe. If military rapprochement with China occurred and Moscow did not demobilize the extra forces, they would become available for allocation to contingencies in the West or the Middle East, radically changing the global balance with the United States and its allies. The second strategic interest is more vigorous encouragement of increases in Japanese military power, to relieve U.S. forces of some burdens in the region. Both of these U.S. policies are mixed blessings, at best, to most of the ASEAN countries, but to Washington, these anxieties are something more to be massaged than to be resolved by compromising other aims. The third interest is continued maintenance of the U.S. deterrent presence in South Korea. Fourth is maintaining access to local air and naval base facilities. This includes facilities in Japan, which are crucial to defense of South Korea and to naval operations throughout the northern Pacific, but access to these bases is not problematic at present. The other principal bases of importance are the huge infrastructures at Clark Field and Subic Bay in the Philipines. The import of Philippine bases now has more to do with global interests than with those in the region. (As Soviet use of Cam Ranh Bay increases, however, the regional rationale for the Philippine bases reemerges.) These bases currently provide the only suitable staging point for operations that would shift forces from the Pacific into the Indian Ocean and Persian Gulf, which superseded Asia as the theater of second military priority (after Europe) following the Iranian revolution and Soviet invasion of Afghanistan.[4] The supply line from Subic Bay to Diego Garcia is 11,000 miles.

In the 1980s, U.S. security policy has been preoccupied with five main politico-military issues:

1. *Improving the overall military balance with the Soviet Union, particularly in intercontinental and European theater nuclear systems, and conventional forces oriented to the Persian Gulf.* Northeast Asia is significant

in this regard, because more Chinese and Japanese strength would weigh heavily in the global equation, enabling Washington to concentrate more on commitments outside Northeast Asia and even beyond the Pacific; the small size of ASEAN military establishments means that even their marked improvement would have little impact.

2. *Nuclear arms control.* Northeast Asia figures indirectly in this problem, because a deal on forces in Europe must not allow Moscow to displace SS-20s to the Far East, increasing the threat to Japan and China. (This is almost an academic point in mid-decade, because serious arms control appears virtually dead for the foreseeable future.) Although Soviet missiles can cover parts of Southeast Asia, this is scarcely ever mentioned, and the problem is subsumed under whatever constraints are obtained because of sensitivities in Tokyo and Beijing.

3. *Marxist-Leninist movements in Central America.* Objectively, hypersensitivity to the U.S. "backyard'" is a bit anachronistic in an era of intercontinental striking power, but it is reinforced by the perception that instability in Nicaragua, El Salvador, and Guatemala is on the verge of exploding out of control. If Communist insurgency threatened to triumph in several Southeast Asian states at once, attention could come to focus on that region again, despite the legacy of the Vietnam War.

4. *The Middle East.* Association with Israel and concern about Gulf oil are problems in their own right, and the region has long been recognized as the superpowers' potential equivalent of the Balkans before World War I— a concern regularly heightened by crises such as events in Lebanon and the Iran-Iraq war.

5. *Repair of the Atlantic Alliance in the wake of controversy over intermediate-range missile deployments.* These tensions are no less manageable than those with Southeast Asian friends, but NATO is the centerpiece of U.S. foreign policy.

To most American strategists, power relationships in Asia are significant primarily for how they inhibit Soviet power and ease U.S. operations on a worldwide scale. China is important for diverting the Russians from Europe and the Middle East; Vietnam is dangerous as a base for Soviet force projection, but by now this is viewed as much in terms of the global "proxy" balance (including Cuba) as in terms of the local balance of power; and the waterways of Southeast Asia are most important as a medium through which U.S. power can pass between the Pacific and theaters to the West. This analysis may appear to exaggerate the indifference of U.S. security policy to purely local interests (and it does not fully define the attitudes of officials outside the Defense Department), but even if it implies a sort of naive callousness toward Southeast Asia, the fact remains that the agenda of high politics is overloaded and top decision makers more often view the region deductively (according to its place on the global chessboard) than inductively (according to internally generated issues). A comprehensive vision of strategy, though, has to appreciate the relationship of more particular local interests to the global framework, even as popular visions in the early 1970s of détente and diffusion of power have given way to the reinvigoration of worldwide containment.

Intrinsic Interests

The biggest American interest in Asia is the security of Japan, the largest market economy in the world after the United States itself and the third most populous democracy (India is the first). American and Japanese interests in the economic sphere are two-edged. Japan and the United State are large trading partners, but they are also competitors irked by each other's protectionist measures, which are limited but provide potent sources of domestic discontent. Economic competition helps fuel U.S. demands that Japan increase its national defense effort, which is less than a sixth of Washington's in proportional terms (percentage of GNP allocated to military functions). This disparity, combined with the one-sided defense commitment (the United States is legally obligated to defend Japan, but the reverse is not true), makes the "free ride" criticism of Tokyo a potent argument; U.S. workers in threatened industries feel that they are subsidizing the economy that is taking their jobs. The best buffer the Japanese have against pressure is that no one argues for a military role fully proportional to economic resources—this would make Japan *the* superpower in Asia. So long as the issue of security burden sharing is about the *degree* of acceptable disparity, it is easier for Tokyo to temporize and fend off criticism by making military increases that are steady and in the right direction, though still grossly disproportional compared to the U.S. burden.[5]

An overwhelming proportion of U.S. interests in Southeast Asia is economic. The fact that trade with nations of the Pacific now outstrips that with Europe—while NATO still remains the primary commitment to Washington—reflects this. The canonical rationale for the huge U.S. military presence in Western Europe has been the combination of economic importance, political and cultural affinity, and the concentration of Soviet military power poised on the inner German border. The continuing import of the last two factors—which are absent in Asia, except for China and Japan in part—overrides the shift in relative economic significance. A subtle resurgence of anti-European "unilateralist" sentiments became visible among some figures in the Reagan administration, but not to the point of revising strategic priorities.

In South Korea, the stakes are mixed. The inertia of tradition since the peacetime stationing of U.S. forces there after the war of the early 1950s plays some role in rationalizing continued military presence despite the fact that the ROK's authoritarian politics make it no more attractive an ally than Franco's Spain was in Europe. Deterrence has worked in Korea for 30 years, a reasonable argument goes, so why change the situation? By now, though, the deterrent function of U.S. troops is exerted not against the major Communist powers but, for the most part, against North Korea. If the Pyongyang regime were to appear as sober and cautious as Moscow or Beijing, Seoul's superiority over North Korea in war potential could seem to be grounds for complete devolution of responsibility for defense on the peninsula. The ROK has more than twice the population of North Korea, almost four times the GNP, and an impressive rate of economic growth (over 7 percent in 1982, whereas that of many NATO nations was negative). These very facts—40 million people (two-thirds the population of West Germany) and a steadily increasing share of the collective economic status of the West—make the security of the ROK arguably a much more direct interest for the United States than has ever been formally acknowledged. Commitment has usually been justified as a derivative interest—to symbolize the solidity of global containment and to prevent Communist conquest from making the peninsula a "dagger pointed at the heart of Japan." (The metaphor has always been more colorful than meaningful. A Communist Korea would scarcely present any greater military threat to Japan than the Soviet possession of Sakhalin already does.) The old strategic rationale that sees South Korea as a domino rather than as a value in its own right has not caught up with economic reality.

In a sense, the population and economic dynamism of Southeast Asia should make the foregoing argument applicable to that region as well as to Taiwan. ASEAN has more than a quarter of a billion people and a GNP of almost $200 billion; from 1979–81, U.S. exports to ASEAN increased about 30 percent, and from 1977–82, total two-way trade more than doubled.[6] In regard to the mainland countries of ASEAN, however, inertia has worked in the other direction, because the United States was so badly burned in its attempt to prop up the dominoes of Indochina. The offshore countries— Indonesia and the Philippines—are virtually secure against external aggression. The New People's Army (NPA) has emerged with frightening speed as a challenge to the government in Manila, but even in the Philippines—and certainly in Indonesia—internal threats to stability are as much non-Communist as the type of subversion that could prompt U.S. military intervention on grounds of containment. Taiwan is comparable to South Korea, though less populous, but the fact that the PRC's stake in Taiwan is very different from its attitude toward South Korea means that the U.S. interest in regard to Beijing compromises its interests in regard to Taipei.

Apart from the economic interest of trade, which is a matter to be handled by American diplomats and businessmen rather than strategic planners, there are two related concerns that overlap with global strategy and lie in the gray area between intrinsic and derivative interests: Indonesian oil and maritime access to straits. Neither of these is a "vital" interest—that is, one of the top few on the list of worldwide interests—and the threats to them are hypothetical and remote.

After 1973, global energy transfers to the industrial democracies became wrapped up in the issue of security. For strategists, however, this was less a global issue than a Middle Eastern one, because both the largest sources of supply and the greatest potential threats to them—from internal instability, Soviet aggression, or both—lay in the Persian Gulf. If supplies from the Gulf were cut off, even in a global war, there would not necessarily be a comparable threat of a cutoff from Indonesia (the Soviet navy's hands would probably be too full with other missions to concentrate on commerce interdiction in that area). In any case, Indonesia has a relatively small proportion of world oil. Oil sources exist around disputed territories, such as the Spratly Islands, but they are not large enough to matter strategically in themselves; for the United States, they are more significant as a potential source of conflict between regional states that could involve Washington against its will. Moreover, the West's adaptation to the rise in oil prices through conservation, reserve storage, and energy diversification—not to mention the oil glut of the early 1980s—has made dependence on oil imports less acute.

Maritime access is more a legal and political issue than a strategic one. The U.S. rejection of the Law of the Sea Treaty, and refusal to recognize Jakarta's full claims to jurisdiction over straits in accord with the Indonesian "archipelagic principle" (*Wawasan Nusantara*) are sources of diplomatic abrasion but are not likely to turn into real impediments to transit.[7] If worse came to worst and commercial voyages were inhibited, circumventing waterways even as crucial as the Malacca Straits would not be a disastrous problem. The West managed to survive quite comfortably for years when the Suez Canal was closed after the 1967 Arab–Israeli War.

Indonesian claims present no practical danger to commerce in any case, because Jakarta has no objection to innocent passage. The United States resists these claims on grounds of principle—the general right of freedom of the seas—but also for pragmatic military reasons. Accepting demands for prior notification of transit by warships is impossible, given the need for flexibility in wartime operations. This is a remote concern, but there is also an immediate day-to-day problem—the use of straits as routes for ballistic missile submarines (SSBNs) moving from Pacific bases to firing stations in the Indian Ocean. Without maintenance of secrecy about their location, the whole purpose of SSBNs—to serve as an invulnerable retaliatory force—is vitiated. Dependence on the Indian Ocean as an area from which to fire, however, declines as older SSBNs with intermediate-range Poseidon missiles are replaced by Trident submarines with long-range missiles, which can cover Soviet targets from areas closer to U.S. home waters.

When Indonesia first promulgated the archipelagic principle in 1957, the Soviets did not oppose it. But that was in an era when Soviet relations with Sukarno were warm and they had no significant "blue water" naval interests. Neither condition now applies. The USSR has as great a stake in freedom of navigation as the United States. It needs the sea routes to supply isolated portions of Siberia, and its navy is far more dependent than the American navy on rights of egress through straits to reach open ocean. The West controls most choke points. Thus, Moscow joined Washington in supporting Article 38 (on free transit) of the United Nations Law of the Sea Conference (UNLOSC) draft convention, whereas China (still lacking a global navy) supported coastal states' demands to regulate passage. Nevertheless, Moscow backed Indonesian claims when Washington insisted that it would consider all major straits to be international waters.[8] Apparently, the Russians see more value in compromising general political principle for diplomatic purposes; given Indonesian assurance of access and inability to detect or identify submarines transiting without notification, and given that in wartime the superpowers would ignore local legal impediments anyway, this sort of pragmatism entails few costs. Moreover, the USSR does have some interest in keeping U.S. naval forces out of certain sea areas, in that it wants to create protected bastions for its own SSBNs.

Soviet economic interests in non-Communist Asia have grown, too, although the significance of this change is not reciprocal to the West. The relative importance of Soviet trade with Asia fell from 1955–78, but this was largely because of the break with the PRC. Initially, Moscow traded almost entirely with Communist countries, but the proportion was down to 45 percent by 1978. This reflected the basic change in policy from fostering a Communist trading bloc to acceptance of an integrated world economy. The largest amount of new trade in Asia has been with Japan. Apart from Vietnam, however, all Southeast Asian countries plus Australia and Japan send less than 4 percent of their exports to the Soviets and receive less than 1 percent of their imports from them.[9] In terms of intrinsic interests in Asia, the Russians' interests are primarily military and—concentrated in border areas with China—outside Southeast Asia. Derivative political and strategic interests in Southeast Asia are, virtually by definition, inverse to those of the United States.

The essential point is that for the United States, intrinsic economic interests in Southeast Asia have been increasing as its military capability in the area has been declining. (This is a potential problem only if the perceived decline in Communist military threats to U.S. clients since the 1960s were to be reversed.) In the early Cold War era, viewing the region as a derivative interest made sense for two reasons: (1) the relative economic interest in

Europe was greater, and (2) the Sino–Soviet alliance made the region an element in the global bipolar balance sheet. Today, the relative economic stakes have shifted, and the regional strategic equation is blurred between tripolarity (the United States, the USSR, and the PRC) and multipolarity (given the rise of nonalignment). In the future, given comparative Asian growth rates and the prospectively greater (and possibly ambiguous) role of Japan, these trends could accelerate. Although the Soviet Union's economic stakes are growing to a lesser degree, its military capabilities have grown more significantly. Though only a modest portion of the USSR's steady worldwide buildup, the relative shift is large because it proceeded from next to nothing in the region, whereas the United States scaled down tremendously from the high level of the 1950s and 1960s. Thus, in short, there is a steadily emerging gap between objective U.S. intrinsic economic interests and derivative strategic interests as perceived by strategic planners in Washington. This may not be especially problematic in regard to the Soviet Union itself, because direct combat is unlikely apart from a war that began elsewhere, but it highlights the import of local political conditions. One reason that the shift in U.S. commercial interests has not produced a comparable shift in strategic commitment to ASEAN as to Europe and Japan is that the other ingredient of affinity—liberal democratic governance—is missing.

Ideological Interests

The United States promotes the spread of democratic regimes as a fundamental part of its foreign policy. This goal is often hampered by and subordinated to the strategic requirements of East–West competition; negative denial of Communist influence or control over pro-Western authoritarian states takes precedence over positive assertions of idealism. Ideological values, however, are not simply humane goals to be dispensed with whenever they fail to coincide immediately with realpolitik. Broadening the ideological affinity of foreign countries contributes to the strength of the Western security coalition and the stability of the balance of power.[10] Indeed, the political democratization of the two greatest industrial nations apart from the superpowers—West Germany and Japan—was the greatest achievement of World War II and the most potent reinforcement of the economic and military power of the Western alliance vis-à-vis the Soviet bloc. Preserving public support for the principle of containment within the West, and within unstable authoritarian regimes allied with the United States, is also easier to the extent that the policy is seen as morally purposive rather than as a cynical lust for power. (Active support for democritization is also a power-oriented hedge against ouster of authoritarian governments—such as in Manila or Seoul—by credibly reducing more popular successors' excuses for animosity toward Washington.) The overwhelming rationale for the revolution in expansion of U.S. power—rejection of isolationism and commitment to containment after 1945—was a reversion to the old Wilsonian ideal: making the world safe for democracy. Two island anchors of Western alliance in the Pacific—Japan and Australia—are liberal democracies, but Japan's military role is restricted to defense of its own territory, and both countries remain peripheral strategic actors in Southeast Asia. The five ASEAN nations and South Korea have authoritarian governments more akin to what Sukarno called "directed democracies" than to forms resembling the American ideal.[11]

Promoting the liberalization of friendly regimes is the long-term American strategic interest, but it does not follow that the current dearth of democracy is palpably damaging to U.S. interests. One reason for promoting democracy is the perception that this would make local governments more stable, although that is more an article of faith to Americans than a demonstrable fact. In any case, preventing realignment or dealignment of those countries—through a change of policy by the regime or a change of regime—is the short-term imperative. The short-term interest does not overwhelm others, however, because in most of Southeast Asia (Thailand excepted) external Communist military threats are potential rather than immediate, and the strategic equation is not starkly bipolar, as it is in other regions of contest. Indeed, the most volatile local antagonisms are between the Communist powers themselves. After 1975, conflict in Indochina was no longer primarily ideological; its essence became classical *raison d'état*.[12] Communism in Southeast Asia is now less a threat to the West than it appeared in the 1960s, because it has been sapped of transnational solidarity. The ideological component of danger is indirect at best. Marxism-Leninism provides a source of discipline, cohesion, and motivation for revolutionaries that can overrun traditional societies where other social forces are particularistic, centrifugal, or lacking in national consciousness. (This was much of the U.S. problem in the Vietnam War, in which the American clients lacked the cooperative qualities for collective action and sacrifice that the Communist Vietnamese exhibited.) Only if internal Communist insurgencies in Thailand, Malaysia, and the Philippines were to fare far better than they have in recent years would this dimension of the political danger loom large. As it is, inter-Communist conflict on the mainland and the island nations' geographically ordained security from invasion present Washington with the chance to pursue a balance of power policy *and*, with some exceptions, long-term political-ideological objectives.

The most obvious limitations are still in Indochina. Thailand's direct exposure to hostile Vietnamese armies on its eastern border, together with the low degree of U.S. involvement (and thus leverage), makes the issue of ideological intervention moot; internal Thai stability, irrespective of whether it is based on authoritarian or democratic forms, will remain the prime concern. American pretensions to promoting human rights are also compromised by association with the Khmer Rouge, although the official U.S. position is that it supports the tripartite coalition, not the Pol Pot forces; Sihanouk and Sonn Sann were received in Washington in 1982, and there has been no official contact with the Khmer Rouge.[13]

Outside of Indochina, the task of combining political and security goals in Asia presents the greatest problems in three countries: Korea, Taiwan, and the Philippines. More than in most of Southeast Asia—where the limits on U.S. military involvement, presence, or aid also constitute limits on leverage—the United States is perceived to have some significant responsibility for the political status of these countries.

Each of the three countries reflects a different form of the problem. Korea and the Philippines both have active, visible, and potentially powerful protest movements as well as a large U.S. military presence and a formal alliance with Washington. Taiwan has none of these; opposition to the Kuomintang regime is more underground, and U.S. bases had dwindled even before the derecognition of 1978. The ROK and Taiwan both face significant external Communist threats. The Philippines does not. (Manila faces an internal Marxist threat, which until recently had been managed off and on for decades and was a less potent challenge to the regime than Moro separatism or the middle-class protestors who identified with Benigno Aquino. In 1983, President Marcos said, "Communism in the Philippines is not getting worse. . . . It is just like malaria.")[14] This nonchalant view is no longer tenable. American military forces in Korea are more a potential lever because their presence is more vital to Seoul than to Washington, but bases in the Philippines are more a hostage because their relative value is reversed.

Domestic political pressure inside the United States to compromise global strategic interests for the sake of local political concerns is not potent in regard to Seoul or Manila (for one thing, there are no significant ethnic constituencies for these countries as there are for, say, Greece and Israel), but it is in regard to Taipei. The Reagan administration has roots in the old China lobby that have been weakened but not severed by the appeal of securing Beijing as a tacitly allied counterweight to Moscow, and Taiwin still has significant support within Congress.

Taiwan no longer plays a direct role in U.S. military strategy since U.S. troops and bases have been withdrawn and normalization of relations with Beijing obviated the old treaty obligation to defend the island. American reservations regarding settlement of the dispute between the island and the mainland by force, however, leave open the tacit possibility of U.S. involvement should Beijing attempt to invade. Moreover, Taiwan retains importance to U.S. strategy in political terms. It is one of the prime symbols of economic success that validates the capitalist model of national development for the Third World, and although its regime is authoritarian (while Beijing's has been loosening), it is freer, with more potential for liberalization, than the PRC. Forcible absorption of Taiwan by the mainland would be a disaster for American diplomacy. So Washington will continue to try to bolster the island's defense capability with military sales but will have great difficulty meeting some of Taipei's requests—such as purchase of F-16 or F-20 fighter aircraft—given commitments to Beijing to limit the quantity and quality of such transfers over time.[15] An uncomfortable degree of tension remains between Washington's de facto stakes in Taiwan and its de jure commitments.

All of these variations make a consistent integration of U.S. security and political policy difficult at any point in time, and inconsistencies are compounded by the volatility of American domestic politics. In one decade, from the mid-1970s to the mid-1980s, there have been four different U.S. administrations, and each has had a different tilt. The Nixon doctrine, linked with a global détente policy toward Moscow, downplayed both ideological issues and military concerns. It scaled down security commitments in Southeast Asia, kept them constant in Korea,[16] and juggled them ambiguously in a diplomatic balancing act between Beijing and Taipei. The Ford administration, beset from the Republican right wing by 1976, remained discreetly indifferent to human rights questions but began moving toward a reinvigorated global security posture, although this shift did not focus on Asia.

Inconsistency and hesitancy reached a peak under the Carter administration. Initially, the administration took a relaxed view in the security dimension and an aggressive stance in favor of internal political reform among friendly authoritarian states. By the middle of the administration, the balance of concern shifted implicitly, although priorities were not consciously realigned (President Carter never being able to admit that not all good things could go together). Reassessment of North Korean strength, along with pressure from Japanese and American hawks, reversed the decision for partial military withdrawal in Korea, and the triple crisis in 1979–80—which focused anxiety on the military balance in the Persian Gulf (the fall of the Shah and the seizure of hostages, the oil price rise, and the invasion of Afghanistan)—placed a higher premium on bases in the Philippines. The liberal human rights policy was also compromised for strategic reasons—in Kampuchea, where Washington accepted the legitimacy of the deposed Khmer Rouge government over the Vietnamese-imposed Heng Samrin regime, and toward Taiwan, when full normalization with the People's Republic was undertaken.

The Reagan administration clearly placed priority on security; Patricia Derian's rhetoric was replaced by Jeane Kirkpatrick's. Human rights concerns complicated the shift, however, in regard to Taiwan, where continued U.S. arms sales to support the island's ability to resist absorption by the mainland damaged relations with Beijing, and tentatively in regard to the Philippines, where unrest after the Aquino assassination made even some of the most conservative U.S. officials worry about a dangerous analogy between Marcos and the Shah.

Of the three countries, the Philippines augurs the greatest danger. Callousness toward Taipei will continue to be overlooked, given the primacy of Beijing in global strategy; ironically for the Kuomintang, Taiwan might gain liberal American allies if it were indeed a political democracy that seemed as much a showcase as its capitalist economy, but sentimental support from the small coterie of right-wing Republicans will be an irritating nettle in U.S. policy rather than a determinant. The immediacy of the North Korean threat not only constrains the priority any U.S. administration will place on liberalization in Seoul; it also keeps a substantial portion of the democratic movement from turning its frustration in a strongly anti-American direction. In the Philippines, however, the lack of external threat means, first, that a future upheaval could indeed undermine U.S. security interests in the country and, second, that political support within the United States for active intervention on behalf of a beleaguered authoritarian clique in Manila would be weak.

There is little prospect for resolution of contradictory security and ideological goals, even if there is less turnover in the U.S. presidency than in the past decade. Consistent priorities can exist only at the extremes of overwhelming or negligible strategic focus on the region, and neither is possible. United States–USSR détente, even in a form as moderate as that of the early 1970s, is not likely to be reconstructed in the foreseeable future, and even then the global strategic competition would endure. And if U.S.–Soviet confrontation worsens, Asia will still remain a secondary or tertiary arena from Washington's viewpoint, so military stakes in the region will not swamp all others.

Military Trends

In the course of the 1970s U.S. military power relative to that of the Soviet Union declined. Both the extent and significance of that decline on a global level have been hotly contested analytically and politically within the United States. The military equation in Korea has not changed much.[17] Although Carter withdrew a small part of the Second Division (which had remained after Nixon withdrew the other division), this makes little difference in the basic function of U.S. forces there—to serve as a tripwire. The biggest problem would be if the United States became engaged in a war elsewhere—for example, the Persian Gulf—which siphoned reserves that would otherwise go to Korea in event of war. In Asia overall, and especially in Southeast Asia, the extent of the U.S. military decline is recognized as clearly greater than that in the world as a whole, yet there is also less anxiety and controversy about it among American strategists. The huge reductions in U.S. deployments in the region resulted in large part from the end of the Vietnam War. Reductions went substantially below prewar levels, but Sino–American rapprochement provided an excuse.

For a brief period after the fall of Saigon, Phnom Penh, and Vientiane in 1975, Asia appeared to be more stable than at any time since World War II. Doubts rose at the end of the decade with the controversy over President Carters' plan to withdraw ground forces from Korea, civil conflicts in the ROK after the assassination of Park Chung Hee, the Vietnamese invasion of Kampuchea, and the punitive Chinese attack on Vietnam, but these events did not materially alter the comparatively relaxed attitude toward the U.S. military role in the region. The decision to withdraw troops from Korea was reversed, taking that controversy off the agenda of debate, and no American policymakers considered direct military action an option for dealing with the Kampuchea problem. Regionally oriented U.S. policymakers were not very concerned with military instruments, and military-oriented policymakers were not very concerned with the region.

In principle, the danger that this situation could change is well recognized, but the buffers against reallocation of military resources remain strong. Soviet military power on the ground is far removed from Southeast Asia and is checked by China in Northeast Asia. The tentative entente between Washington and Beijing holds the potential for risk in the event of Sino–Soviet conflict, but the uncertainty of the U.S. intent to aid China leaves room for maneuver. Vietnam's military power is alarming to the extent that it is seen as a surrogate for Soviet expansion. So long as Vietnam remains focused on Kampuchea, however, this challenge will not be seen as significant enough to override the reluctance instilled by the experience of the 1960s about using U.S. military power in Indochina. Soviet use of Vietnamese facilities at Cam Ranh Bay and Danang worries U.S. strategists, but exploitation has remained below the objective potential of the bases. The Soviets' use of the facilities, however, has been gradually expanding in a fashion that suggests a more daunting Soviet presence as time passes. The bases markedly improve Soviet reconnaissance and intelligence collection capability, roughly doubling aerial coverage in the Western Pacific. A few TU-16 bombers were stationed at Cam Ranh at the end of 1983, and several more in late 1984, as well as MIG-23 fighters for air defense and midair refueling aircraft. Access to Cam Ranh has enabled Moscow to station attack submarines in the South China Sea for the first time. More extensive use of operating bases in Vietnam would do much to alleviate the Soviet navy's problem of exit through narrow straits around Japan.[18]

This potential, along with the general burgeoning of the Soviet navy, represents a challenge to the Reagan administration's shift toward a maritime strategy based on offshore firepower. Such a strategy is of questionable military utility, even with unimpeded use of the sea. In another Korean War, the balance of ground forces and land-based airpower would be most critical. Air bombardment and naval gunfire can support allied troops on land and can damage the logistical train for enemy ground forces (such as Vietnamese armies invading Thailand), but they cannot be decisive. Massive air war in the 1960s hampered but did not stop North Vietnamese reinforcement and supplies for combat in South Vietnam. And if it faced Soviet naval forces in combat, the U.S. Seventh Fleet would have to allocate most of its assets to self-defense, with little to spare to support friendly armies on land.

These constraints suggest that a maritime strategy offers meaningful help to mainland countries—particularly Thailand—only at the lowest of three levels of conflict: a limited Vietnamese probe that is not aimed at decisive defeat or occupation of Thailand. With fewer than 200,000 troops now in Kampuchea and tied down by guerrilla warfare, a Vietnamese attack on Thailand *might* be contained by Thai forces with U.S. fire support. At the other extreme, though, the problem would not be much of a concern—in a direct U.S.–Soviet military conflict, Communist advances on the ground in Southeast Asia would be near the least of Western worries. Perhaps the most problematic contingency, therefore, is the intermediate one: a major war between Vietnam and Thailand, without a Soviet combat role, in which U.S. commitment to Bangkok is brought into play but naval and air firepower is insufficient to save the day. The best hope in this instance is that the Chinese threat in the north would prevent Vietnam from transferring the bulk of its army westward. Considering the Chinese attack in 1979, subsequent allusions to the possibility of a "second lesson," and artillery exchanges in the mid-1980s, it is entirely plausible that Beijing would launch another offensive against Hanoi if it struck into Thailand.

Changes in military technology are not likely to bear much on this problem. The Reagan administration is changing the tactical capabilities of U.S. forces relevant to this sort of contingency only in incremental ways, and not with the dramatic innovations that could lie on the horizon for other elements of strategic power. One is the planned expansion of the navy to 600 ships, including additional aircraft carrier task forces. Another is the recommissioning of battleships, which—if unthreatened by Soviet bombers—can add to power projection by coastal gunfire and long-range cruise missiles. Cruise missiles are a useful technical innovation, but they offer decisive firepower only when they carry nuclear ordnance. Conventionally armed cruise missiles can help strike fixed targets that are too well defended for manned aircraft to attack, but otherwise cruise missiles' per-unit cost unit makes them unattractive substitutes for manned aircraft, and their low numbers (they cannot be reused, as aircraft can) mean that in a prolonged war, they would be quickly exhausted.[19] The development of various other sorts of precision-guided munitions makes prospective use of tactical airpower more effective than it was in previous wars, but not enough to replace the ability of ground forces to take and hold territory. Though poorly equipped, the Vietnamese army dwarfs not only Thailand's but all of ASEAN's combined, and with a million men it is even larger than the entire U.S. Army and Marine Corps.

Unless Washington were to repeal the Nixon doctrine and prepare for a combat role in Southeast Asia comparable to what it undertook in the 1960s, purely military considerations would appear to recommend a major buildup of ASEAN military forces. This could be unwise in the full context of local economic and political conditions.[20] However, although the Reagan administration's global policy has been dominated by military resurgence, its Southeast Asia policy has not. This again reflects the extent to which the region is seen as a strategic backwater and the probability that strategic problems in the area will probably continue to be addressed by muddling through rather than by an ambitious new master plan.

Local Interests and U.S. Aims

In Northeast Asia, local friends' strategic interests coincide fairly closely with what Washington wants to provide. There are tensions between Tokyo and Washington over economic issues—trade and defense burden sharing—but no basic disagreements over security objectives (barring the views of Japanese socialists, who have never been able to gain power). Seoul's security policy is completely aligned with U.S. commitment, and almost all freedom of maneuver in the strategic relationship belongs to the Americans. There is less identity of overall interests between Washington and Beijing, but the USSR provides the basis for cautious tacit alignment. Neither the Americans nor the Chinese want to be fully committed to each other's support to retain some room for maneuver with Moscow, and the Taiwan problem represents future grounds for conflict. The common interests of the present, though, argue against precipitate action by either side to resolve underlying sources of disagreement.

Because U.S. security interests in Southeast Asia are largely derivative, they overlap only partially with those of friendly local countries. For most of the regional states—Thailand being a conspicuous exception—the divergences are only a latent source of tension in the relationship for the same reason that the area is a low military priority for the United States: the low level of external Communist threat. In the late 1970s, Southeast Asian governments realized, as three observers note:

. . . that American intervention is most likely to occur in the least likely contingencies, such as large-scale conflict among major powers and is least likely to materialize in the most likely contingencies, such as insurgencies or local armed conflict between neighboring countries. In other words, the United States is still seen as a formidable global power, but is no longer considered the custodian of a particular regional order in Southeast Asia.[21]

The image of American skittishness has receded more recently, but there is still little reason to expect conventional military intervention against domestic threats. The relaxed American view of the international military equation was reflected in statements by Secretary of Defense Weinberger during a trip in late 1982. Though representing the most hawkish U.S. administration of the postwar era, Weinberger said that defense expenditures by ASEAN countries were high enough and that there was no need to press them (as the administration was pressing other allies) on security matters.[22] There is a latent tension in this situation, however. Washington has positive relations with ASEAN and can afford to remain strategically relaxed because the area is relatively stable. Residual concern about containment in the area is covered by vague faith in China's deterrent role; but if that role has to be exercised, strains would arise between U.S. and ASEAN interests. Therefore, if the stability of regional order is challenged, the destabilization may be compounded. In short, the congruence of U.S. and local interests could be most compromised when it is most needed.

Coordinating Strategic Objectives

The anti-Soviet powers in Northeast Asia share the U.S. view of an appreciable Soviet threat in that region, so coordination of military aims has been relatively close. The fact that most of the Southeast Asian states share the relaxed view of external military threat in that region is reflected in the tentativeness and ambiguity of local defense cooperation measures that could substitute for formal alliance with Washington, although this low-profile approach also results from the desire to maintain a nonprovocative image toward the Communist powers. A network of bilateral cooperation is substituting for multilateral forms that would appear too much like a revivified SEATO. This involves "sharing intelligence, efforts to standardize command systems and bilateral exercises."[23] Other ASEAN states resisted Singapore's suggestion of expanded cooperation because it would seem too close to a pact. Since 1971, a formal Five Power Defense Arrangement has linked Malaysia, Singapore, Australia, New Zealand, and Britain, but it is weak—characterized by the U.S. Defense Department's Richard Armitage as "dormant" since inception and "a relatively innocuous grouping."[24] Cooperation among the member-countries did increase in the early 1980s, but more in bilateral terms than under the formal aegis of the Arrangement.[25]

In terms of military strategy in the region, the U.S. shift to an offshore posture based on air and naval firepower recalls the Eisenhower administration's stance, although that was different in terms of both its applicable power and its target. Strategy in the 1950s was directed against China and was based on early resort to nuclear weapons, although U.S. conventional capabilities deployed in the region were also far greater then than today. The lesser amount of U.S. firepower now deployed is linked to the changed role of China; Washington has implicitly ceded the role of deterrence on the ground (against Vietnam) to the PRC.

The U.S. withdrawal from the Vietnam War was less worrisome to Indonesia than to Thailand because a "blue water" strategy covered the island nations. In the Philippines, Marcos did not feel the need for the Mutual Security Treaty to deter conventional attack, but he did want it to cover territorial claims that conflict with other countries, such as in the Spratly Islands.[26] (The fact that Washington would not agree is related to Marcos's irritating jockeying over renewal of base agreements.) American strategic interests are not identical to those of the archipelagic countries, but they generally complement the interests of these countries and especially other offshore countries relevant to the region—including Japan, Australia, and New Zealand (though not Taiwan). The offshore countries are both more important and less vulnerable. None have intense conflicts with Communist states or "irreconcilable differences among themselves. Thus, although the United States has formal security treaties with all but Indonesia, the potential demand for military help in defending against external attack is low."[27]

This is far less true on the mainland. Thailand has the least assurance of outside assistance commensurate with the security threats it faces. After U.S. disengagement from Vietnam, Thai leaders sought to combine non-provocation of Hanoi and balance of power diplomacy. Initially, this involved phasing out SEATO, proclaiming an independent foreign policy, and seeking Soviet intercession with Vietnam; Kriangsak's visit to Moscow in March 1979 was the first ever by a Thai prime minister. As Michael Leifer put it, this was a policy of "flawed neutrality."[28] The Thais could not accept the Soviet proposal for a collective security arrangement because this would alienate the PRC; and after the Vietnamese border incursion in June 1980, Chinese support was needed all the more as a deterrent. Yet decisive reliance on Beijing was not a comfortable option: "China is a permanent factor in the region, and while the Soviet Union continues to support Vietnam, Thai efforts to benefit from Chinese protection in the absence of countervailing U.S. support, entail a subordination that has previously been temporary."[29] Moreover, although greater political distance from Washington was required to reassure Hanoi in the late 1970s, fastening the residual U.S. security commitment under the Manila Treaty was important as Vietnamese troops probed in the early 1980s; Washington sent an emergency consignment of weapons after the border crossing, although it was more a token gesture than a meaningful boost to Thai capabilities. And in 1983, the Soviets reportedly gave

Bangkok assurances that the Vietnamese would not attack.[30] So Thailand has reason to continue pursuing multiple avenues of support, and each avenue is likely to produce only limited or tentative results: diplomatic pressure from Moscow on Hanoi, military pressure from Beijing on Hanoi, and military assistance from Washington.

From the U.S. point of view, the only country in Indochina that does not pose difficult choices for balancing acts is the one that is least important—Laos. This was the only one of the fallen "dominoes" in 1975 with which Washington retained diplomatic relations. Vientiane poses no aggressive threat and is buffeted by two insurgent movements (supported by China and Thailand), so the United States can stand back and offer "proper" relations, sweetened by token assistance. (Congress banned foreign aid, but the Reagan administration used exempted disaster relief funds for a hospital and offered to find buyers for T-28s flown to Thailand after the 1975 Pathet Lao victory.[31]) There is an unpleasantly heavy Vietnamese and Soviet presence in the country, but this is almost a superfluous threat to China and Thailand given their borders with Vietnam. Any degree of civility between Washington and Vientiane is worse for Moscow and Hanoi than for any other countries involved. Laotian weakness facilitates a welcome but scarcely significant bit of diplomatic amity.

It is impossible for the United States to establish a similar diplomatic relationship with Hanoi so long as the Vietnamese occupy Kampuchea and threaten Thailand, but the desire to avoid military entanglement in Indochina has led the United States to take a position that gives friendly local states mixed feelings. The United States has refused to give overt military aid to Sonn Sann's forces, the stronger non-Communist element of the tripartite anti-Vietnamese coalition in Kampuchea. (At this writing proposals are afoot in Congress to provide small amounts of aid.) Singapore reportedly has supplied Sonn Sann and Sihanouk's National Army with light arms, but the U.S. position, by default, gives greater weight to the PRC's support for the Khmer Rouge. For most of ASEAN, solving the Kampuchean problem must not be done in a way that increases Beijing's power position in the area.[32] American diplomacy may dance around this issue, but it does represent a conflict between U.S. global anti-Soviet interests and local ASEAN interests.

Malaysia and especially Indonesia are the most opposed to a Chinese role in regional security, seeing Vietnam as a lesser threat. Not only does Jakarta blame the PRC for the coup attempt and upheaval of 1965, but animosity toward domestic Chinese populations is present throughout Southeast Asia. It was well noted that the Chinese attack on Vietnam in 1979 was provoked in part by Hanoi's actions against indigenous Chinese. Although Beijing reduced support for Communist insurgent movements after the 1970s, continued insistence on separating state-to-state and party-to-party relations leaves local capitals wary and thus unenthusiastic about U.S. inclinations toward de facto alliance with the PRC.[33] Reconciliation between China and Hanoi would have ambiguous implications for both the United States and ASEAN. If it happened by weaning Hanoi away from Moscow, this would be beneficial for Washington in global terms but might be worrisome locally if the two Communist states could then turn cooperatively toward supporting subversion in the region.

In the near term, some regional observers have seen a silver lining in the Indochinese cloud. To court ASEAN, Vietnam gave up support for insurgencies in Thailand and Malaysia; and to compete, China muted its support, too, even though the insurgent Communist parties favored Beijing in its conflict with Hanoi. Especially in Thailand, the rebel forces declined markedly.[34] The "appeasement option"—allowing Vietnam to satisfy itself with domination of Indochina—also appealed to some. But if absorption of the neighboring countries were accomplished, Vietnam "would assume a different kind of interest in the political fortunes of Thailand than if Kampuchea and Laos had assumed the role of genuine buffer states. In other words, for Vietnam, Thailand would then come to assume the role of buffer state."[35] So long as Hanoi and Beijing are in conflict, ASEAN remains in a bind, though, because uncompromising resistance could lead not only Vietnam to aid insurgents again, but also its patron, the USSR. The Soviet deputy foreign minister reportedly dropped warnings to this effect in Singapore.[36]

If Chinese–Vietnamese détente happened as part of a Sino–Soviet reconciliation, this would be a negative development for both U.S. and ASEAN interests, as multipolar equilibrium reverted toward a more challenging bipolarity. On balance, though, U.S. and ASEAN interests converge in a compromise status for China: sufficient weakness to preclude an independent and aggressive military posture, but sufficient strength to resist Moscow and inhibit Hanoi. If Chinese military development shortchanges naval power and airpower and strengthens ground forces without providing the mobility and logistics necessary for long-range operations, such a reasonable compromise would be feasible. But it would still be an unstable equilibrium; the line between too little and too much Chinese strength is impossible to draw, and the uncertainty is tolerable only so long as China's potential is not called into play.

Other alternatives to U.S. power for bolstering the Western security position are Japan and Australia. (New Zealand could offer little even if it had not cracked the alliance in 1985 by refusing visits of nuclear-powered U.S. ships.) Three problems limit this option. First, it would supplement only the U.S. offshore strategy, leaving the issue of deterrence on the ground. Second, only Japan has enough potential power to weigh significantly against major

Communist states, and to ASEAN an enhanced role for Japan is far preferable to one for China only so long as Japan's potential is not fully developed. One Australian official's proposal for a joint peacekeeping force with Japan to allow removal of Vietnamese troops—though promising as a symbol of Australian willingness to accept wider responsibilities—is neither feasible nor desirable to most local nations. Singapore's foreign minister approved a Japanese buildup for purposes of *self*-defense because it would relieve the United States of some missions, allowing it to redeploy resources elsewhere in the Pacific. As Weatherbee notes, however, most of ASEAN fears that U.S. rhetoric about Japanese burden sharing is "a euphemism for 'burden-shifting. No Southeast Asian country wants to see Japan become a surrogate for absent American power."[37] When the dimensions of the new 1,000-mile Japanese defense perimeter were clarified—by stating that it extends from Tokyo and Osaka, rather than from the lower tip of Japan, and southward but not westward—Southeast Asian anxieties were muted. But a much greater Japanese military role will be acceptable only if it is integrated in a broader western alliance and subordinated to U.S. forces' command. This could be the "JANZUS" solution, utilizing Japanese strength while controlling it, in a manner similar to the full integration of West Germany in NATO, which was necessary for European acceptance of German rearmament. But such integration is not feasible for Tokyo for domestic political reasons, because it constitutes formal alliance.[38] Ironically, the arrangement that would assuage fears of Japanese activism is resisted by the Japanese polity precisely because it wants to avoid activist entanglements. And the realistic domestic political limits on prospective Japanese military buildup are such that the likelihood of a radical increase in Tokyo's security role in the foreseeable future is a moot question.

The basic problem blocking full congruence of ASEAN and American interests is that local strategic reality is more multipolar than the global overlay that dominates U.S. concerns. China is not a formal ally in the Western coalition against the USSR, but coincidence of interests makes it tacitly so. This coincidence is less significant for some of ASEAN because the USSR does not threaten them noticeably more than China does. Even those facing the Vietnamese threat have a stake in not provoking Moscow, which can help restrain Hanoi, when the alternate choice of Chinese help would offer either too little (failing to deter Vietnam) or too much (replacing Vietnam as the hegemonic threat). Although ASEAN resists the Soviet collective security proposal, the ASEAN scheme for a neutrality zone (ZOP-FAN) therefore has a natural appeal, and it could be acceptable to Washington if feasible. A ZOPFAN, however, could only *reflect* a prior solution to the problems that could motivate external intervention, not cause it, and the feasibility of isolating the region is dubious.

Domestic Security and International Security

In Northeast Asia, doubts about internal stability affect U.S. interests in regard to Korea and China. If Washington has much leverage on either government or opposition in Seoul, it is hard to discern how it has been used. Pyongyang, on the other hand, has often acted recklessly, and it is difficult to predict how that pattern might change under Kim Il Sung's successors. The potential for change in PRC politics that affects U.S. policy is not any danger to the regime itself, but the question is whether Deng Hsiao-ping's moves toward liberalization and good relations with Washington will endure or the old guard might succeed in reasserting itself.

Alan Goodman has persuasively argued that there are four sources of instability in Southeast Asia—a Western power vacuum since U.S. withdrawal from Vietnam, Vietnamese adventurism since then, insurgent movements, and societal change—and that the last of these is the greatest problem. Elements of this problem include urbanization reaching the point of severe strain on government services and legitimacy; fragmenting racial, religious, and ethnic tensions that could accelerate dangerously at any time in several countries; and trends in elite competition and exclusion.[39] The United States faces three difficulties. First, it has little reason to become involved in these problems other than indirectly through economic aid. Second, Americans could do little to affect the course of these developments even if they tried to intervene politically, through covert operations or otherwise. But third, some of these developments could metastasize to the point that they spill over into the East–West conflict dimension that does interest Washington or produce worrisome forms of non-Communist nationalism. Interstate conflicts in ASEAN have declined in recent decades, but some have not been fully or permanently resolved (such as the Philippine claim to Sabah). New aggressive nationalists in power, whether rightist or leftist, could resurrect such antagonisms.

Weak leadership in Thailand and aging strongmen in Singapore, the Philippines, and Indonesia make the issue of succession important, which in turn makes the diverse insurgent or protest movements that are now manageable potentially more problematic.[40] Autonomist Islamic groups in Thailand and the Philippines or prospective Muslim unrest in Indonesia[41] might worry U.S. policymakers more than they should because of facile analogies to the threat of "Islamic fundamentalism" as it is seen in Iran or the Middle East. But in combination with the large number of Communist and other insurgent movements in the region—the NPA in the Philippines, five different groups in Indonesia, more than can be counted in Burma, and residual

Communist guerrillas in Malaysia and Thailand—the variety of threats to government control in the event of a regime crisis is substantial.

The dangers represent the prime security threat to local states and thus a current divergence between their principal strategic concerns and Washington's. For reasons of comparative disinterest or importance, Washington cannot deal with potential threats of this sort and can only file them away until a point at which the potential may be actuated. The only realistic hedge would be to modify support for present governments, in case their replacements blame Washington for the sins of the *ancien regime,* but this contradicts the aim of cooperation and solidarity (against external Communist powers) with the governments that now determine the regional order. In short, in regard to the most likely sources of change, the United States is in the position that always makes strategists uncomfortable: the reactive position. Analytical consciousness of potential threats does not necessarily offer a basis for policy change when interests at different levels conflict. Perhaps correctly, but in any case probably, U.S. political initiatives will remain focused on the regional international order and on the external Communist powers, both of which mean continuing to develop positive relations with local governments.

Working at the Margins

So long as current common interests in Northeast Asia endure (strategically, with China and South Korea, and more generally, with Japan), compatible strategic stances should also endure. The most visible potential complication is how the Taiwan tangle is handled. In Southeast Asia, so long as U.S. posture and commitments in the region do not revert to those of the 1950s and 1960s—confronting *all* the Communist powers in Asia—some divergence between U.S. and ASEAN strategies will endure. This makes the integration of political and security goals in U.S. strategy in both parts of Asia more a diplomatic challenge than a military one. This should involve a discreetly discriminatory approach to the local states—for example, not expecting much from Indonesia (which is more independent vis-à-vis the U.S.–Soviet conflict and more anti-Chinese) and seeking more from Singapore (which also has the potential for partially offsetting reduced access to Philippine bases).

Managing Strategic Competition

Containing Soviet power appears to be a relatively manageable task in Southeast Asia, because that region is no greater a priority for Moscow than for Washington. The Soviet military buildup in the area has been impressive, but it is not proportionally larger than elsewhere; Moscow, too, has a "Europe first" principle, and now, more than Washington, it has a "China second" requirement for deterrence. In earlier times, the principal Soviet interest in the area was an extension of the global move to exploit neutralism and Third World nationalism to circumscribe Western power whenever possible. This was consistent with Moscow's June 1969 proposal for a regional collective security system. The USSR still faces a network of bilateral and multilateral anti-Communist treaties—between the United States, Japan, Australia, New Zealand, the Philippines, and Thailand, and between Britain, Singapore, Australia, New Zealand, and Malaysia—as well as extensive U.S. bases in Japan and the Philippines. The collective security scheme would break up this Western coalition and give the USSR regional access as a security guarantor, thereby giving it the chance to inhibit operation of U.S. conventional forces between the Pacific and Indian Oceans. When it was reiterated in 1972, the proposal was explained as similar to Soviet treaties with Egypt, Iraq, and India.[42]

The Soviet collective security proposal has not fared well. After 1975, ASEAN governments tentatively saw some balance of power value in limited Soviet presence because it would induce the United States to remain involved and, together, would limit Chinese influence. But the collective security proposal excluded other external actors and thus the possibility of a real balance of power.[43] Unilateral Soviet moves have not produced dramatic results either. Lack of economic and political influence make the overall superpower balance—the "correlation of forces" in Soviet terms—still unfavorable to Moscow, despite military gains. The military progress, Indochina aside, has not yielded comparable politial advances because of the enduring pro-Western character of the regional equilibrium.[44] This is due to the following factors:

> (1) The new cold war among the Communist states, (2) China's dramatic turn to the West, (3) the gradual reassertion of Japan, (4) the end of the period of American "drift," (5) the development of ASEAN, (6) the Korean stand-off, and (7) the dynamic economic growth in the region that could lead to a new Pacific-Asian trading-community. . . . The Soviets are faced in the Asia-Pacific region with countervailing military power, regional cohesion, and socio-economic resilience. . . . The main Soviet interests in the region are likely to remain essentially conservative ones. Moscow's principal goal will be to prevent the emergence of an anti-Soviet coalition in the region.[45]

Indochina is an important exception to this reassuring equilibrium. Vietnam is the linchpin of Soviet influence in Southeast Asia: it is by far the most militarily powerful state in the region, it is a southern bulwark against China, and it provides valuable access to facilities at Cam Ranh and Danang.

Vietnam's value is mitigated by its drain on scarce Soviet resources—$3 million to $4 million in aid each day, as of late 1983[46]—and by some modest tensions with Hanoi. Vietnam has still not formally granted the Russians permanent bases, it embarrassed them with incursions into Thailand, and it has opposed attempts to extend their influence in Laos and Cambodia.[47] These tensions are of minor significance, however, compared to the tightening of alignment since the late 1970s and the joint interests Moscow and Hanoi share against Washington and Beijing.

Putting a wedge between Vietnam and the Soviet Union would be attractive, but even if it were feasible, it could involve potential problems for the regional balance of power. Before the conflict between Hanoi and the Khmer Rouge regime and the PRC, there may have been some chance for fostering distance between Vietnam and the Soviet Union. In the first couple of years after the fall of Saigon, the Socialist Republic of Vietnam (SRV) maintained some visible independence from the USSR, did not castigate ASEAN as an imperialist surrogate, did not support the Soviet collective security proposal, and still had hopes of securing Western aid for national reconstruction; but by 1978, Vietnam was a member of COMECON and had a friendship treaty making it a regular member of the Soviet bloc.[48] In the interim, which was still painfully close to the humiliating debacle of 1975 that had climaxed decades of U.S. effort to preserve the independence of South Vietnam, it was impractical for the Carter administration to move swiftly toward rapprochement, especially since it was expending some domestic political capital in doing so toward Cuba—and after hostility between Hanoi and Beijing intensified, a U.S. initiative toward Vietnam could have upset negotiations on normalization with the PRC. Washington no longer holds the main chips in the game; détente with Hanoi depends on resolution of the Kampuchea problem and on détente between Hanoi and Beijing.

The Soviets might be able to pressure the Vietnamese toward concessions on Kampuchea, but this is scarcely conceivable unless it is part of a Sino–Soviet reconciliation, which would not serve U.S. interests in the overall strategic competition. To the extent that the inter-Communist conflict creates the potential for crisis and escalation, however, such a deal could have some benefits that would partially offset the losses on the global chessboard. It is easy to forget, after the fact, that the Chinese attack on Vietnam in 1979 was potentially far more dangerous than was generally recognized, in that it raised the specter of war between the USSR and the PRC. In retrospect, Soviet restrain in the amount of support it gave its client was more prudent than Americans had a right to expect. When China struck, Moscow noted its treaty obligations and urged Beijing to stop. The PRC stated publicly that the war was limited and punitive, and Soviet officials indicated to diplomats that they would refrain from intervention so long as the Chinese effort did, indeed, remain so limited.[49] In effect, keeping the crisis from reaching the flashpoint required keeping Chinese intervention from forcing a resolution of the Kampuchean situation. In this respect, China holds more of the cards than either of the superpowers in regard to Indochina, even though the United States became the "pivot" in the overall triangular relationship after 1969.[50] And the embarrassing ineffectiveness of the Chinese attack did as much to tarnish its perceived deterrent role as to reinforce it. Yet to have done better would have heightened the risks of global conflagration. China cannot function as a U.S. proxy to reverse Vietnamese hegemony in Indochina without threatening wider U.S. interests in stability; at best, it may contain Vietnam within Kampuchea. Thus, there is no practical active strategy to keep that local sore point from festering.

Unhappily, then, it could be that continuing instability in Kampuchea goes hand in hand with wider stability in Asia and between the superpowers. (For example, the unsettled situation in Kampuchea inhibits the outbreak of conflict over claims in the Spratly and Paracel Islands, because "neither China nor Vietnam wish to alienate any claimant member states" of ASEAN.[51]) For the United States, in these respects as in others previously noted, the extent of global strategic interests and the limits of desired strategic entanglement in the region indicate an interest in being able to "use" the region without being fully "responsible" for it. The Philippine base issue highlights this ambiguous aim.

Philippine Bases

Controversy about U.S. military bases in the Philippines is an old story. Even Filipino arguments that the bases endanger the country's security by making it a nuclear target go back a long way.[52] The United States manages the latter problem by resorting to a general policy of neither confirming nor denying the presence of nuclear weapons at overseas bases, although circumstantial evidence suggests that such weapons may indeed be stored in the Philippines. (In March 1978, for example, the U.S. commander at Subic Bay issued orders about what to do in the event of nuclear materials accidents, although this instruction could relate to ship reactors.[53]) In brief, the nuclear storage question reflects the objective difference—beyond symbolic sensitivities about national sovereignty—in Philippine strategic interests in the base.

Washington has justifications to offer for the bases in terms of regional interests, but these interests are weak compared to the wider role of the bases.[54] The Marcos government thus has more than just mercenary reasons for driving a hard bargain in renewal of the base agreements (a $900 million aid proviso was the price tag in the 1983 revision). Some of the tactics used are worrisome, however, at least symbolically. Less than a week after Marcos told visiting U.S. congressmen that they could remove U.S. bases if the Philippine price was too high, Foreign Minister Carlos Romulo released a

Soviet letter seeking closer relations. Manila's shift to a more independent policy toward the Third World and its greater stake in the Arab world for overseas jobs and oil raise doubts about whether Washington would be assured the free use of Subic and Clark in the event of a Middle East crisis (use of Clark was barred for offensive missions during the Vietnam War).[55] The 1979 agreement provided for review and revision every five years, which could make bargaining a near-constant ordeal for the United States.

Some have argued that removing the bases would be not only feasible but strategically advantageous, increasing U.S. freedom of action as much as constricting it. George Kahin wrote that the Reagan administration committed the United States to supporting Philippine forces anywhere in the Pacific, which could make Washington complicit in Philippine claims in the South China Sea that conflict with Vietnam, the PRC, and Taiwan. (This overstated the U.S. commitment, but there is certainly some potential relationship between reliance on Philippine territory and entanglement in Philippine policy.) He also argued that operational constraints from shifting to facilities in Guam, Tinian, and Australia would be manageable.[56] Political access to such alternative locations would indeed probably be more reliable, and there have been moves in that direction already; in 1981, Australia agreed to let U.S. B-52s and KC-135s operate out of Darwin into the Indian Ocean. But antinuclear sentiments in the Australian Labour Party raise questions about how permanently secure such arrangements might be under future conditions. And there are political impediments even on Guam.[57] So long as U.S. stakes in bases are primarily for Middle East contingencies or global conflict with the USSR and local stakes are regional in nature, the balance of potential risks and benefits for *any* host to U.S. bases could seem uncertain; the assurance of sufficient American help in regional conflicts may not seem much greater than the possibility that the host country could be attacked in a wider conflict.

Uncertainties work against spending $2 billion to $3 billion to build new facilities elsewhere when they would pose operational constraints—even if manageable—greater than those in the Philippines. As a former U.S. commander in chief in the Pacific, Admiral Long, put it: "In the end we would have less capability for more money than we have now."[58] The natural inertia that goes with high sunk costs in the Philippine infrastructure makes a large change in Pacific basing unlikely, even under a different U.S. administration that might be more concerned with the political issues. The danger in such inertia is that a crisis could force hasty and ineffective adaptation. The base issue could explode if Filipino politics degenerate, or use of the facilities could be most impeded just at the time they were most needed—for example, in a U.S.–Soviet confrontation in the Persian Gulf. The most prudent and realistically imaginable compromise between inertia and reform is not an immediate decision to close shop in the Philippines but creeping reorganization. Infrastructure might be gradually diversified, shifting some functions to other locations to distribute political risk, thereby incrementally reducing the concentration at Subic and Clark. This would entail some penalty in peacetime operational efficiency, but that is outweighed by greater reliability for the wartime contingencies that matter. Even small skeletal new installations, if sprinkled around, would provide a useful hedge by creating a basis for expansion if need arose. This course is budgetarily attractive as well (limiting cost and spreading its impact over a longer period), and it would provide counterleverage against Filipino compensation demands (demonstrating willingness to readjust). This would preserve the connection with Manila while also attenuating support for the Marcos government, which offers some hedge against a change of regime.

Diffusion of Deterrence

There is little reason to believe that the gap between increasing economic interest and reduced military presence in Southeast Asia will be closed in advance of a crisis that would make the advisability of such a shift too obvious for overloaded American policymakers to ignore. The change in relative economic importance of Asia and Europe will not yield any decisive shift of U.S. stratgic focus, because the underlying historical and cultural sources of the priority of Europe are overwhelming. To the extent that policymakers focus on a linkage between economic interests and military strategy, the focus will be on the Middle East and Persian Gulf, where political ignition points for crisis are clearer than anywhere else. To the extent that more military attention and effort are devoted to Asia, it will be more in Northeast Asia, where power on all sides is more concentrated and the inertia of tradition reinforces recognized strategic interest to maintain U.S. presence on the ground (in Japan and Korea). There is still too much strategic urgency to go around in the world for Southeast Asia's military and political priority to come into line with its economic priority. Although this conservative view will appear to be an irresponsibly misbegotten curse if a great regional crisis eventuates, it reflects the current blessing of relative stability. Stability and conservatism (and thus lack of major change in U.S. policy) are sides of the same coin. Dangers that are potential more than actual have to take second place to current challenges elsewhere.

Two countries on the Asian periphery, however, should have a different view. In strategic terms, Japan and Australia are naturally more oriented to the region than the United States is.[59] They are also politically in concert with most U.S. goals. And because the rising economic importance of Southeast Asia to the United States is a reflection of the global diffusion of power, it is reasonable to consider adapting through diffusion of strategic responsibility. As noted earlier, there are ample barriers to shifting U.S. military burdens to these countries. Japan is inhibited by the feelings of its own citizens as well as those of Korea and ASEAN. Australia lacks the capacity, let alone the will, to become a great power.

Consistent with the characterization of the regional situation as relatively stable and of prospective changes in U.S. posture as probably modestly incremental, it helps to think in terms of incrementalism in the diffusion of strategic functions. This could mean steady encouragement of Japan to increase its foreign aid, to the point that it could help improve indigenous Korean and ASEAN defense capabilities. Tokyo has already used its foreign aid in Southeast Asia as an excuse for resisting U.S. pressure for higher Japanese defense expenditures. Washington might embrace the principle that such aid is indeed a security function, point out that total Japanese aid is still trivial in terms of overall U.S. and Japanese security spending, and counter citations of domestic sensitivity against building national military power by accepting a radical increase in subsidies for friendly Asian forces as a substitute for Japanese military increases beyond those already planned by Tokyo. For Australia, the U.S. aims might be, first, to encourage a more assertive leadership role for Canberra in the Five Power Defense Arrangement and, second, to cooperate in the creeping diversification of U.S. base facilities suggested earlier. If these aims are diplomatically too ambitious, one can only conclude that the two U.S. allies in the Pacific that represent the greatest combination of political stability, economic development, and compatibility of purpose do not see more reason to bolster the Western position in Asia than Washington does.

Notes

1. Donald S. Zagoria and Sheldon W. Simon, "Soviet Policy in Southeast Asia," in Donald S. Zagoria, ed., *Soviet Policy in East Asia* (New Haven: Yale University Press, 1982), p. 172.

2. Desmond Ball, *Politics and Force Levels: The Strategic Missile Program of the Kennedy Administration* (Berkeley: University of California Press, 1980), pp. 190–91. In 1960, the commandant of the Marine Corps, General David Shoup, was considered a disruptive gadfly when he protested to the secretary of defense, "Sir, any plan that kills millions of Chinese when it isn't even their war is not a good plan. This is not the American way." Quoted in Fred Kaplan, *The Wizards of Armageddon* (New York: Simon and Schuster, 1983), p. 270.

3. See Charles A. Stevenson, *The End of Nowhere: American Policy Toward Laos Since 1954* (Boston: Beacon Press, 1972), pp. 118–49.

4. In recent years, Central America and the Caribbean have become an important area of concern, but geographic proximity and relative weakness of adversary conventional forces in the area preclude the need to divert a large portion of logistical or combat resources from other commitments.

5. For more extensive discussion, see Richard K. Betts, "Washington, Tokyo, and Northeast Asian Security: A Survey," *Journal of Strategic Studies* 6 (December 1983): 5–30.

6. *U.S. Department of State Bulletin*, October 1982, p. 33.

7. See Michael MccGwire, "The Geopolitical Importance of Strategic Waterways in the Asian-Pacific Region," *Orbis* 19 (Fall 1975): 1058–76.

8. Yaacov Vertzberger, "The Malacca/Singapore Straits," *Asian Survey* 22 (July 1982): 609, 613, 615; Susumu Awanohara and Rodney Tasker, "Indonesia's Golden Pond," *Far Eastern Economic Review*, 6 January 1983, pp. 12–13.

9. Ed. A. Hewett and Herbert S. Levine, "The Soviet Union's Economic Relations in Asia," in Zagoria, ed., *Soviet Policy in East Asia*, pp. 203–6.

10. Although he takes the point too far, Michael Doyle presents an intriguing analysis of the historical spread of democracy. He notes: "Even though liberal states have become involved in numerous wars with nonliberal states, constitutionally secure liberal states have yet to engage in war with one another" (italics deleted). Doyle, "Kant, Liberal Legacies, and Foreign Affairs," *Philosophy and Public Affairs* 12 (Summer 1983): 213.

11. "Southeast Asia's Boom Belt," *World Press Review* 30 (February 1983): 31 (reprinted from *Wirtschaftswoche*).

12. Michael Leifer, *Conflict and Regional Order in South-East Asia*, Adelphi Paper No. 162 (London: International Institute for Strategic Studies, Winter 1980), p. 2.

13. U.S. Department of State, "Kampuchea After 5 years of Vietnamese Occupation," *Current Policy*, no. 514 (15 September 1983): 3.

14. Quoted in "Philippines: A Fighting Stance," *Asia Week*, 22 July 1983, p. 12.

15. See Peter Samuel, "A Wary Eye Towards China, Taiwan Asks for U.S. Arms," *Defense Week*, 12 March 1984, pp. 10–11; and A. Doak Barnett, *The FX Decision* (Washington, D.C.: Brookings, 1981). Taiwan analysts have gone to great lengths to make a case for their need (see *Military Requirements for Advanced Aircraft*, Parts I–IV, Institute of International Relations, National Chengchi University, Republic of China, June 1983), and Taipei has indicated the possibility of undertaking manufacture of sophisticated planes on its own (Michael Weisskopf, "Taiwan, Nearing Limits of U.S. Arms Supply, to Build Own Jets," *Washington Post*, 31 March 1984, p. A13), but the latter course will be an extraordinary economic and technical challenge.

16. Nixon did withdraw a division, in consonance with the Guam Doctrine's overall emphasis on emphasizing arms aid to allies and reducing their reliance on U.S. military manpower, but the pledge to commit American forces against a North Korean attack was not modified.

17. See Charles Sorrels, *Planning U.S. General Purpose Forces: Related to Asia* (Washington, D.C.: Congressional Budget Office, June 1977); and Stuart E. Johnson with Joseph A. Yager, *The Military Equation in Northeast Asia* (Washington, D.C.: Brookings, 1979).

18. Michael Leifer, "The Security of Sea-Lanes in South-East Asia," *Survival* 25 (January/February 1983): 20; Richard Nations, "The Reason Why," *Far Eastern*

Economic Review, 9 May 1985, p. 44; "Admiral Crowe on Defending the Pacific," *Pacific Defence Reporter,* November 1983; Karen DeYoung, "New Arms, Troops Expand Soviet Military Role in Southeast Asia," *Washington Post,* 21 December 1983, pp. A1, A34.

19. See Richard K. Betts, "Complexities, Uncertainties, and Dilemmas," in Richard Betts, ed., *Cruise Missiles: Technology, Strategy, Politics* (Washington, D.C.: Brookings, 1981), pp. 513–16, 537–40.

20. See William Overholt, "Progress and Politics in Pacific Asia," *International Security* 7 (Spring 1983): 190.

21. Guy J. Pauker, Frank H. Golay, and Cynthia E. Enloe, *Diversity and Development in Southeast Asia* (New York: McGraw-Hill, for the Council on Foreign Relations, 1977), p. 45.

22. William Branigin, "Weinberger Tries to Allay Fears of Japan," *Washington Post,* 4 November 1982, p. A32.

23. Michael Richardson, "ASEAN Extends Its Military Ties," *Pacific Defence Reporter,* November 1982.

24. U.S. Congress, Senate, Committee on Foreign Relations, Subcommittee on East Asian and Pacific Affairs, *Hearings: U.S. Policy in Southeast Asia,* 97th Cong., 1st sess., 1981, p. 40. The Arrangement "has sometimes seemed preoccupied with keeping Singapore and Malaysia on sensible terms." Bruce Grant, *The Security of South-East Asia,* Adelphi Paper No. 142 (London: International Institute for Strategic Studies, Spring 1978), p. 2.

25. See Warwick Beuther, "On Parade Down Under," John McBeth, "A Cosy Relationship," Susumu Awanohara, "The Ties That Bind," and V.G. Kulkarni, "Room for Manoeuvre"—all in *Far Eastern Economic Review,* 21 July 1983, pp. 40–42— and W.B. Pritchett, "Defending Australia and Its Interests," *Pacific Defence Reporter,* July 1982, p. 59.

26. Sheldon W. Simon, *The ASEAN States and Regional Security* (Stanford, Calif.: Hoover Institution Press, 1982), p. 114.

27. Leslie H. Brown, *American Security Policy in Asia,* Adelphi Paper No. 132 (London: International Institute for Strategic Studies, Spring 1977), p. 11.

28. Leifer, *Conflict and Regional Order in South-East Asia,* p. 29.

29. Leszek Buszynski, "Thailand: The Erosion of a Balanced Foreign Policy," *Asian Survey* 22 (November 1982): 1041, 1038.

30. Nayan Chanda, "Fueling New Hopes," *Far Eastern Economic Review,* 3 March 1983.

31. Martin Stuart-Fox, "National Defence and International Security in Laos," in Martin Stuart-Fox, ed., *Contemporary Laos* (New York: St. Martin's Press, 1982), pp. 240–41; Paul Quinn-Judge, "Picking Up the Pieces," *Far Eastern Economic Review,* 14 July 1983, p. 14.

32. William Branigin, "Noncommunist Rebels reportedly Attack Vietnamese in Cambodia," *Washington Post,* 12 October 1982, p. A15; Justus M. van der Kroef, "Kampuchea: The Diplomatic Labyrinth," *Asian Survey* 22 (October 1982): pp. 1019–22.

33. Donald S. Weatherbee, "The View From ASEAN's Southern Flank," *Strategic Review* 11 (Spring 1983): 58–59; Juwono Sudarsono, "Security in Southeast

Asia: The Circle of Conflict," in Robert A. Scalapino and Jusuf Wanandi, eds., *Economic, Political, and Security Issues in Southeast Asia in the 1980s,* Research Papers and Public Policy Studies No. 7 (Berkeley: University of California, Institute of East Asian Studies, 1982); Overholt, "Progress and Politics in Pacific Asia," p. 187; William R. Heaton, "China and Southeast Asian Communist Movements: The Decline of Dual Track Diplomacy," *Asian Survey* 22 (August 1982): 779–800.

34. Nayan Chanda, "Indochina Shot ASEAN on to the World Stage," *Far Eastern Economic Review,* 13 August 1982, p. 44.

35. Leifer, *Conflict and Regional Order in South-East Asia,* p. 27.

36. Marian K. Leighton, "Soviets Still Playing Dominoes in Asia," *Wall Street Journal,* 14 October 1983, p. 30.

37. "Australian Asks Cambodia Peace Force," *New York Times,* 16 May 1983, p. A3; "Straight-Talking Shogun," *Asiaweek,* 20 May 1983, p. 29; Weatherbee, "The View From ASEAN's Southern Flank," p. 60.

38. William W. Tow, "The JANZUS Option: A Key to Asian/Pacific Security," *Asian Survey* 18 (December 1978); Simon, *The ASEAN States and Regional Security,* p. 124.

39. Remarks at a conference at the Johns Hopkins University School of Advanced International Studies, 16 April 1982.

40. "Insurgency has deep roots in South-east Asia and utopianism a respected place in its folklore." Grant, *The Security of South-East Asia,* p. 28.

41. See "Thais Press Attacks on Guerillas," *New York Times,* 22 April 1982, p. A3; and Sidney R. Jones, " 'It Can't Happen Here': A Post-Khomeini Look at Indonesian Islam," *Asian Survey* 20 (March 1980): pp. 311–23.

42. Leszek Buszynski, "The Soviet Union in Southeast Asia: Motives, Limits, and Opportunities," *Contemporary Southeast Asia* 4 (December 1982): 273–74, 278–79; Zagoria and Simon, "Soviet Policy in Southeast Asia," pp. 154–55.

43. Les Buszynski, "The Soviet Union and Southeast Asia Since the Fall of Saigon," *Asian Survey* 21 (May 1981): 549.

44. Evelyn Colbert, "Changing Relationships in Southeast Asia: ASEAN, Indochina, and the Great Powers," *Contemporary Southeast Asia* 4 (June 1982): 84; Donald S. Zagoria, "The Soviet Dilemma in East Asia," in Scalapino and Wanandi, eds., *Economic, Political, and Security Issues in Southeast Asia in the 1980s,* pp. 208–9.

45. Zagoria, "The Soviet Dilemma in East Asia," pp. 209, 215–16.

46. U.S. Department of State, "The Soviet Role in Asia," *Current Policy,* no. 521 (October 1983): 3.

47. Buszynski, "The Soviet Union in Southeast Asia," pp. 284–85. See also Leif Rosenberger, "The Soviet-Vietnamese Alliance and Kampuchea," *Survey* 27 (Autumn/Winter 1983).

48. Simon, *The ASEAN States and Regional Security,* pp. 50–51.

49. King C. Chen, "China's War Against Vietnam, 1979: A Military Analysis," *Journal of East Asian Affairs* 3 (Spring/Summer 1983): 249–52.

50. On the evolution of the controlling power in triangular diplomacy, see Gerald Segal, "China and the Great Power Triangle," *China Quarterly,* no. 83 (September 1980): 493–99.

51. Leifer, "The Security of Sea-Lanes in South-East Asia," p. 16. See also Marwyn S. Samuels, *Contest for the South China Sea* (New York: Methuen, 1982), chapters 5–6, 8.

52. George E. Taylor, *The Philippines and the United States: Problems of Partnership* (New York: Praeger, for the Council on Foreign Relations, 1964), pp. 234–46.

53. "Asia's Horizon of Terror," *Asiaweek,* 27 May 1983, pp. 39, 41.

54. For criticisms of standard arguments, see Robert Pringle, *Indonesia and the Philippines: American Interests in Island Southeast Asia* (Ithaca, N.Y.: Cornell University Press, 1980), pp. 67–75.

55. "Philippines, After Rebuff to U.S., Wooed by Soviets," *Baltimore Sun,* 15 July 1983, p. 2; William Branigin, "Manila's Policy Shift Brings Bases' Value Into Question," *Washington Post,* 15 September 1982, p. A20.

56. George McT. Kahin, "Remove the Bases From the Philippines," *New York Times,* 12 October 1983, p. A23.

57. Robert Trumbull, "U.S. Military Plans for Guam Run Into Snags," *New York Times,* 21 April 1985.

58. Quoted in Jack Cushman, "Relying on Marcos," *Defense Week,* 6 September 1983, p. 12. There are problems beyond finance or distance in relocating in Micronesia, such as doubts about sufficiency of local labor forces. See "Admiral Crowe on Defending the Pacific." See also Alvin J. Cottrell, "Key U.S. Bases in the Philippines," *National Defense,* December 1982, pp. 35–36.

59. For a contrary view, see Harry Gelber, "Australia's Role in the Years Ahead," *Pacific Defence Reporter,* December 1982/January 1983, p. 43; for optimistic reflections on a Pacific concert, see Gelber, "Australia, the Pacific, and the United States in the 1980s," *Comparative Strategy* 3 (1981): 97–116.

3
Japan: Regional Stability

Masashi Nishihara

Since about 1977—for the first time after it regained independence in 1952—Japan has emerged as a visible political actor in the Asia Pacific region. In that year, Prime Minister Fukuda Takeo proclaimed the "Fukuda Doctrine" in a speech in Manila. The doctrine was designed to define Japanese policy directions toward Southeast Asia and suggest playing a positive political role there. In the following year, Tokyo changed its long-standing policy of equidistance toward its giant Communist neighbors, opting for closer political ties with Beijing than with Moscow. And in the wake of the Vietnamese invasion of Kampuchea later that year, the Japanese government sought to help restore the regional balance of power by supporting the ASEAN criticism of Hanoi and acquiescing in February 1979 to China's "punitive action" against Vietnam. Then, in 1979, Prime Minister Ohira Masayoshi expressed interest in promoting the concept of Pacific Basin cooperation. This was another new move to demonstrate Japan's active diplomacy. The Soviet invasion of Afghanistan led Tokyo to seek an enhanced political role "as a member of the Western camp," by strategically cooperating with the United States and Europe.

Fukuda's trip to Southeast Asia, symbolized by the Fukuda Doctrine, was an epoch-making event for Japanese diplomacy. A high-ranking diplomat who was involved in Fukuda's trip wrote: "Perhaps for the first time in the postwar years our country with the Prime Minister's trip this time took a positive diplomatic initiative."[1] A high-ranking U.S. State Department official remarked in 1980:

> In the past four years, Japan's role in the world has begun the transformation from one of caution, with almost total attention to pragmatically-centered economic activity, to political activism, partnership and leadership. This change was first evident when Prime Minister Fukuda traveled to Southeast Asia in 1977.[2]

Tokyo's political role has become even clearer since the beginning of 1983 with the rise of a hawkish and articulate prime minister, Nakasone

---

All the views expressed herein are strictly personal and do not necessarily represent those of the Japanese government.

Yasuhiro. In his visit to Seoul in early January, following his inauguration, Nakasone talked about the importance of security consultation, quickly settled the economic aid disputes and Japanese textbook controversies, and gained President Chun Doo Hwan's endorsement of Japan's plan to expand its "self-defense" capability. Then, in April and May, he toured the five ASEAN capitals and Brunei, again successfully gaining local endorsements for Japan's military improvement plan. After his travel in Southeast Asia, the Japanese prime minister attended the Seven Nations' Summit in Williamsburg, asserting Japan's more positive security role in the non-Communist world.

Why has Japan begun to change since 1977? What are the current strategic interests of the Japanese government in the non-Communist Asian region—South Korea, Taiwan, the six ASEAN nations (Brunei, Indonesia, Malaysia, the Philippines, Singapore, and Thailand), and Burma? How are they different from Japan's past? Are there any patterns of Japanese relations with those countries? And what are the prospects of Japanese strategy? I will attempt here to respond to these questions.

The Concept of Stability

What does Japan want to achieve by playing an active political role in the non-Communist region of Asia? In his keynote policy speech at the National Diet in January 1977, Foreign Minister Hatoyama Iichiro stated: "The Asian region is the most important area with which our country shares *peace* and *prosperity*" (emphasis added).[3] In January 1983, Foreign Minister Abe Shintaro declared in the Diet: "For our country to develop close friendly relations with Asian countries, based on mutual trust, is highly important as a member of the Asian community and as a basis for the conduct of our positive diplomacy elsewhere." He then went on to say: "I would like to make efforts in increasing mutual understanding with Asian countries, responding to their confidence in and expectations of Japan, contributing to their *progress* and *prosperity* and thus promoting the *peace* and *stability* of Asia" (emphasis added).[4] A quick survey of Japan's foreign policy statements reveals that the key words referring to Japan's strategic interests in Asia and, for that matter, in other regions, are *peace, stability, progress,* and *prosperity*. In short, Japan wants to promote a politically stable and economically viable Asia.

Political stability and economic viability are expected to go hand in hand. The sustained economic growth, with controlled inflation and unemployment, is a key to containing political and social unrest and depriving Communist subversives of the chances to exploit the unrest. Domestic economic and political frustrations constitute major sources of national security threats for many Asian developing countries. Economic progress is likely to promote political stability. Inversely, political stability serves as the basis for economic growth, whereas political instability generates room for external powers' intervention, leading to further economic and political instability. The politically stable non-Communist areas are important for Japan, because they create stable markets for Japan's exports and suitable environments for its investments. With a total population of 327 million, the non-Communist countries of Asia in 1982 imported 20.1 percent of Japanese exports in value and contributed to 19.5 percent of Japanese imports. Thirty-three percent of Japan's private direct investment went to the same region in 1982.[5] At the same time, non-Communist countries that interact economically with Japan are likely to be friendly and thus advantageous to its national security. Like many other nations, Japan needs friendly neighbors, which are a more assured source of security than its own military reinforcements would be.

Thus, in Abe's words in 1983, "*stable* Japanese–ROK relations have been established" by Prime Minister Nakasone's visit to Seoul in January 1983, and "Japan should spare no efforts in contributing to the reduction of tensions in the Korean peninsula, if there were something which Japan could contribute in its capacity."[6] With regard to Southeast Asia, Abe said that the ASEAN nations, deepening their sense of solidarity and achieving steady progress, were an important element of stability for Southeast Asia and all of Asia. He said: "It is encouraging, and our nation should continue to support such efforts by the ASEAN nations in order to attain long-term *peace* and *stability* in Asia and should make efforts in further developing cooperative relationships with them" (emphasis added). He then stated: "The Cambodian problem remains unsolved and is an element of *instability*," and "our nations should make every effort in solving the problem by cooperating with each of those nations concerned such as the ASEAN countries and by maintaining dialogue with Vietnam."

Political stability can be achieved under either a democratic government or an undemocratic one. The Tokyo government certainly prefers the former to the latter but finds it difficult to favor political instability under a democratic government over political stability under an authoritarian government. On the whole, it has accepted the latter. In the past, the Japanese government has rarely raised the issue of political freedom and other basic human rights in Asian countries. Nor has it used economic leverage to improve human rights situations—for instance, in South Korea, the Philippines, and Indonesia—as Washington and Canberra often did. In fact, Tokyo maintained close relations with both the Sukarno and the Suharto governments in Jakarta, when Washington expressed displeasure with Sukarno's pro-Communist stands in 1962–65 and Canberra sharply criticized Suharto's repressive measures against East Timor's independence movement leaders after 1970. Tokyo also chose to stabilize its relations with Seoul's authoritarian military government rather than support Kim Dae Jung's "democratization" moves after the Korean intelligence organization kidnapped Kim in Tokyo in 1973. Tokyo–Seoul relations improved while President Carter hardened U.S.–Korean relations over the human rights issue. When Manila, under President Marcos's martial law, emerged after 1972 as a safer and more orderly city than before, it induced more foreign, especially Japanese, investors to go in. Former Senator Benigno Aquino's assassination in August 1983 and subsequent political and economic unrest have apparently brought Tokyo even closer to the Marcos government, with the view that he is the only leader strong enough to lead the Philippines.

Starting with a basic interest in promoting the political stability of *non-Communist* Asia, Japan attempts to approach the Communist nations of the region in somewhat similar ways. First, Japan wants to support and improve China's political stability and economic productivity, for such a China would be likely to pose no military threat to the non-Communist areas. Foreign Minister Yoshio Sakurauchi mentioned in January 1982: "China, attempting to build a *stable* and *prosperous* nation, contributes to the peace and stability of Asia, and it is important for our country to continue to cooperate with China as much as possible in the future."[7] China's steady economic development would continue to promote the flow of Western capital, goods, technology, and would keep the country at a certain distance from Moscow. So long as its assertive nationalism supports this distance, China can function as a buffer for Japan and the non-Communist region against the Soviet Union. The 1978 Treaty of Peace and Friendship between Tokyo and Beijing and subsequent numerous bilateral agreements to promote various forms of economic and technological cooperation appear to be advancing these Japanese interests. Since 1972, when the two countries normalized their relations, Prime Ministers Suzuki Zenko and Nakasone Yasuhiro visited Beijing, and Deng Xiaoping, Hua Guofeng, and Hu Yaobang came to Tokyo. (In contrast, no Japanese prime minister has visited Moscow since 1973.)

Second, Japan wishes to promote a stable North Korea. An unstable and aggressive North Koera is not in Japan's security interests, for this would destabilize Seoul–Pyongyang relations, which in turn is likely to threaten Japanese security and upset Tokyo–Seoul economic and political relations. Stable and controlled, if tense, relations between North and South Korea would encourage Pyongyang to maintain its own political stability, handling Kim Il Sung's succession carefully. Japan has no control over such issues, but it hopes that low-level contacts with North Korea will help the North Koreans become aware of the benefits of establishing a stable and friendly policy toward their non-Communist neighbors, especially Japan. As Foreign Minister Abe stated: "Japan would like gradually to accumulate exchanges with North Korea in the trading, economic, and cultural fields."[8]

Third, Japan seeks a moderate and stable Vietnam, which can live peacefully with the ASEAN nations. Vietnam, having close economic and military ties to Moscow, threatens the ASEAN nations—Thailand in particular. To the extent that they become preoccupied with this threat, the ASEAN nations will have to allocate more of their resources for national security and will tend to reduce the level of Japanese investment and trade activities in their countries. Vietnam, with 50 million people, presents itself as a potentially attractive market for Japan. A Vietnam more independent of Moscow, coexisting with the ASEAN nations, and friendly to Japan would also meet Japanese interests in ensuring the safety of trade routes that pass through the South China Sea. In 1979, Japan depended on the Strait of Malacca for 78 percent of its crude oil imports and 41 percent of its iron ore imports, as well as 35 percent of its steel exports, 63 percent of its cement exports, and 38 percent of its automobile exports, to name a few major items.[9] In August 1977, as part of the aforementioned Fukuda Doctrine, the Japanese government pronounced a policy of seeking mutual understanding with Indochina and thus stable relations with it. A stable and moderate Vietnam, if achieved, would also stabilize relations with China and would facilitate Japan's political and economic relations with both Communist countries. The stability of Indochina is a key to the stability of the whole region, as the post-1945 history of the region has amply demonstrated.

Fourth, although the Soviet Union poses a major security threat to Japan, Tokyo still has no choice but to live with Moscow. Moscow's strategy seems to be to intimidate and blackmail Japan with force, strongly condemning the Japan–United States Security Treaty, U.S. bases in Japan, and binational military consultations and exercises, thus attempting to weaken Japan's relations with the United States. Japan has to cope with Moscow's intimidation. It boycotted the Moscow Olympics and joined the West in imposing economic sanctions in 1980 to protest the Soviet invasion of Afghanistan. Japan has also taken an adamant position against Soviet occupation of the disputed northern territories. Yet Tokyo's ultimate interest is to "establish *stable* relations based on true mutual understanding," as Foreign Minister Abe remarked in 1983.[10] It is in the Japanese interest to have dialogue with the Russians and to learn where both sides stand, even if the tense relations continue. To "stabilize" relations with Moscow, the Japanese government has continuously emphasized an early settlement of the territorial issues, which it claims as the precondition for closer economic relations—such as investment and technological assistance for Siberian development. So far, no early settlement is in sight.

The Japanese strategy for promoting stability in Asia presupposes the American presence. Because of its limited military capabilities, Japan alone cannot play a decisive role in maintaining a stable regional balance of power. It is the United States that ensures an overall regional balance of power favorable to the non-Communist Asian nations. Sharing basic political and security interests of Asia, the two Pacific powers have good reasons to strengthen their collaborative efforts. Whereas Japan needs the American presence in Asia, the United States can take advantage of the economic capabilities of Japan, which can be used for the region's economic development, which, in turn, benefits Washington.

There are many past cases of Japanese–American collaboration in Asia. For instance, the Asian Development Bank, established in 1966, started with an agreement between the two countries in which each would contribute one-third of the starting capital. The multinational consortium for post-Sukarno Indonesia was also formed in 1966. Originally named the Tokyo Club and later renamed the Inter-Governmental Group on Indonesia (IGGI), it began with exactly the same arrangement between the two countries. The ideas of the binational joint efforts in Asia historically date back at least to 1948, when the United States disclaimed its rights to Japan's war reparations and instead saw the advantage of utilizing the recovery-bound Japanese economic potential for the economic development of Asia. Watanabe Takeshi, the first president of the Asian Development Bank, recalls that in June 1950, he and a few other Japanese quietly met U.S. special envoy John Foster Dulles in Tokyo and discussed the possibility that Japan, with U.S. financial aid, would be able to serve as "a factory" for East Asia's development and thus solidify the region against Communist manipulations.[11]

A clearer statement favoring joint operations in the region came out in March 1977, when Prime Minister Fukuda and President Carter agreed that "the two countries are prepared to continue cooperation and assistance in supporting the efforts of the ASEAN countries toward regional cohesion and development."[12] Similarly, the Suzuki-Reagan joint communique issued in May 1981 stated that their countries agreed "to continue their cooperation in support of the solidarity of ASEAN and its quest for the greater resilience and development of its members."[13] This shows that the U.S. factor occupies an important position in Japan's Asian policy.

Determinants of Japan's Strategy

Although the style of Japan's strategy changed from passivity to activity in the late 1970s, basic Japanese interests in the region have remained the same throughout the postwar period. Indeed, Japan's interests in the Asia Pacific region have a longer history than that as demonstrated in its colonization of Taiwan (1895–1945) and Korea (1910–45) and its occupation of Southeast Asia (1942–45), as well as in the prewar and wartime ideology of pan-Asianism, culminating in the concept of the Greater East Asia Co-Prosperity Sphere.

Many people have asserted that, unlike prewar Japan, postwar Japan has lost its political interests and objectives in Asia. These analysts typically say that Japan has no foreign policy other than economic diplomacy.[11] For many years after World War II, it is true, the Japanese government refrained, in principle, from taking stands on Asian issues; its utmost interest was to promote export trade. It feared that any political stands, if taken, would jeopardize its economic activities overseas. In 1952, when Japan regained sovereignty, Prime Minister Yoshida Shigeru decided to leave political and military matters to Washington, thus minimizing Japan's defense burden; hence, "economic diplomacy." This basic policy, which may be most fittingly called the Yoshida Doctrine, was a success, as was demonstrated in the subsequent growth of Japan's economic strength.[14] Because of this intensive emphasis on economic diplomacy, it has been widely perceived that Japan actually had no political interests in Asia. Nothing could be more misleading. Although Japan refrained from an explicit expression of its political concerns in the region, it actually retained clear political and strategic interests there. Several examples will illustrate this.

As early as April 1952, Japan opted to sign a peace treaty with the Republic of China in Taipei rather than the new Communist government in Beijing. Although this option was strongly influenced by the U.S. policy, Tokyo nevertheless made a strategic decision that affected its foreign policy for the subsequent two decades. In December 1954, for example, Prime Minister Yoshida stated in a Diet speech that "the largest challenge to the free countries today is how to combat Communism. . . . For our defense against Communism, it is urgent to promote the economic development of Southeast Asia and to enhance the livelihood of their peoples." With regard to war reparations, he then stressed that "by settling negotiations we should promote economic cooperation and friendship with the Southeast Asian countries, thereby in part minimizing the room for Communist offensives."[15] Starting in Burma in 1954 and ending in South Korea in 1965, Japan agreed to pay war reparations or their equivalent only to the non-communist states. Japan thus had political interests in the region, but it refrained from a clear expression of them and avoided playing a more direct role until about 1977.

Many factors account for the positive change in Japan's foreign policy stance in the late 1970s. It appears that external factors had a more direct impact on this change than internal ones did. Japan's economic power, for instance, which assumed more than 7 percent of the total world GNP in the mid-1970s, forced the Japanese to feel the need to share international political responsibilities as well. There was a growing demand by the American and European members of the Organization for Economic Cooperation and Development (OECD) for Japan to give more official development aid to the developing countries and to take appropriate measures to reduce Japan's continuing favorable balance of trade with the United States and the European Community nations, which failed to recover from the oil shortage of 1973 and suffered a rising rate of unemployment.

That Japan had been a member of the Economic Summit since its inception in 1975 also contributed to the Japanese awareness of international responsibilities. In the 1977 summit, held in London, the argument prevailed that Japan, together with the United States and West Germany, should play the role of an engine, pulling the world economy out of recession. A similar stimulus may have come from Japan's association in the Trilateral Commission, a nongovernmental policy-oriented forum of distinguished private individuals from Western Europe, North America, and Japan, launched in 1973.[16]

The expansion of the Soviet military in the Western Pacific also contributed to the formulation of the new Japanese strategy. The increase in Soviet military flights near Japanese airspace plus the expansion in Soviet naval activities in waters near Japan were seen as posing an incremental threat to Japanese security. In 1970, Japanese jet fighters scrambled against approaching Soviet military planes 370 times; in 1976, they scrambled 528 times. In 1982, the frequency had increased to 929 times.[17]

In contrast to the Soviet military buildup was the relative decline of American military power in Asia. Between 1973 and 1977, the United States withdrew its troops from Vietnam and closed down its bases in Thailand, while Democratic presidential candidate Jimmy Carter advocated the policy of withdrawing U.S. troops from South Korea. As the Japanese perceived it, the vacuum of power that resulted negatively affected the regional balance of power. The ASEAN leaders who visited Tokyo one after another in the period following the fall of Saigon in 1975 also made the Japanese leaders more aware of their expected new role in Southeast Asia: that of a political actor in maintaining the regional balance of power.

An equally important factor was Washington's incremental encouragement or pressure on Tokyo to assume a larger diplomatic role, commensurate with its economic power. These pressures, in part, forced Japan to begin to define and identify its security interests in the region and to formulate the kind of political role it could play in Asia.

Although the external factors were important for the change in the Japanese policy toward non-communist Asia, it was, after all, the Japanese perception of what they should and could do for their own security that affected the Japanese strategy. Various international events, such as the oil shock of 1973 and the Soviet military buildup, helped the Japanese recognize the international impact of their own national power. By being a relatively more active player, they felt they should be able to bring about an international environment more favorable to their own national security.

Prime Minister Fukuda remarked in 1980, after he left office, that his basic foreign policy posture had been determined by the thought that Japan's peace and prosperity were and would be possible only to the extent that the world enjoyed peace and prosperity, and that "Japan must contribute to the peace and prosperity of the world by its own economic capabilities."[18] A high-ranking diplomat who was deeply involved in planning Fukuda's trip to Southeast Asia in 1977 wrote that he had felt that Japan should no longer remain simply as a passive observer, adjusting to the changing international environment, but that it should actively contribute to the establishment of a stable regional order in post-Vietnam Southeast Asia.[19] This feeling was first given expression by Foreign Ministry officials engaged in Southeast Asia affairs, meeting in Hong Kong in March 1976. This meeting led to a policy recommendation that Japan should extend positive support for the resilience of ASEAN nations and should make an active contribution to building a harmonious relationshp between ASEAN nations and Indochina. In December 1976, this recommendation was further examined at a conference of all Japanese ambassadors serving in Southeast Asia; and the following year it became the basic framework for the Fukuda Doctrine.[20]

The growing consciousness among diplomats of the need for an active diplomacy also eventuated in 1979 and 1980 in the concept that Japan should act positively as a member of the Western camp, strongly criticizing the Soviet invasion of Afghanistan. In January 1980, Foreign Minister Okita Saburo remarked:

> Japanese foreign policy is currently undergoing an important revolution. Very briefly, we are moving into a new phase of heightening awareness of Japan in the international political context and increasing willingness to act in accordance with that awareness.[21]

This awareness was also reflected in a new, comprehensive approach to national security, recognizing that security depended not just on military security but also on economic and energy security. The Nomura Research Institute, a leading think tank in Tokyo, issued a report in late 1977 that introduced the concept of "comprehensive national security," recommending that the cost of national security should consist not only of defense cost but also of the cost of such items as economic aid and research and development of alternative energy resources.[22] This added a new dimension to the thinking about Japanese diplomacy, causing many Japanese, for the first time, to conceive of economic assistance to Asian countries to promote their economic and political stability as an instrument for improving Japan's stability and security as well.[23] Hence, it was a positive diplomacy.

Let us see now how Japan has been expressing this new thrust in its strategic policies toward selected countries in the Asia Pacific region.

Relations with South Korea

The basic importance of South Korea to Japanese security has remained unchanged throughout the postwar period. Japan needs a stable and resilient anti-Communist or at least non-Communist government in South Korea, one that depends upon Washington and Tokyo. So far, Seoul has met Japan's interests. Seoul's strong defense posture has served as a buffer between Japan and Communist forces on the Asian continent. The American military presence in South Korea is essential for the security of Japan, for it plays a critical role in balancing North Korea's continuous military buildup. All of the postwar South Korean governments have accepted the U.S. role in the peninsula. Japan's pro-Washington policy is also important for South Korea's security, for it allows for U.S. bases, which in turn are indispensable for South Korean security.

Although the two Asian nations depend on each other somewhat symmetrically in security areas, their economic interdependence has been asymmetrical. In 1977, Japan's exports to and imports from South Korea were U.S.$4.080 billion and U.S.$2.113 billion, respectively. This imbalance of U.S.$1.967 billion widened further until 1982, when the size of the imbalance shrank slightly. But Japan still had U.S.$1.627 billion surplus in its trade with that neighbor.[24] In 1981, 16.5 percent of the ROK's exports went to Japan and 24.4 percent of its imports came from Japan. Japan has been the largest exporter and the second largest importer for South Korea. But South Korea was Japan's fourth largest export market in the world; it was also the third largest source of Japan's imports in Asia after Indonesia and China and its ninth largest source in the world. In 1981, 3.7 percent, or U.S.$5.658 billion worth, of Japanese exports went to South Korea, and 2.4 percent, or U.S.$3.389 billion worth, of Japanese imports came from South Korea. Though asymmetrical, their economic relations are highly important for both countries. South Korea has based its industrial modernization largely, if not primarily, on Japanese capital and technology and thus finds continued reliance on Japanese economic power to be indispensable. At the same time, Japan considers that the economic progress of South Korea is a key to its political stability.

Despite the recognition by both sides of the importance of their bilateral relations, they continue to face political tensions. Other than tensions stemming from the aforementioned trade imbalance, two incidents that occurred in the early 1970s severely damaged Tokyo–Seoul relations: the Kim Dae Jung incident, in which the presidential aspirant was abducted from Japan by Korean intelligence agents in August 1973, and the Mun Sae Kwang affair, in which President Park barely escaped assassination by a Korean dissident residing in Japan and the First Lady was gunned down by mistake. What was worse, Japanese critics and mass media subsequently created the image that the Park government was as authoritarian and oppressive as its northern rival.

Under these circumstances, although the Japanese government began to take a more positive approach in Southeast Asia after the fall of Saigon, it faced numerous difficulties in improving its relations with Seoul. In July 1979, for instance, Minister of State for Defense Yamashita Ganri of the Japanese Defense Agency (JDA) became the first Japanese ever to visit Seoul in such a capacity. Prior to that, the highest-ranking officials of the JDA who had visited Seoul were the chairman of the Joint Staff Council and the chiefs of staff of the three services. Yamashita's visit itself meant a positive move from Japan. However, his proposals, such as the exchange of mutual visits of naval training ships, apparently received a cool response from the Korean government.[25] Yet in February 1979, Prime Minister Ohira had met with Deng Xiaoping in Tokyo, and he met in December with Hua Guofeng in China and discussed the problem of peace in the Korean peninsula. Here one can observe the Japanese government's efforts to strengthen relations with Seoul in security fields, while also communicating with Beijing about the importance of peace and stability in Korea.

President Park's assassination in December 1979 halted Japan's diplomatic efforts for a while. The rise of Chun Doo Hwan as his successor opened new possibilities, but when the Korean government requested $6 billion in 1981 as Japanese aid for the security of South Korea, new tensions were produced. While Seoul argued that Japan was a "free rider" on South Korea's difficult efforts for national defense, Tokyo refused to say that it had contributed to the security of South Korea by nonmilitary means. The Japanese government had hitherto maintained a policy of not giving economic aid that might be construed as a contribution to South Korea's defense. It is true that by 1981, the Ohira leadership was using the concept of comprehensive national security to argue that Japan should consider economic aid to developing countries as part of Japan's security policy. This concept might have been applied to the aid of Seoul, but it was not.

Seoul's adamant attitude in demanding $6 billion as a "charge" for its contribution to Japanese security continued to irritate the binational relations for some time. Added to this tension was the so-called textbook incident, which occurred in 1982. The revision of school history textbooks allegedly undertaken under the Education Ministry's instructions to tone down and justify Japan's past militaristic deeds raised quick and strong condemnation from Koreans. The Suzuki government had to promise that it would see to it that textbooks would be written so as not to impede the friendly bilateral relations.

It was Prime Minister Nakasone Yasuhiro who came to office in late November 1982 and skillfully mended the fences with Korea by taking positive action. Through back channels, he settled with the Korean side on $4 billion to be loaned over the following five years.[26] The loan was to be used for nonmilitary projects; but in his joint communique with President Chun at the time of his visit to Seoul in January 1983, the prime minister said that he greatly appreciated the fact that South Korea's defense efforts were contributing to the maintenance of peace in the Korean peninsula.

Since these events, the Koreans have also shown positive attitudes toward Japan. President Chun accepted Nakasone's invitation to visit Japan as the first Korean head of state to come to Japan. In September 1983, a member of the Korean–Japanese Parliamentary Association proposed low-level security cooperation between the two countries, reviving the Yamashita proposal of four years before, including the exchange of military cadets and naval training ships;[27] and in late 1983, for the first time in postwar history, three Japanese cadets from the National Defense Academy were sent to Korean counterpart schools for short goodwill visits. It appeared that the Koreans were moving gradually toward accepting the idea of binational talks with Japan in the security field.

Tokyo has yet to state exactly what role it would play in another Korean crisis. It has not even given blank-check permission for U.S. bases in Japan to be used for military operations in the Korean peninsula. The issue is still too politically sensitive. This reluctant posture has naturally annoyed Seoul. But here again, since January 1982, Japanese and American officers have been working together to produce scenarios for their cooperation in future Korean crises.[28]

Several positive efforts from both sides notwithstanding, there are still more than a few sources of tension between the two countries. First, a continuing trade imbalance remains as a serious diplomatic issue. To correct the imbalance, the Japanese have to buy more Korean commodities. At the same time, the Koreans are calling for an extensive technology transfer from Japan to help them produce their own high-quality manufactured goods. But the Japanese government is not enthusiastic about technology transfer, because Japanese businessmen are concerned about what they call the "boomerang effect." They have lost the competition with their Korean counterparts in textiles, and they are apprehensive that a greater transfer of technology may cause them to lose in other sectors as well, including automobiles, shipbuilding, television, and computers.

Second, a gap in threat perception tends to create political strains. For Seoul, the major threat is North Korea, whereas for Tokyo the primary security threat is the Soviet Union. In fact, most Japanese consider the tottering world economy and the unstable supply of oil equally serious sources of threat. The South Koreans have obtained a U.S. guarantee of their energy supply, but the Japanese have not. To the consternation of South Korea, the lack of a perceived threat to Japan from North Korea has led Tokyo to have informal, though troubled contacts with that country. By 1983, North Korea had accumulated U.S.$770 million in debts to Japan, payment of which it had deferred three times since 1976.[29] With the indispensable help of pro-Pyongyang Korean residents in Japan, who number roughly 300,000, North

Korea can use Japan as the base for its intelligence and subversive activities aimed at South Korea. Yet the Japanese consider that keeping informal channels of communication open with North Korea helps stabilize North–South relations in the peninsula, because it exposes North Korean leaders to the attractions and merits of the industrial achievements and political freedoms of the West. The Japanese–North Korean Friendship Association, headed by a Liberal Democratic Party member of the Diet, occasionally sends a group of conservative members to Pyongyang. In March 1981, a Socialist Party mission, headed by party chairman Asukata Kazuo, issued a joint statement for the establishment of a nuclear-free peace zone in Northeast Asia. Quite a few journalists, and some scholars as well, have been invited to North Korea in the recent past. North Korea's invitation diplomacy is probably designed to obtain more sympathy from the Japanese public, and these moves certainly disturb Seoul. The Rangoon incident of October 1983, in which many members of President Chun's entourage were assassinated by Pyongyang-directed terrorists, cooled down Japanese–North Korean relations. Sanctions were imposed, only to be lifted on January 1, 1985, following the opening of a North Korean–South Korean dialogue.

Third, mutual animosity is still strong and makes binational political relations difficult.[30] Nakasone's visit in January 1983 marked the first occasion for the Japanese flag to be hoisted in Seoul in the postwar period, but it will be many years before the two peoples can be expected to overcome their antagonistic feelings. The undercurrent of anti-Korean or anti-Japanese nationalism can surface quickly, as it did in the textbook incident of 1982. Yet, ironically, the number of people who have visited each other's country has risen sharply in the last ten years. Korean visitors to Japan increased from about 72,000 in 1970 to 137,000 in 1982, and Japanese visitors to Korea increased from 45,000 in 1970 to 414,000 in 1982.[31]

Gradually, the Koreans appear to be making a more emotion-free assessment of Japan–ROK relations. More programs on Japan are being shown on Korean television. Reciprocally in Japan, where many individuals have been persistently prejudiced against Koreans, there is an increase in respect for Korea's economic success. These developments on both sides are conducive to closer cooperation in the future.

Fourth, there have been frequent charges that Japanese economic aid has been misused by Japanese and Korean firms and that certain political leaders on both sides have colluded for corrupt purposes. Political kickbacks are alleged to have benefited some members of the "pro-Korea lobby," notably the members of the Japan–Korea Cooperation Committee.[32] The committee, formed in 1969, is a private group consisting of members of the Liberal Democratic and Democratic Socialist parties and representatives of big business. This committee and the Japanese–ROK Parliamentary Association seem, from the Japanese side, to play a central role in the nongovernmental and often even governmental areas of the bilateral relations.[33]

Finally, the lack of Japan's appreciation of South Korea's defense efforts will continue to annoy Seoul. In the past, Japan has been reluctant to admit in public the importance of South Korea to Japan. In 1969, the Sato-Nixon joint communique, referring to the Korean peninsula, included one of the rare specific statements that a Japanese leader has made concerning the security linkage between Japan and South Korea. It stated that "the security of the Republic of Korea is essential to Japan's own security."[34] On most other occasions, Tokyo has referred to the linkage much less specifically. Although Nakasone, in his visit to Seoul in January 1983, expressed an implicit appreciation of South Korea's defense efforts, his joint statement with President Chun went no further than to say that "the maintenance of peace on the Korean Peninsula is imperative for the peace and stability of East Asia, including Japan."[35] This exactly same wording had appeared in several previous white papers of the Foreign Ministry.[36] More positive wording would be required to improve the binational relations.

Relations with Taiwan

Since the derecognition of the Republic of China in 1972, Japan has pursued a policy toward that country of separating politics from economics, as it did toward the continent before then. Despite these new relations between Tokyo and Taipei, their economic relations are in fact better today than in years past. After the 1978 Treaty of Peace and Friendship between Tokyo and Beijing put their relations on a firmer ground, Tokyo began to take an even more positive policy toward Taipei of separating politics from economics.

Japanese exports to Taiwan increased from U.S.$1.049 billion in 1972 to U.S.$4.255 billion in 1982, which made Taiwan the fourth largest market for Japanese exports in Asia—after South Korea, Indonesia, and Singapore. Japanese imports from Taiwan during the same period grew from U.S.$381 million to U.S.$2.443 billion, which made Taiwan also the fourth largest source for Japan in Asia—following Indonesia, China, and South Korea. Japan is still the number one trading partner for Taiwan: in 1982, 11 percent of Taiwan's exports and 28 percent of its imports were traded with Japan.[37]

The number of visits by Japanese to Taiwan similarly increased from 114,000 in 1970 to 558,000 in 1982, while visits by Chinese from Taiwan to Japan swelled from 47,000 to 289,000.[38] In 1970, 2,852 Japanese, most of whom undoubtedly were businessmen and their families, were registered as residents in Taiwan; by 1980, the number had increased to 5,022, which was fewer than the number of Japanese living in mainland China by only 1,177.[39] The Japanese Chamber of Commerce and Industry in Taipei has as many as 181 corporate members.⁴⁰ Japan Asian Airways and China Air Lines both make frequent flights between the two countries, and business and tourism are extremely active.

Even semidiplomatic relations continue. Since derecognition, the Association of East Asian Relations, which has a few offices in Japan, acts as the de facto representative office of the Republic of China—issuing visas, for instance. The Interchange Association, in turn, functions from the Japanese side as an overall agency to facilitate Japan–Taiwan relations. The Interchange Association has its head office in Tokyo and maintains an overseas office in Taipei. Its chairman, Horikoshi Teizo, is a noted businessman and a former vice-chairman of Keidanren (Federation of Economic Organizations). Its president, Uomoto Tokichiro, is a former ambassador to the USSR. His predecessor, Nishiyama Akira, served as ambassador to Indonesia. The current head, Hara Fukio, is also a retired diplomat, having been ambassador to Poland. Most of the top officers of the association are retired government officials of the Foreign Ministry and the Ministry of International Trade and Industry (MITI), thus maintaining a loose, semigovernmental liaison between the Tokyo and Taipei governments.⁴¹

Among several parliamentary groups that are sympathetic to the ROC is the Diet Members' Association for Japanese–Chinese (Taiwanese) Relations, which is headed by Nadao Hirokichi, a conservative leader who served as the Speaker of the House of Representatives, and which has Kishi Nobusuke, a former prime minister, among its advisors. As of 1983, according to an official source, the association had 126 Lower House and 80 Upper House members, all from the ruling party.⁴² Another group is the much smaller Japan–China (Taiwan) Group, consisting of thirty-two Democratic Socialist Party members of the Diet and chaired by Nakamura Masao, vice-chairman of the party. Nadao's group visited Taipei in April 1982 and October 1983. In July 1982, Ezaki Masumi, chairman of the LDP Special Research Council on International Economic Measures, also headed a mission to Taiwan to find ways to reduce the trade imbalance. Earlier that year, Ezaki also headed another mission to Europe and the United States to solve trade frictions there. Ezaki's Taipei mission, therefore, was an important move, closely linked to the Suzuki government's concerns. In September 1982, a mission led by Anzai Hiroshi, chairman of the Tokyo Gas Company, visited Taipei to promote imports from that country.

In the academic field as well, the number of scholars and critics sympathetic to the ROC is not insignificant. Almost all of them are conservatives and professed anti-Communists who often travel to Taiwan to attend international conferences, although some of them, it should be noted, have also visited the mainland. While agreeing to the strategic importance of Japanese relations with Beijing, these scholars, together with politicians and businessmen, emphasize the importance of Taiwan for the security of the Western Pacific.

Thus, except for the issue of Japan's relations with the PRC, Japan seems to share basic political and economic interests with the Taipei government. Both endorse the American military presence in the Western Pacific, and Taipei needs a stable Japanese economy and a stronger Japanese defense capability, which can help deter Soviet attacks. In fact, Japanese economic aid to the PRC is also helping Taiwan, by contributing to Beijing's moderate posture on external relations.

The government in Tokyo understandably avoids making any official reference to the security link between Taiwan and Japan. For instance, Japanese defense white papers, diplomatic bluebooks, and foreign ministers' speeches, do not discuss Taiwan. Unlike United States–Taiwan relations, Japan–Taiwan relations involve no problems of arms transfer and defense commitment. Yet the Japanese capital and technology being used in Taiwan are contributing to Taiwan's national security indirectly. Higher technology, which may thus be developed in Taiwan, may have a direct influence on the quality of arms development in the future.

In this sense, Japan continues to hope for a stable government in Taipei. Although it is difficult to foresee Taiwan's future political and economic system, the island is not likely to follow Hong Kong in acceding to Beijing's sovereignty. A Taiwan that will have some kind of political understanding with the Beijing government and will peacefully coexist with it is plausible. It is also plausible, though perhaps less so, that Taiwan will declare its independence. Either alternative will suit Japan's interests, so long as the island retains political stability and continues to prosper economically.

Relations with the ASEAN States

As Americans were compelled to leave Cambodia and South Vietnam in 1975 and Thailand in 1976, the political and military vacuum created in Indochina encouraged Hanoi and Moscow to hurry to step in despite Beijing's opposition. Under these circumstances, the ASEAN capitals attempted to balance these Communist moves by encouraging Tokyo to play a greater role in the region.

Earlier in the period from 1972 to 1974, Japan faced several serious student demonstrations against its economic "overpresence," particularly in Bangkok and Jakarta. In January 1974, Prime Minister Tanaka Kakuei could leave Jakarta only by having Indonesian authorities fly him by helicopter straight from the presidential palace to the airport; but three and a half years later, in August 1977, Prime Minister Fukuda Takeo was warmly welcomed. More eager at that time to bring Japan in, the ASEAN governments were gratified by Fukuda's promise of $1 billion for ASEAN industrialization projects.

In the early 1980s, Japan's economic presence in Southeast Asia was still large, but very few people criticized this, at least openly. In 1982, Japanese official and private economic aid to the ASEAN region amounted to U.S.$1.741 billion, or 84 percent of Japan's total aid to Asia.[43] Japan's favorable trade imbalance with the ASEAN region widened from U.S.$1.526 billion per annum for the first half of the 1970s to U.S.$2.496 billion in 1981 and U.S.$1.888 billion in 1982.[44] Yet Prime Minister Mahathir of Malaysia advocates the "Look East" policy, and Lee Kuan Yew of Singapore has long promoted the introduction of the Japanese work ethic, bureaucratic efficiency, and other aspects of Japanese social relations. In 1970, there were only about 35,000 Japanese visitors to the region; by 1982, the number had increased to 529,000.[45] Japan's enhanced diplomatic role has lowered the level of the ASEAN nations' criticism of Japanese economic behavior to a great extent.

The aforementioned Fukuda Doctrine, announced in 1977, had three points: (1) Japan will not become a military power; (2) Japan will seek "a heart-to-heart understanding" with the ASEAN nations, working with them as equal partners; and (3) Japan will continue to give importance to the ASEAN region, while also trying to have cooperative relations with Indochina.[46] The last point was particularly significant, because it implied that Japan would help the ASEAN nations coexist with Indochina. But Vietnam's invasion of Cambodia in early 1979 changed the Japanese policy expressed in the Fukuda Doctrine. Japan sided more closely with the ASEAN states, particularly with Thailand in its stand on the Cambodian issue. Tokyo considers that Thai security and political stability should be given top attention, believing that in the immediate future, the security of ASEAN is likely to be determined by Thai security. Prime Minister Suzuki's selection of Bangkok as the last stop in his ASEAN tour in early 1981 underlined this belief.

Japan has so far taken fairly clear positions on the Cambodian issue, siding with ASEAN and condemning Vietnam's militant actions. Japanese assistance to Indochinese refugees was originally extended in monetary terms, rather than by inviting them to settle in Japan. Tokyo provided one of the largest financial contributions to this cause (a total of about $340 million in 1979–82) and helped process 6,700 refugees in Japan, 2,300 of whom were helped to settle in Japan by the end of 1982.[47] This is so low in comparison to the number of refugees who entered the United States and some European countries that it has been severely criticized by those governments and by various international institutions. In 1980, as one way to compensate for its deficiency, the Japanese government set up a medical center near the Thai–Cambodian border. In addition, it has extended economic aid to assist the relocation of border-area Thai villagers.

Japan has played an active role in the United Nations as well, joining those nations that introduced several joint resolutions in the General Assembly supporting Democratic Kampuchea. Japanese foreign ministers attend the special sessions of annual ASEAN foreign ministers meetings. In 1981, Foreign Minister Sonoda proposed a plan for a Cambodian solution, including a demilitarized zone along the Thai–Cambodian border and a U.N.-supervised free election.[48]

Although this was the first time Japan had taken a clear political stand on Indochina issues, one should not forget its precedents. From 1963 to 1966, Japanese leaders, including Prime Minister Ikeda Hayato, acted to mediate between Jakarta and Kuala Lumpur over the former's "Crush Malaysia" or confrontation policy.[49] Ikeda twice invited President Sukarno and Prime Minister Tunku Abdul Rachman to Tokyo to have private meetings to reach settlements. Ikeda also visited Jakarta in September 1963 to persuade Sukarno to reach a compromise settlement of the issue. Because of the payment of war reparations and additional credits extended to Indonesia— and perhaps because one of Sukarno's wives was Japanese—Japan was the only major Western power that retained adequate diplomatic communications with Sukarno in the 1963–65 period. The Indonesian president accepted the Japanese mediation role, although the mediation was not successful. Then, in early 1966, Prime Minister Sato Eisaku offered a financial loan to Indonesia on the condition that Indonesia would quickly terminate its militant policy toward Malaysia. Although the mediation role was not successful, the political leverage was.

Another earlier political move by Tokyo was its active participation in the Asian Conference on Cambodia, held in Jakarta in May 1970. Several Asian powers expressed concerns about Cambodia's future, and from among the ten nations that attended the meeting, Malaysia, Indonesia, and Japan were selected to form a task force to urge all foreign forces to withdraw from Cambodia and to press the International Control Commission on Cambodia, originally set up by the 1954 Geneva Conference, to be reactivated. In the following month, the representatives of the three countries visited five capitals, including London and Moscow. Earlier, in 1968, Japan had expressed its interest in serving on an international peace observation team for Indochina, although this did not materialize. Thus, Japan's positive diplomacy after 1977 was not a sudden development.

The question is how far Japanese security relations with the region will develop. Since Prime Minister Fukuda made his famous speech in Manila in 1977, declaring that Japan will not be a military power, Japanese leaders have consistently repeated this pledge. But they continue to face suspicions from Southeast Asian government leaders and intellectuals that "Japanese militarism" is reviving. In support of this contention, they cite Japan's defense spending ($10.36 billion in 1982) as the eighth largest in the world,

Japanese military hardware (such as F-15 and P3C airplanes and destroyers) as formidable, Japanese economic and technological power as able to transform the current small defense industry into an impressive mass-production capacity for sophisticated weapons, and so on. It is true that Japan's 1982 defense budget was larger than the combined total of those of the five ASEAN governments, which was $8.17 billion.[50] On the other hand, Southeast Asians are inclined not to appreciate fully the domestic political constraints on a faster expansion of Japan's defense capability.

They may also be somewhat less concerned than appearances suggest. In fact, when certain Southeast Asian leaders, such as President Suharto and Ferdinand Marcos, warned about a Japanese "military buildup," commentators suggested that their true purpose was to persuade the United States to retain and restore its own military presence in Southeast Asia and to use criticism against Japan as a bargaining chip to draw more Japanese economic aid. If they really feared Japanese militarism, it has been argued, the leaders would have taken some concrete military steps to cope with it. Instead, some ASEAN governments are known to have expressed interest in obtaining Japanese arms or arms technology. The Thai military have been interested in buying Japan-made military equipment. President Suharto asked Nakasone in May 1983 if Japan would be willing to assist Indonesia's defense industry.[51] Singapore's Lee Kuan Yew at one time proposed a joint fleet organized by Western powers, Japan included, to patrol the Straits of Malacca. None of these proposals has yet been implemented, in large part because of Tokyo's prohibitive policy on arms transfer (except for transfer to the United States) and on the overseas dispatch of its own armed forces.

Thus, the security cooperation that has taken place so far has been on a very limited scale. Under the 1958–60 reparations payment program for Indonesia, which totaled $223 million, Japan provided, among other things, 1,500 trucks and 1,300 jeeps, some of which were used by the military for transportation of equipment and troops.[52] Some jeeps were later equipped with anti-aircraft guns. The government has given permission for small-scale arms, such as hand grenades and pistols, or their parts, such as fuses and cartridges, to be exported to Southeast Asia, so long as they are registered to be used for training and police purposes.

Japanese defense attachés and police attachés serve in all the ASEAN capitals. The Japanese Police Agency works with its ASEAN counterparts in control of drug traffic, international terrorists, and other subversives. Since 1982, the Japanese Maritime Safety Agency has begun to hold annual meetings with the Philippine Coast Guard to exchange intelligence regarding maritime safety and drug traffic.[53] Singapore has adopted a Japanese police box (*kōban*) system, under which police officers are stationed in congested apartment complexes to control urban crimes. Malaysia and Indonesia are reportedly interested in following suit.[54]

Quite a few ASEAN military personnel visit Tokyo, and ASEAN states maintain military attachés in Tokyo. Several officers have come to the schools of the Japanese Self-Defense Forces for a short period of training.[55] But there have been no joint military exercises and no significant arms transfers.

In the early 1980s, on the whole, there appear to be no particular sources of political conflict between Japan and the ASEAN region. There seems to be a growing understanding on the part of the ASEAN leaders that Japan's expanded defense capability will actually improve the security of the ASEAN region. Malaysian Prime Minister Mahathir indicated in January 1983 that "Japan is a forward base for ASEAN against Soviet expansionism."[56] By that he meant that by deterring Soviet military movements, Japan was serving as a buffer for the ASEAN states. Philippine Foreign Minister Carlos Romulo spoke along the same lines in the ASEAN foreign ministers' meeting held in June 1983.[57]

A possible source of future tension may lie in approaches to the Indochinese issue. Japan is inclined to think that an economic interdependency between Vietnam and the non-Communist countries will eventually moderate Vietnam's "hegemonic" moves and thus that Japan may be wise to de-freeze its economic aid to Hanoi at some point in the near future. Some ASEAN members, such as Indonesia, seem to share this view, but Japan and the ASEAN nations differ on the correct timing.

In a similar vein, Japan feels that increasing economic aid to Laos may encourage Vientiane to become less dependent on Hanoi. Foreign Minister Abe stated in May 1983 that Japan would increase its economic aid to Laos. He was later criticized by the Indonesian foreign minister, although he apparently was supported by the Thai government.[58] Thus, so far, Japan has been so loyal to ASEAN's position that it tends to be a hostage to ASEAN's Indochinese policy. Japan may find it in its own national interest to disassociate itself slightly from ASEAN's position, thus gaining greater freedom of action in the region. Such a move would probably displease the ASEAN leaders.

Future Prospects

Japan has many actual and potential issues with non-Communist countries in Northeast and Southeast Asia, but its overall relations with them appear healthy and constructive. Japan's strategy of stability and its insistence on a positive diplomatic role, as expressed symbolically in the Fukuda Doctrine, has more or less been accepted in Asia. The general nature of Japan's emerging relations with the region is that, with caution, Japan seeks an enhanced political and economic presence there. Although the non-Communist nations have found the growth of Japan's power useful, they are uneasy that it might become excessive. These states increasingly accept Japan's self-defense capability as a buffer against the growing Soviet military presence in the Asia Pacific region, but they oppose the development of a capability of projecting Japan's military power abroad. They are also critical about Japan's current lack of concern for correcting the trade imbalances and for increasing technology transfer.

Will Japan find it necessary to change its strategy of stability toward the region and its positive stance? What factors might affect such a change? The Japanese are likely to continue to give importance to the Asia Pacific region. Indeed, because the region's dynamic economic growth is drawing more and more attention from the extra-regional powers—including the United States, the Western European countries, and the Soviet Union—it seems likely that the importance of the region in Japanese diplomacy is likely to grow.

There are additional factors to support this speculation. First, Japan's relations with Communist Asian nations, which affect its relations with non-Communist Asian countries, are likely to improve gradually as these states, too, find it beneficial to use Japanese economic power for their national development. Such improved relations between Japan and the Communist nations of Asia would encourage Japan to use its economic leverage in moderating the external conduct of those Communist nations. This is likely to enhance Japan's role in the non-Communist region.

On the other hand, Japan's contacts with Communist Asian countries could impair its relations with non-Communist countries. North Korea, for instance, seems to be losing in a diplomatic competition with South Korea for establishing trade and political relations with the Third World; and South Korea is becoming active in hosting numerous international conferences, including some to which Chinese and Soviet delegates are invited. One unlikely scenario would be for North Korea to express its concern by adopting more terroristic activities against the south, possibly in connection with the 1986 Asian Games and 1988 Olympic Games, both to be held in Seoul and both symbolizing South Korea's diplomatic triumph. If South Korea then perceives that such activities are being assisted by North Korea's supporters in Japan, Tokyo–Seoul relations would be severely strained.

If mainland China should succeed in managing its modernization programs and should start securing more Japanese capital and technology than Taiwan, Japan–Taiwan relations may prove to be more frail than they are generally thought to be. Japanese businessmen might shift their attention to the mainland rather quickly, as they once did during the first half of the 1970s—that is, the initial postrecognition period. But such a situation is not likely to happen in the near future, because the PRC has many internal problems to solve before making itself attractive to foreign capital.

Another possibility is that Japan might disagree with the ASEAN nations about approaches to the Indochinese issue. Both may consider a moderate

Vietnam to be in their interests, but if Japanese efforts for a moderate Vietnam were to produce a Vietnamese–Chinese rapprochement, it would threaten the ASEAN capitals more than Tokyo. Again, such a possibility is very unlikely at the moment.

A second factor that is likely to encourage Japan's positive diplomacy is the change in mutual perceptions that may result from the generational change in both Japanese and other Asia Pacific leaders. Most of the present leaders experienced wartime Japanese occupation and have varying degrees of bitter memories. President Marcos, born in 1917, was a guerrilla fighter against Imperial Army intruders. President Suharto, born in 1921, went through a Japanese-run military training school. Prime Minister Lee Kuan-yew was in Singapore and was 19 years old when the Japanese army invaded. Leading Japanese figures today also spent their youths under military rule, which advocated the Greater East Asia Co-Prosperity Sphere. Their mutual perceptions, which tend to have been colored by wartime experiences, will soon be replaced on both sides by those of the younger generations, who are much less affected by wartime relations. Many upcoming leaders in South Korea, Taiwan, and the ASEAN nations were trained in Western countries in the postwar period and are more comfortable in international dealings than their predecessors have been. They may have a more detached view of Japan than their predecessors do. New Japanese leaders, likewise, are more free of the old ethnocentric view of their country's role in international society. Aided by their own economic growth, these Asian countries will gain more equal status with Japan, which would strengthen their relations with Japan. Naturally, the reverse may be true, too, if the two sides should mismanage their mutual relations—for example, by not cooperating on technology transfer. One must also be aware that as non-Communist Asian countries become economically stronger by achieving higher industrialization, their economies will become more competitive with Japan, thereby creating political tensions.

A third factor that is likely to facilitate the continuation of Japan's positive diplomacy is the welcome the United States is giving such a Japanese role. Whereas Japan's strategy of stability works only under the assumption that the United States maintains its military presence, the United States also benefits from Japan's role of providing economic aid, not just to promote Japanese trade but also to increase the political stability of the region. Since Japan and the United States share the same political objectives, these roles supplement each other. Thus, as long as Washington supports Japan's efforts to increase its defense capabilities and play an active political role, these efforts are likely to continue.

A corollary to this proposition is that if Japan's growing active diplomacy should be seen by the region as a substitute for U.S. commitment to the region or as competitive with Washington rather than cooperative, Tokyo would find it difficult to proceed. It would also find it difficult to proceed if the level of U.S. activity were to change drastically. A much stronger U.S. presence, as in the 1950s and 1960s, would deprive Japan of the need for a positive diplomacy, whereas a much weaker U.S. presence would make Japan's positive conduct fruitless. The South Koreans particularly are in a dilemma. A militarily weak Japan with a strong U.S. presence may not help South Korea's security position to the extent needed if the United States were to divert necessary resources away from South Korea for Japanese defense. But a strong Japanese military power with a weak U.S. presence would remind the Koreans of their prewar unhappy experiences with domineering Japan.

Tokyo–Washington relations are thus important not only for themselves but also for Japanese–Asian relations and for the security of non-Communist Asia as a whole. The proper sharing of the two Pacific powers' roles in the region should be considered in a regional rather than a bilateral context.

In a wider regional context, what is emerging now is an informal, loose coalition of Pacific Basin countries—Japan, South Korea, Taiwan, the six ASEAN nations, with Australia, New Zealand, the United States, and Canada, plus China, although China's position is more than precarious. It is not a tight political alliance, much less a military alliance, but there is a broad consensus about three points: all of the countries are interested in attaining a higher level of economic prosperity through coordination of their respective economic and industrial policies; they all share the view that East Asia and the Western Pacific is an economically dynamic region, which they all wish to use for their respective economic growth; and they all share the growing threat of Soviet military power.

Although this coalition is primarily intended as a device for joint economic progress, it currently assumes an anti-Soviet character. That character appeared particularly salient in 1977–80, when China, advocating "an international united front against Soviet hegemony," actively courted Japan and the United States. However, the anti-Soviet stance has now been slightly weakened by China's changed position, whereby it seeks to be more independent of the U.S. strategic position while seeking transfer of modern U.S. military hardware. This fluctuation in the saliency of its anti-Soviet character seems to strengthen the merit of a loose coalition, allowing for freedom of action for each member within broadly shared political and economic objectives.

Quite a few countries in the Pacific rim have expressed interest in the notion of Pacific Basin cooperation beyond a private, nongovernmental level. In 1979, Prime Minister Ohira commissioned a private study group to look into the framework for Pacific Basin economic cooperation. Ohira's visit to Canberra in early 1980 produced a semigovernmental scheme in the region to continue studies on the same subject. South Korea is a member, but China and Taiwan are not. In July 1982, President Chun Doo Hwan proposed a

Pacific summit conference, which, unlike ideas proposed by Japan or Australia, had connotations of security cooperation. In a way, his proposal is a modified revival of the old Asia-Pacific Council (ASPAC), which had the political objective of combatting Communism, primarily Chinese Communism. Organized on Seoul's initiative, it came into being in 1966 and lasted until early 1973. Australia and New Zealand were among the members, but not the United States. The new proposal may still have anti-Communist objectives, but it does not stress that aspect; and unlike the old one, it includes the United States as a member. An institution actually quite close to President Chun's proposal is the annual ASEAN foreign ministers' meeting, which invites European Community representatives and foreign ministers from Canada, the United States, Australia, and New Zealand, as well as Japan. Although the subjects discussed have been limited to Southeast Asian issues—the Vietnamese military presence in Cambodia, Indochinese refugees, and some economic development issues—the participants share a common concern about the Soviet threat. This meeting represents a loose coalition of like-minded nations in the Pacific Basin region. Future meetings may well be expanded to include South Korea and even China.

As it stands now, however, any formal institutionalization of Pacific Basin cooperation faces membership issues. The difficulty becomes particularly insurmountable in the security field. Thus, the informal coalition that is evolving today as a network of basically bilateral security arrangements between the United States and various Asian partners seems to be the most viable security structure under current conditions and the one under which Japan can most effectively play a more positive role—compatible with the United States and other non-Communist nations in the region—in checking the threatened dominance of Soviet power and in promoting the stability and prosperity of the region.

Notes

1. Nishiyama Takehiko, "Fukuda Sōri no Tōnan Ajia Rekihō" [Prime Minister Fukuda's visit to Southeast Asia], *Gaikō Jihō*, no. 1148(October 1977): 6. See also Watanabe Kōji, "Japan and Southeast Asia," *Asia Pacific Community*, Fall 1980, pp. 83–97; and Bernard Gordon, "Japan, the United States, and Southeast Asia," *Foreign Affairs*, April 1978, pp. 579–600.

2. Richard C. Holbrooke, *U.S.–Japanese Relations in the 1980s*, American Policy Series No. 24 (Tokyo: U.S. Embassy, 1980), p. 3. This was a speech given at the Japan Society, New York, 21 November 1980.

3. Japan, Foreign Ministry, *Waga Gaikō no Kinkyō, 1978* [Recent conditions of our diplomacy, 1978], p. 288.

4. Japan, Foreign Ministry, *Waga Gaikō no Kinkyō, 1983* [Recent conditions of our diplomacy, 1983], pp. 285–386.

5. Japan, Ministry of International Trade and Industry (MITI), *Tsūshō Hakusho, 1983* [White Paper on Trade, 1983], p. 267.

6. *Waga Gaikō no Kinkyō, 1983*, p. 386.

7. *Waga Gaikō no Kinkyō, 1982*, p. 381.

8. *Waga Gaikō no Kinkyō, 1983*, p. 386.

9. *Bōei Nenkan, 1983* [Defense Yearbook, 1983] (Tokyo: Bōei Nenkan Kankōkai, 1983), p. 44.

10. *Waga Gaikō no Kinkyō, 1983*, p. 387.

11. Watanabe Takeshi, *Senryōka no Nihon Zaisei Oboegaki* [Memoranda on Japanese finance under the Occupation] (Tokyo: Nihon Keizai Shinbun Sha, 1966), pp. 294–95.

12. *Public Papers of the Presidents of the United States*, Carter, 22 March 1977, p. 480.

13. Ibid., Reagan, 8 May 1981, p. 414.

14. Nishihara Masashi, "How Much Longer the Fruits of the 'Yoshida Doctrine'?" in Han Bae-ho and Yamamoto Tadashi, eds., *Korea and Japan* (Seoul: Korea University, Asiatic Research Center, 1978), pp. 150–67.

15. Yoshida Shigeru, *Kaisō Jūnen* [Ten Years in Recollection] (Tokyo: Shinchō Sha, 4 vols.), Vol. IV (1958), pp. 264–65; and Vol I (1957), p. 271.

16. Miyazawa Kiichi gave a keynote speech in the annual meeting of the Trilateral Commission, held in London in March 1980, emphasizing Japan's political responsibilities in the trilateral world. See his "To Meet the Challenge," *Trialogue*, no. 23 (Spring 1980): 5–9.

17. Obtained from Public Information Division, Air Staff Office, Air Self-Defense Force, Japan.

18. Fukuda Takeo, "Waga Shushō Jidai" [My Prime Minister years], *Chuo Koron*, October 1980, p. 292.

19. Nishiyama, "Fukuda Sōri no Tōnan Ajia Rekihō," p. 9. Nishiyama also argued that Japan's ASEAN diplomacy was not a substitute for U.S. diplomacy. See his "Waga Kuni no tai-ASEAN Gaikō" [Our Diplomacy Toward ASEAN], *Gaikō Jihō*, no. 1146 (August 1977): 3–8.

20. Nishiyama, "Fukuda Sōri no Tōnan Ajia Rekihō," p. 9.

21. Okita Saburō, "Japanese Foreign Policy in the 1980s," in his *Ekonomisuto Gaishō no 252 Nichi* [Economist Foreign Minister's 252 Days] (Tokyo: Tōyō Keizai Shinpo Sha, 1980), p. 232. This was a speech given at the Foreign Correspondents Club of Japan, 23 January 1980.

22. Nomura Research Institute, *Kokusai Kankyō no Kenka to Nihon no Taiō; 21-Seiki e no Teigen* [Changes in the international environment and Japan's responses; Recommendations for the 21st century] NRC-77-4a, pp. 145–49. The concept was then adopted by Prime Minister Ohira in 1979, when he established a private study group with that name. See Comprehensive National Security Study Group, *Report on Comprehensive National Security*, July 1980.

23. This led to the Foreign Ministry's report, *Keizai Kyōryoku no Rinen* [The doctrine of economic cooperation], December 1980.

24. Unless otherwise mentioned, trade figures here and hereafter are from Japan, Foreign Ministry, *Waga Gaikō no Kinkyō*.

25. *Mainichi Shinbun,* 21 July 1979, morning edition. Although his proposal was apparently accepted by the Korean side, it has never since materialized.

26. *Asahi Shinbun,* 30 January 1983, morning edition. Regarding Nakasone's emissary, Ryōzō, see also Hong N. Kim, "Politics of Japan's Economic Aid to South Korea," *Asia Pacific Community,* no. 20 (Spring 1983): 94–95.

27. Anh Kyo-tuk, "Bei-So no Kyokutō Shinryaku to Kan-Nichi kan no Anzen to Heiwa" [The Far Eastern strategies of the United States and the Soviet Union and security and peace between Korea and Japan], *Ajia Kōron,* October 1983, pp. 64–68.

28. Japan Defense Agency, *Bōei Hakusho, 1983* [White paper on defense, 1983], p. 244.

29. *Asahi Shinbun,* 22 September 1984, morning edition.

30. An opinion survey conducted by the Prime Minister's Office in April 1983 reveals that, when asked which country Japan should become friendly with, only 1 percent chose South Korea, as compared to 39 percent favoring the United States. *Asahi Shinbun,* 19 November 1983, morning edition.

31. Japan, Ministry of Justice, *Shutsunyūgoku Kanri Tokei Nenpō, 1970* and *1982.*

32. Nikkan Kankei o Kirokusuru Kai, ed., *Shiryō Nikkan Kankei II* [Data on Japanese–Korean relations, II] (Tokyo: Gendaishi Shuppan Kai, 1976), pp. 235–77.

33. Yamamoto Tsuyoshi, "Nikkan Kankei to Yatsugi Kazuo" [Japanese–Korean relations and Yatsugi Kazuo], *Kokusai Seiji,* No. 75 (October 1983): 114–29.

34. *Public Papers of the Presidents of the United States,* Nixon, No. 453, 21 November 1969, p. 954.

35. Japan, Foreign Ministry, *Gekkan Kokusai Mondai Shiryō,* February 1983, p. 18.

36. See, for instance, Japan, Foreign Ministry, *Waga Gaikō no Kinkyō, 1980,* p. 17; *1981,* p. 19; *1982,* p. 23.

37. *Japan 1983: An International Comparison* (Tokyo: Keizai Koho Center, 1983), pp. 32–33.

38. Japan, Ministry of Justice, *Shutsunyūgoku Kanri Tokei Nenpō.*

39. Japan, Prime Minister's Office, *Statistical Yearbook of Japan, 1982,* p. 36.

40. Taiwan Kenkyujo, *Chūka Minkoku Sōran, 1983* [Comprehensive survey of the Republic of China, 1983] (Tokyo: Taiwan Kenkyujo, 1983), pp. 799–813.

41. Ibid., p. 814.

42. Ibid., pp. 814–815.

43. Japan, Foreign Ministry, *Waga Gaikō no Kinkyō, 1983,* pp. 558–59.

44. Calculated from *Japan 1983: An International Comparison,* p. 29.

45. Japan, Ministry of Justice, *Shutsunyūgoku Kanri Tokei Nenpō.*

46. Japan, Foreign Ministry, *Gekkan Kokusai Mondai Shiryō,* September 1977, pp. 51–55.

47. Japan, Foreign Ministry, *Waga Gaikō no Kinkyō, 1983,* p. 101.

48. *Waga Gaikō no Kinkyō, 1982,* pp. 405–407; and "Sonoda Steals the Show," *Far Eastern Economic Review,* 10 July 1981, pp. 26–27.

49. Nishihara Masashi, *The Japanese and Sukarno's Indonesia* (Honolulu: University Press of Hawaii, 1976), pp. 128–50.

50. The figures here are based on *The Military Balance 1983–84* (London: International Institute for Strategic Studies, 1983).

51. *Asahi Shinbun,* 12 May 1983, morning edition.

52. Nishihara, *The Japanese and Sukarno's Indonesia,* p. 105.

53. Japan, Maritime Safety Agency, *Kaijō Hoan Hakusho, 1983* [White paper on maritime safety, 1983], p. 339.

54. *Sankei Shinbun,* 1 November 1983, evening edition.

55. Since 1975, thirty-three Singaporean and forty-seven Thai officers have been trained in Japan. Japan, Defense Agency, *Bōei Hakosho, 1983* [White paper on defense, 1983], p. 339.

56. *Asahi Shinbun,* 1 January 1983, morning edition.

57. *Asahi Shinbun,* 30 June 1983, morning edition.

58. *Asahi Shinbun,* 29 June 1983, morning edition.

4
South Korea and Taiwan: Local Deterrence

Byung-joon Ahn

South Korea

For more than thirty years, the primary task of South Korea's international security policy has been to deter North Korea from resuming the attack. Unable to accomplish this alone, especially in view of the support China and the Soviet Union give to their northern partner, the government of South Korea has striven to augment its power internationally by maintaining its alliance with the United States, strengthening its economic and political ties with Japan, and developing more enduring relations with the non-Communist countries of Southeast Asia.

Of these relationships, those with the United States and Japan are absolutely vital. At the same time, they are not free of strain. As Koreans see it, the basic problem is that Americans and Japanese tend to view the situation in the Korean peninsula as different from their own situations. To most Koreans, these powers too often seem to treat South Korea as not important in itself but as a sideshow to their own relationship. To a certain extent, the South Korean government has learned to live with this, recognizing that the differences in its weight and theirs in world affairs may make such a relationship not entirely avoidable. It has even been able, on occasion, to utilize this relationship to advantage, at times turning to the United States for help in its relations with Japan and at other times calling on Japan for help in its relations with the United States.

Nevertheless, South Korea has never been happy with the situation. For some time, it has been groping for ways to overcome these asymmetries by demonstrating a capacity for a more active and independent foreign policy—for example, by hosting the Asian Games in 1986 and the Olympic Games in 1988. Its hope is to persuade its big partners to lift their eyes from their own relationship and pay greater attention to the specific needs of South Korea. Backed by its growing strategic and economic power, South Korea is thus working to redefine the partnerships on which it relies so heavily.

Managing the U.S. Alliance

For now, the dependability of the U.S.–South Korean alliance rests, as it has for the past thirty years, on the extent to which America's regional concern for the big powers—the Soviet Union, China, and Japan—is in accord with South Korea's local concern for North Korea.

When South Korea and the United States have shared a strategic consensus, they have been able to work together smoothly. When they have diverged in their strategic thinking, the deeper differences between the more open and competitive American political process and the relatively closed and controlled Korean political process have come to the fore. Attempts by each side to influence the other have been clumsily handled, and the relationship has fallen into serious strain.

The first time under the alliance that the solidarity of security views was broken was in 1969, when President Nixon enunciated the Guam Doctrine, calling upon Asian countries to assume the primary responsibility for providing the manpower for their own defense.[1] In 1971, the United States proceeded to pull the Seventh Division out of South Korea. Compensation was pledged in the form of a $1.2 billion force modernization program, but Seoul's anxiety was high. It rose even higher when the United States withdrew from Vietnam and the North Koreans were discovered to have dug a series of tunnels beneath the DMZ.

Facing this direct evidence of North Korea's aggresive intent and what he feared was the strategic withdrawal of the United States, President Park searched vigorously for domestic alternatives. He began to develop a defense industry. At the same time, believing that widespread domestic unrest would undermine the capacity of South Korea to withstand a military attack, he issued a series of emergency decrees designed to consolidate unity and stability at home. With these, he began to crack down on a number of dissident leaders, including Kim Dae Jung.

The side effect of these actions on the United States was dramatic. South Korea became one of the principal targets when the U.S. Congress amended the Foreign Assistance Act to require that the State Department report on the status of human rights in countries receiving aid. Subsequently, congressional committees conducted critical hearings on the human rights situation in Korea.

By this time, the level of disagreement had begun to worry leaders in Washington as well. In August 1975, President Ford tried to relieve Korean fears by sending Secretary of Defense James Schlesinger to Seoul to hint at the possible readiness of the United States to use nuclear weapons in the case of another North Korean assault.[2] In November, he took the additional step of quietly urging President Park to be more lenient toward his opponents and warned that, otherwise, public and congressional support for Korea would erode.[3]

Throughout this period, the South Korean government had been looking for a change in American policy that would restore its confidence in the U.S. tie. Instead, the election of Jimmy Carter served only to intensify the crisis. "It is a new world that calls for a new American foreign policy," he proclaimed, "a policy based on constant decency in its values and on optimism in our historical vision."[4] Human rights would be given an even higher priority. Moreover, in March 1977, he justified the worst of Korean fears, announcing that all U.S. ground troops would be phased out of South Korea in four or five years. Like Nixon, he promised a force improvement plan—this one worth $800 million—to compensate for the loss.

But to the Korean government, nothing could substitute for the presence of American ground forces. The nation grew panicky, and a risky expedient was allegedly attempted. Tongsun Park, a Korean businessman residing in Washington, and his associates are widely believed to have distributed some $750,000 to various U.S. congressmen in an effort to buy their support for Korea, particularly for blocking the troop withdrawals. The American press, inflamed by the Watergate affair, quickly dubbed this "Koreagate" and conducted a zealous investigation. The U.S. Congress followed up with an investigation of its own, even attempting to get the former Korean ambassador to the United States, Don-jo Kim, to testify, despite his diplomatic immunity. It was a sordid business, and it severely damaged the image of South Korea in the eyes of the American public.

Meanwhile, however, opposition to the troop withdrawal began to gain ground in the U.S. Congress and among the American military, so that when the U.S. intelligence community revised upward its estimate of North Korean strength, President Carter was forced to reconsider.[5] He visited Seoul in July 1979 and announced that he would shelve the plan, at least until 1981. He also agreed on that occasion with President Park that an American military presence was necessary to preserve peace and stability in Northeast Asia. In return, Seoul promised to increase its military spending from 5.5 to 6 percent of GNP from 1980 on.[6]

But before a significant thaw could take place in Korean–American relations, the U.S. government's confidence in the stability of the Korean government was shocked in October 1979 by the assassination of President Park and the political turmoil that followed. The uprising that took place in Kwangju was graphically reported in the cover stories of *Time* and *Newsweek*. The political situation remained unsettled until General Chun was elected president in September 1980.

It was not until February 1981, in fact, that this dangerous trend in Korean–American relations was reversed. A new U.S. president, Ronald Reagan, had just been elected, and one of his first acts in office was to proclaim that security interests would again receive priority in the U.S. policy toward South Korea. First persuading President Chun to issue a pardon, commuting the life sentence of Kim Dae Jung, he then invited the Korean president to Washington for high-level talks on security, policy planning, and economic cooperation.

At the thirteenth Korea–United States Security Consultative Meeting in San Francisco in March 1981, Secretary of Defense Weinberger promised that the United States would sell South Korea 38 F-16 fighter planes and would provide a military sales package of $327 million for 1981–82 with somewhat eased credit terms. At the fourteenth meeting in Seoul the next year, Secretary Weinberger strongly reaffirmed the American commitment to render "prompt and effective assistance to repel armed invasion" of Korea.[7] The Korean government, for its part, responded with efforts to close the political gap as well. In March 1982, it further reduced the life sentence of Kim Dae Jung to 20 years, and in December he was allowed to go to the United States. Referring to these political issues in the joint statement issued in November 1983, President Chun joined President Reagan in affirming "the importance of defending and strengthening freedom and the institutions that serve freedom, openness and political stability."[8]

Since that time, South Korea and the United States have been working smoothly to strengthen their security relationship. Once more, the two countries agree on the essentially aggressive and dangerous character of the North Korean regime and on the superiority of its armed forces to those of the south. According to the latest estimate by the London-based International Institute for Strategic Studies, North Korea maintains an army of more than 784,500 men, while South Korea forces number only 622,000. Richard Armitage, U.S. assistant secretary of defense, points out that Pyongyang still has an advantage over Seoul in all capabilities, as follows: two to one in maneuver battalions, two to one in artillery, three to one in tanks, two to one in fighter aircraft, and three to one in naval combatants.[9] Such comparisons are somewhat inconclusive, in that they do not take into account differences of quality; but they testify to the very important fact that the United States and South Korea agree that Pyongyang's forces are far larger than necessary for purely defensive purposes.

There is no disagreement between them, either, on the need for the United States to maintain ground forces in the peninsula. The reason, as Henry Kissinger pointed out, is the same in Korea as it is in Europe: to deter the would-be aggressor.[10] Less understood but vitally important is the American surveillance and intelligence-gathering mission, which can only be effectively performed when foot soldiers are present.

At the same time, the United States and South Korea continue to agree on the need to increase South Korea's fighting capabilities. Washington allotted $180 million worth of foreign military sales to South Korea for 1983 and envisioned $230 million for 1984 and 1985, respectively. Moreover, in Seoul in November 1983, President Reagan promised that the United States would continue to make available the weapons systems and technology the South Koreans may require.[11] These actions are supplementary, of course, to the Republic of Korea's own force improvement efforts. Since 1971, when the United States pulled out the Seventh Division, Seoul has worked steadily to develop its own defense industries. It now produces ammunition, rifles, artillery, and light tanks. Its aim is to achieve a self-sufficient military balance with North Korea—excluding its Chinese and Soviet supporters, of course— by the early 1990s. If South Korea can sustain a high level of economic growth and continue to improve its science and technology, it should be able to accomplish its goal.

Although the strategic consensus seems to have restored a sense of solidarity to the Korean–American relationship, two other subjects have the potential for mischief. One is the appropriate negotiating stance to be taken toward North Korea. After being virtually closed since the failure of the Geneva Conference in 1954, the subject was reopened in 1975 by Henry Kissinger, when he proposed at the thirtieth U.N. General Assembly that the two Koreas, the United States, and China hold an international meeting to explore the possibility of securing a "cross recognition" of the two Korean states by the four powers, including Japan and the Soviet Union. This idea had Seoul's support, but Pyongyang immediately rejected it—branding the proposal a scheme to perpetuate "two Koreas"—and instead demanded direct talks with the United States alone for the purpose of replacing the current armistice with a peace agreement.[12]

South Korea has always opposed official, bilateral talks between the United States and North Korea, insisting that only South Korea itself would be the appropriate party for such negotiations. In deference to this stance, Washington has always rejected any official contact with Pyongyang unless Seoul is fully represented. It did so this time as well. But the idea that there might be a time or a formula for bringing North Korea to the bargaining table is one that has continued to tantalize Washington.

In July 1979, it was the Carter administration that took up the issue, this time suggesting a tripartite conference of only Washington, Seoul, and Pyongyang. President Park reluctantly accepted the idea and in effect made a joint proposal with President Carter, but Pyongyang rejected it again. In March 1983, it was the Reagan administration's turn. The U.S. Department of State this time issued new guidelines to permit U.S. diplomats in certain capitals to have informal contacts with North Korean diplomats. It also relaxed rules on issuing visas to North Koreans who might wish to attend academic conferences in the United States. The case of a North Korean diplomat at the United Nations who was charged with sexual abuse interrupted this effort; but in September, as soon as the case was settled, the State

Department resumed the exploration of negotiating possibilities, informing the North Koreans, through the Chinese, that the United States would be willing to participate in any talks in which South Korea was represented on an equal basis.[13]

On October 8, 1983, Pyongyang responded by proposing a tripartite conference of Washington, Seoul, and itself, but the terrorist bombing that killed seventeen South Korean high officials in Rangoon the following day made it impossible to follow up on this initiative. South Korea insisted that North Korea would have to admit its responsibility for the affair before talks could begin. In any event, Seoul and Washington were agreed that the Pyongyang formula was unacceptable. They were not willing to enter a conference for the narrow purpose Pyongyang had enunciated—to replace the armistice with a "peace agreement." Nor did they wish to enter one without the participation of the Chinese. Washington, too, returned to this formula. In Seoul in November, President Reagan rephrased the American position of September, explaining that, in his view, any step toward North Korea that was not reciprocated toward South Korea by North Korea's principal allies would not be conducive to promoting stability in the area.[14] He also explained this position to Zhao Ziyang in Washington in January 1984 and reaffirmed it when he visited Beijing in April of that year.[15] As this position was unacceptable to North Korea and its allies, the conference issue, at least for the time being, appeared to be dead. The South Korean government then returned to its older call for a direct North–South dialogue. The U.S. government cooperated by conveying, through the Chinese, South Korea's readiness to engage in such confidence-building measures as exchanges of sports, mails, and people.

Another issue that has the potential for opening up rifts between the two allies is trade policy. The government in Seoul is increasingly worried by the restrictions Washington is placing or threatening to place on South Korea's exports of steel, television sets, and other manufactured goods. But if past experience is a guide, it seems reasonable to suppose that this issue, like those of political reform and negotiating posture, can be prevented from rupturing the alliance so long as the strategic consensus holds.

Striving for Japanese Support

South Korea and Japan are often said to be near and yet far from each other. Although they are separated only by a narrow sea and although both are closely allied with the United States, they are constrained by history and domestic politics from forging any direct military security links with each other. It was not until 1965 that they established diplomatic relations, and it was not until the early 1980s that they began as a normal procedure to take up bilateral issues directly, rather than through their American ally.

Thus, how to secure Japanese support for South Korea's deterrence policy has been a pressing and difficult problem. What Seoul desires is clear enough. Realizing that deep, popular sentiments in both countries rule out any direct military security link, it at least wants the government of Japan to recognize unambiguously that the security of South Korea is vital to the security of Japan and, in consequence, to give South Korea its unwavering political and economic support.

To achieve these objectives, the leaders in Seoul have concentrated their attention on the officials in Tokyo, particularly on certain influential members of the ruling Liberal Democratic Party and of the business community, using such organizations as the ROK–Japan Parliamentary Association and the Korea–Japan (Private Economic) Cooperation Committee. Opposition parties in both countries have been critical of this close interaction. Seoul's leaders have also relied heavily on the United States to persuade the authorities in Tokyo to affirm Japan's security interest. The United States, with its own substantial commitment to South Korea, has worked hard for the same objective. In November 1969, for example, President Nixon persuaded Prime Minister Sato to accept a strong "Korean clause" in their joint communique, which read: "The security of the Republic of Korea is essential to Japan's own security." At the time of the return of Okinawa to Japan, President Nixon secured a public pledge from the prime minister that U.S. bases in Japan would be available for use in the conventional defense of South Korea and Tawian.[16]

It seems likely that the Japanese government took these positions partly to appease the U.S. government. It is certain that it did so, in part, because it felt that it was in Japan's interest for the United States to guarantee the security of South Korea and that, without these pledges, the United States might weaken. Several times during the era of détente in the 1970s, when South Korea became a principal target of America's limited disengagement policy, the Japanese government spoke up in protest. In August 1975, for example, Sakata Michita, the Director-General of Japan's Self-Defense Agency, asked U.S. Defense Secretary Schlesinger not to withdraw the U.S. ground forces from South Korea. When, in spite of this, President Carter announced his withdrawal plan in 1977, Prime Minister Fukuda quietly told him that, in his view, the plan was a mistake that would seriously jeopardize South Korea's security.[17]

There is also reason to believe that the government of Japan is beginning to take more seriously the desirability of some kind of security cooperation with South Korea. At the foreign ministerial conference held in August 1981, Foreign Minister Sonoda said that he had come to "appreciate the defense efforts" made by South Korea.[18] At the United States–Japan Security Consultative Committee meeting in January 1982, the Japanese side even agreed to carry out a joint study of contingency planning for an emergency situation that might break out in areas outside Japan. In January 1983, Prime Minister Nakasone selected Seoul for his first foreign trip; there, he endorsed the thesis that peace and stability on the Korean peninsula are essential to the peace and stability of East Asia, including Japan. In the present atmosphere, any direct security cooperation between South Korea and Japan, such as might be involved in joint staff planning and military exercises, is still out of the question; but possibilities do exist for formal cooperation, mediated by the United States, such as might be involved in the exchange of intelligence or parallel action to close the Tsushima Strait.

And yet, to the chagrin of the South Korean government during these same years, the Japanese government has often seemed more committed to the United States than to South Korea. Part of the explanation may be found in the vicissitudes of domestic politics; but for whatever reasons, Japan has at all times sought to avoid confrontation with North Korea. It has consistently permitted trade with North Korea, and on occasion, various Japanese officials and political leaders have hinted at a willingness to accommodate it even further.

In 1974, for example, Foreign Minister Kimura Toshio seemed to be moving toward a "two Koreas" policy, stating that "the peace and security of the entire Korean peninsula"—not of South Korea alone—"is essential to Japan's security."[19] In March 1981, Foreign Minister Ito even told U.S. Secretary of State Alexander Haig that, in his view, North Korea posed no military threat to South Korea.[20] In June the Asia–Africa Study Group of Japan's ruling party invited a North Korean politician, Hyun Chun-Guk, to Tokyo; and in November, Kuno Chuji, a leading parliamentarian of that party, organized a Leage of Japanese Diet Members to Promote Friendly Relations with North Korea and recruited more than 240 members for it.

In 1983, in apparent coordination with the U.S. demarche to explore North Korean attitudes, the government of Japan admitted a delegation from Pyongyang to the twenty-third Asian–African Legal Consultative Conference, held in Tokyo in June, and Foreign Minister Abe went out of his way to meet with delegation members at a diplomatic reception. The Japanese Foreign Ministry subsequently publicized some old guidelines authorizing its diplomats to make contact with North Koreans at social gatherings. In July 1983, with the tacit understanding of the Japanese government, Mr. Kuno went to Pyongyang and, upon returning, advocated an exchange of reporters between Japan and North Korea and the establishment of trade offices in both capitals.[21] Such Japanese behavior has inevitably provoked a strong reaction in Seoul.

Relations have also been seriously strained on occasion by Korean behavior, notably by domestic political upheavals in South Korea, which has fed the opposition in Tokyo and has caused the government there to pull back its support, at least temporarily.[22] The abduction of Kim Dae Jung from a hotel in Japan in 1973, allegedly by South Korean agents, and his subsequent treatment in South Korea are cases in point. So, too, were the political unrest in South Korea in 1980 and the arrest of Kim Dae Jung. Japan's Prime Minister Suzuki Zenko responded that November by warning the Korean ambassador, Choi Kyung Nok, that Japan might halt its economic aid and might even open relations with North Korea if Kim were to be executed. Only after Kim's sentence had been commuted did Tokyo resume its regular consultations with Seoul. The activities in Japan of the North Korea-backed General Federation of Korean Residents (Chōsōren) have also caused problems for Seoul.

The shooting down of KAL-007 on September 1, 1983, and the bomb blast at the Aung San Mausoleum on October 9 seems to have put a halt, at least temporarily, to the antagonistic trends in Japanese policy. Tokyo condemned Moscow for the airline incident and joined the United States in imposing sanctions against Soviet civilian flights. After the Burmese government confirmed North Korean involvement in the Rangoon incident, Tokyo decided to curtail contact with and travel to Pyongyang. When Hu Yaobang visited Tokyo in November, Prime Minister Nakasone complained to him about North Korean terrorism; and when Nakasone visited Beijing in March 1984, he supported the South Korean and U.S. position vis-à-vis the North Korean proposal for tripartite talks. He even went so far as to persuade Zhao Ziyang to allow visits by Korean relatives between South Korea and China.[23]

In this way, although there have been serious blocks to South Korea's achieving the political and economic partnership with Japan it feels its security requires, it has been making steady progress, with the help of the United States. Its success in the 1982–83 negotiations with Tokyo for economic assistance illustrate how far it has come. In 1982, Seoul asked Tokyo to acknowledge directly the contribution South Korea makes to Japan's security by providing it with $6 billion of governmental credits. This was a bold move by the government under President Chun to attempt to restructure the relationship with Tokyo, independent of the United States–Japan bilateral ties. Initially, Tokyo rejected outright any idea of linking economic cooperation with security; but it gradually moderated its stand, indicating its willingness to offer some economic aid on the basis of merit and available funds. When negotiations became deadlocked, Washington discreetly intervened to encourage an early settlement for the sake of stability in the Northeast Asian region.

The two sides were in the process of edging toward an agreement when, in the summer of 1982, the furor over the revision of Japanese high school textbooks caused the negotiations to be suspended. Distortion of historical facts about Japan's rule over Korea triggered a series of street demonstrations in South Korea against the Japanese government. When the Japanese Education Ministry promised to have the textbooks corrected, the anti-Japanese campaign subsided. This gave Prime Minister Nakasone the opportunity to settle the issue decisively. In January 1983, Seoul reached an agreement with him on a $4 billion package, including $1.85 billion in official development aid and $2.15 billion in Export-Import Bank credits.

Whatever the conception of this unprecedented credit may be in Tokyo, the understanding in Seoul is that because it serves to ease somewhat the heavy burden of defense expenditures borne by Seoul, it is an unpublicized but nevertheless real acknowledgment by Japan of the role South Korea plays in Japan's defense. As such, it symbolizes the political and economic partnership Seoul would like to see.

"Correct" Relations with Taiwan

South Korea has had a long and intimate relationship with Taiwan. The two countries have much in common. They share Chinese culture and a colonial past under Japan. Each engages in a "soft authoritarian" form of government that is currently testing the waters of liberalization. The current South Korean government is pledged to transfer power according to its constitutional procedure in 1988. If this is accomplished, one may expect that some kind of interest politics will emerge as a result of rapid industrialization and the growth of the middle class.

The Nationalist political system in Taiwan is also loosening its controls, seeking to base its legitimacy on something other than the pretension that it will liberate the mainland from the Communist regime. Martial law continues to be enforced, but a policy of "Taiwanization" is in progress. This is a process through which more and more native-born islanders are being brought into both the government and the ruling party. Over 70 percent of the party's 2 million members are now said to be native-born; and the number of Taiwanese appointed to the party's thirty-one-member Central Committee has recently increased to twelve. In March 1984, President Chiang Ching-kuo nominated Lee Teng-hui, a native Taiwanese, as his vice-president for the 6-year term beginning in May 1985, thus making him the first Taiwanese who can take over the presidency should President Chiang fail to complete another 6-year term.[24] At the same time, more and more political opposition is being allowed. In the local elections held in November 1981, for example, non-Kuomintang elements, referred to as *tangwai,* or persons "outside the party," captured 25 percent of the seats.

The two governments also find themselves in similar international predicaments as regimes in divided territories, facing formidable foes against whom they cannot hope to defend themselves alone. They have maintained diplomatic relations since 1948, when the Republic of Korea was founded. So long as both have confronted the same foes—China and the Soviet Union— and both have received similar support from the same friends—especially the United States and, at least economically, Japan—the two countries have pursued an intimate and supportive relationship. South Korea's recent efforts to open a door to China, however, have inevitably strained the relationship.

In 1983–84 two incidents occurred that highlighted this new problem. The first incident was the forced landing of China's Trident airplane in May 1983. Contrary to its earlier handling of the two Chinese pilots who had defected to South Korea and whom it allowed to resettle in Taiwan, Seoul decided in the Trident case to deal with the six hijackers cautiously, in accordance with the Hague Convention. By so doing, Seoul was able to achieve its objective of entering into direct negotiations with Beijing officials. In the end, Seoul returned the hijacked plane to Beijing and subjected the six hijackers to South Korean laws, sentencing them to 6-year prison terms. Beijing protested the punishments as too light, whereas, Taipei protested their being tried at all and demanded, to no avail, that they be released as "freedom fighters."

The second incident took place during the eighth Asian Youth Basketball Championships, held in Seoul in April 1984. The Korean Basketball Association, which was hosting the occasion, did not allow Taiwan's teams to carry their national flag at the opening ceremony, although it did allow the Chinese teams to carry theirs. This prompted the Taiwanese teams to go home. After the Taiwanese teams had returned to Taipei, there were a series of demonstrations and protests against Seoul's action. Some Taiwanese leaders called for cuts in trade, shipping, and airline activities with South Korea. Taipei indeed decided not to grant a new quota for Korean automobile imports.

Nevertheless, the Seoul–Taipei relationship has remained "correct" and in all probability will continue to be so through the 1980s—provided that the United States maintains the deterrence on which the external security of each country depends and provided that each finds an effective path to the political stability and institutionalization required for its security at home.

The Opening to Southeast Asia

South Korea has no historic connections with the countries of Southeast Asia on which to draw. It would like to have their political support for its policy toward North Korea, and it would like to play a larger role on the regional scene, but for the time being, it has had to be content with an expanding economic relationship.

South Korea's first openings to the south were diplomatic. It began early with the Philippines in 1949, then gradually normalized relations with other countries until it now enjoys full diplomatic relations with each of the six ASEAN states, as shown in the table below. This is in contrast to the efforts of North Korea, which still has no diplomatic relations with the Philippines or Brunei.

Country	Date
Philippines	May 16, 1949
Thailand	October 1, 1958
Malaysia	February 23, 1960
Indonesia	September 8, 1973
Singapore	August 7, 1975
Brunei	January 1, 1984

Trade relations have followed. In 1970, for example, South Korea's exports to the ASEAN countries were valued at only $22 million; they rose to $1.13 billion in 1980. Its imports in 1970 totaled $136 million; in 1981, they rose to $1.61 billion.[25] Although the exchange has been in favor of the ASEAN countries, it rests on a great deal of complementarity—South Korea being a manufacturing country and the ASEAN states largely vendors of resources. In a very short period of time, the subregion has become South Korea's fourth largest trading partner, after Japan, the United States, and the Middle East. In addition, capital has begun to flow. Several large South Korean firms are making substantial investments in construction and in exploration projects for oil and natural gas, especially in Indonesia and Malaysia.

Success in these efforts has encouraged South Korea to offer its leadership to the non-Communist countries of the Asia Pacific region for the formation of some kind of cooperative, multilateral economic structure. Since South Korea is a member of neither ASEAN nor OECD, it has been anxious to break out of its diplomatic isolation by exerting its influence in the Third World in general and in Southeast Asia in particular. It has hoped, also, that such evidence of diplomatic initiative and capability would encourage the United States to remain in the region. In addition, as a former Japanese colony and yet a middle-level industrializing country, South Korea is genuinely interested in fostering mutually beneficial economic relations with the ASEAN countries.

With these objectives in mind, South Korean representatives have been active from the beginning in the semiprivate, semiofficial Pacific Economic Cooperation Conferences. Since 1980, these conferences have been providing a forum for interested businessmen, academics, and government officials from each of the non-Communist countries of the Asia Pacific region to examine the possibilities of multilateralism. For example, at the fourth meeting, which took place in Seoul in April 1985, a South Korean task force presented a report on the trade of manufactured goods within the Pacific region. Through this body, South Korea is exploring ways to establish some institutional access to ASEAN.

At an official level, when President Suharto visited Seoul in 1982, President Chun renewed his call for a summit meeting of Asian leaders to discuss trade and economic cooperation. Suharto and other ASEAN leaders have agreed in principle on the need for such cooperation, but they have taken rather cautious positions, apparently fearing that any larger organization for Pacific cooperation might well dilute the integrity of ASEAN itself.

Understanding these attitudes, South Korea has been concentrating its political efforts on deepening its political relations with each ASEAN state individually. In June and July 1981, President Chun made state visits to each of the ASEAN countries. Though designed to strengthen economic and political relations generally, these visits also served to project the image of a politically stable state with an independent foreign policy. Significantly, the leaders of these countries not only agreed to expand economic cooperation, but also endorsed South Korea's call for dialogue with North Korea and the simultaneous admission of both Koreas to the United Nations. From this time on, an official cooperation committee of some form has been established between South Korea and each ASEAN country. In 1982, Thai Prime Minister Prem Tinsulanond and Indonesian President Suharto paid reciprocal visits to Seoul. In August 1983, Malaysian Prime Minister Mahathir bin Mohammad also visited Seoul and took the occasion to tell President Chun that his country would like to learn from South Korea as part of its "look East" policy. In March 1984, Sultan Muda Hassanal Bolkiah visited Seoul as the king of the newly independent Brunei.

Taiwan

Although Taiwan is similar to South Korea in many ways, its international position is substantially different in at least one important particular. Since the normalization of China's relations with the United States and Japan and China's admission into the United Nations, Taiwan has suffered a serious diplomatic setback. Of all the states in the Asia Pacific region, only South Korea continues to maintain diplomatic relations with it. Yet Taiwan has not only survived, but prospered, although the repeated calls by China for its "liberation" and China's success so far in coping with the Hong Kong problem cast some uncertainty over its future.

Taiwan's external security depends primarily on the state of Sino–American relations in general and the American defense commitment in particular. So far, in spite of Chinese pressure, that commitment has been kept. It rests today on the Shanghei Communique of 1972, which included a statement of U.S. interest in a peaceful settlement of the Taiwan question by the Chinese themselves. In more specific terms, under the Taiwan Relations Act of 1979, the United States has promised to sell arms of a defensive nature to Taiwan so that Taiwan can maintain the capacity to resist any resort to force that threatens its security and social and economic system. During the presidential campaign in 1980, Ronald Reagan divulged his intention to upgrade the unofficial relationship when he became president; but after he assumed office, his secretary of state, Alexander Haig, continued the policy of seeking a strategic partnership with Beijing. Haig visited Beijing in June 1981 and agreed to sell U.S. arms to China. At the same time, Washington was considering the sale of the FX aircraft to Taiwan. At that point, Beijing demanded that Washington limit all arms sales to Taiwan, and in September 1981, it tried to persuade Taiwan to return to China on the basis of a nine-point program that promised Taiwan autonomy as a special administrative region, with the right even to retain its own armed forces. Deeply distrustful of Beijing's intentions, Taipei rejected the offer.

But Washington eventually came to endorse it and after a prolonged negotiation on the arms transfer question, issued a joint communique with Beijing on August 17, 1982, stating that "it does not seek to carry out a long-term policy of arms sales to Taiwan, that its arms sales to Taiwan will not exceed, either in qualitative or in quantitative terms, the level of those supplied in recent years," and "that it intends to reduce gradually its sales of arms to Taiwan, leading over a period of time to a final resolution."[26]

After this agreement was reached, Sino–American relations regained some momentum, as shown by U.S. Secretary of Defense Caspar Weinberger's visit to Beijing in September and Chinese Foreign Minister Wu Xueqian's visit to Washington in January 1984. When President Reagan himself made a state visit to Beijing in April 1984, Taipei could not help but be deeply worried. It was somewhat relieved by the fact that the Chinese reportedly did not raise the Taiwan issue on Reagan's visit and by assurances reportedly given by President Reagan that he would not abandon an old friend for a new one.[27]

But the trend troubles Taiwan deeply. The second Sino–American communique made the status of Taiwan somewhat tenuous by allowing China to establish a connection between U.S. arms sales and Taiwan's responses to Beijing's call for negotiation. The United States insists that it places a constraint on China to seek its objectives peacefully; but Taiwan is more conscious of the pressures on itself to negotiate.

There is some basis for such negotiations. Both sides across the Taiwan Strait agree that there is only one China. Both sides also would not tolerate any attempt by the native Taiwanese to form an independent Taiwan. Neither side, however, is ready to give up its independence or its claims. So long as the United States insists on a peaceful resolution of the difficulties, neither side has the force to compel the other to do its bidding. Many observers believe that in the long run, a negotiated settlement is inevitable; but for now, the stalemate is not wholly unsatisfactory to any of the powers. So long as China can get the economic and technological cooperation it wants from the United States, it seems content not to press the Taiwan issue too far. So long as Taiwan is able to maintain its political stability and support a healthy economy, it presents no insurmountable problem for its Asia Pacific neighbors.

The United States has been Taiwan's largest export market. In 1982, for example, Taiwan exported $8.9 billion worth of goods to the United States and imported goods valued at $4.3 billion from it. Since 1979, the American Institute in Taipei and the Coordination Council for North American Affairs in Washington have handled the unofficial and economic contacts between Taiwan and the United States. Even without diplomatic relations, the United States remains the most important friend for the survival of Taiwan.

Taiwan has also been successful in securing what it requires from Japan. It was the Japanese, in fact, who first worked out a way to maintain the economic relations both sides desired in spite of the dissolution of diplomatic relations, which in Japan's case took place in September 1972. At that time, Tokyo felt compelled to recognize Beijing as the "sole legal government of China" and Taiwan as an "inalienable part of the territory of China." With this declaration, the peace treaty of 1952 between the Republic of China and Japan ceased to function; however, an institution known as the Interchange Association was set up in Tokyo and another called the East Asia Relations Association was established in Taipei to continue to conduct the practical business of the relationship.

It is through these unofficial relations that Taiwan has been able to expand aviation and trade with Japan. Taiwan's trade volume with Japan in 1982 reached $2.4 billion in exports and $4.8 billion in imports.[28] This imbalance in favor of Japan prompted Taiwan to ban imports of more than 1,500 items in February 1982. Tokyo sent a trade mission headed by Ezaki Masumi, an LDP Diet member, to Taipei in July. After a series of private-level talks, the Taiwanese government lifted its ban on imports in 1983. Taiwan still sends roughly 11 percent of its exports to Japan and takes 27 percent of its imports from Japan.

There is little doubt that Taiwan wants Japan to support its position vis-à-vis China. Many Nationalist leaders expect that Tokyo will continue to make serious efforts for Taiwan's viability as an independent entity. A number of Japanese conservative politicians still support the Taiwanese cause in Sino–Japanese relations. These people have been active in the Japan–Taiwan Cooperation Committee, which serves as a pressure group for Taiwanese interests. The Institute of International Relations and the Society for Strategic Studies in Taiwan often invite friendly Japanese leaders and academics to Taipei as a way to influence Japanese foreign policy in Taiwan's favor.

It is not difficult to see that Taiwan does have significance for the security of Japan, because Japan not only values the economic relationship with Taiwan but also depends heavily on the security of the sea-lanes that pass its shores. But Japan has no taste for antagonizing China and has long since opted out of the security game in the Taiwan Strait theater.

The non-Communist states in Southeast Asia are in a similar situation. Like South Korea, Taiwan has been cultivating them assiduously. It has been conducting its commercial activities through its chamber of commerce or airline office in each of the ASEAN countries. Taiwan's relations with Indonesia in particular are warm, because Jakarta has not resumed diplomatic relations with Beijing since 1967. In December 1981, Taiwan's Premier Sun Yun-suan led a delegation of cabinet ministers and generals to Jakarta and met President Suharto and other officials. There are rumors that Taiwan agreed to sell weapons and to provide military training to Indonesia.[29]

Even though Malaysia recognized China in 1974 and Thailand and the Philippines did so in 1975, Taiwan has continued to expand its economic ties with these countries, too. Its investments in Singapore, which recognizes neither Beijing nor Taipei, are also substantial, as are its cultural ties through the overseas Chinese who are friendly to it.

Again like South Korea, Taiwan has seen the value of being as active as it can in regionwide developments. For example, its representatives have taken a strong interest in the semiprivate, semipublic efforts in support of the Pacific Community concept and at the Bali meeting in November 1983 secured observer status in the Pacific Economic Cooperation Conference.

Notes

1. Richard Nixon, *RN: The Memoirs of Richard Nixon* (New York: Grosset & Dunlap, 1978), pp. 394–95.

2. *Asahi Shinbun*, 28 August 1975.

3. Gerald R. Ford, *A Time to Heal* (New York: Harper & Row, 1979), p. 213.

4. Jimmy Carter, *Keeping Faith* (New York: Bantam Books, 1982), p. 141. For the rationale for this policy, see Zbigniew Brzezinski, *Power and Principle: Memoirs of the National Security Advisor, 1977–1981* (New York: Farrar, Straus and Giroux, 1983), pp. 124–28.

5. Cyrus Vance, *Hard Choices, Critical Years in America's Foreign Policy* (New York: Simon and Schuster, 1983), p. 129.

6. Harold Brown, *Thinking National Security, Defense and Foreign Policy in a Dangerous World* (Boulder, Colo.: Westview, 1983), p. 126.

7. *New York Times*, 30 March 1982.

8. *Korea Herald,* 15 November 1983.

9. *The Military Balance, 1983–84* (London: International Institute for Strategic Studies, 1983), pp. 93–94; and *Korea Herald,* 10 March 1983.

10. Henry Kissinger, *Years of Upheaval* (Boston: Little, Brown, 1982), p. 308.

11. *International Herald Tribune,* 14 November 1983, p. 1.

12. Byung-joon Ahn, "Unification of Korea: Reality and Policy," *Journal of Northeast Asian Studies* (March 1982): 71–88.

13. *Far Eastern Economic Review,* 31 May 1984, pp. 40–41.

14. *International Herald Tribune,* 20 October 1984, p. 1.

15. Byung-joon Ahn, "North Korea's Proposal for a Tripartite Conference and Changes in Four Power Relations in East Asia," *Korea and World Affairs* 8 (Spring, 1984): 17–47.

16. Henry Kissinger, *The White House Years* (Boston: Little, Brown, 1979), pp. 334–35.

17. Vance, *Hard Choices,* p. 128.

18. *Korea Herald,* 21 August 1981.

19. *Asahi Shinbun,* 20 August 1974.

20. *Japan Times,* 21 and 22 August 1981.

21. *Korea Herald,* 31 July 1983.

22. Byung-joon Ahn, "The United States and Korean–Japanese Relations," in Gerald L. Curtis and Sung-joo Han, ed., *The U.S.–South Korean Alliance: Evolving Patterns in Security Relations* (Lexington: Lexington Books, D.C. Heath, 1981), pp. 143–47.

23. *Korea Herald,* 30 March 1984.

24. *International Herald Tribune,* 23 May 1984, p. 8.

25. Ibid., 8 December 1982, p. 5.

26. "U.S.–PRC Joint Communique, August 17, 1982," in Martin L. Lasater, *Taiwan: Facing Mounting Threats* (Washington, D.C.: Heritage Foundation, 1984), pp. 73–74.

27. *International Herald Tribune,* 27 April 1984, p. 1.

28. *Japan 1983: An International Comparison* (Tokyo: Keizai Koho Center, 1983), p. 32.

29. *Asia 1983 Yearbook* (Hong Kong: Far Eastern Economic Review, 1983), p. 126.

5

ASEAN: Subregional Resilience

Chan Heng Chee

S
ince its formation on August 8, 1967, the Association of Southeast
Asian Nations (ASEAN) has been subject to conflicting evaluations,
ranging from enthusiasm to disappointed and skeptical criticism. The
differences in assessments of the role and achievements of ASEAN stem
partly from the intellectual assumptions of the critics. It may be inevitable
that once a subregional approach to the creation of international order has
been widely favored by scholars and practitioners—especially because the
regional integration movement has been so powerful and demonstrably successful in Europe after World War II—the ideal of integration would become
the hidden yardstick by which subregional efforts would be judged.[1] Consequently, ASEAN, like so many multilateral organizations, may be unfairly
criticized for not having accomplished what it did not intend to accomplish.
To arrive at a realistic assessment of the role and prospects of ASEAN as a
subregional organization, it is first necessary to isolate it from this sort of
intellectual ambush.

ASEAN began as an effort in subregional cooperation, and although the
processes of cooperation have advanced considerably in the past 16 years,
member-states show no intention of divesting themselves of their sovereign
powers or individual identities. Subregional integration, in the economic and
political sense, has never been an expressed goal.

But even if subregional cooperation need not logically or inevitably lead
to subregional integration, ASEAN—through years of cooperative experience—has overcome divergent national interests arising out of difference in
history, geography, cultures, and internal political dynamics to forge a political community of shared values and outlook, shared vulnerabilities, and
a sharpened appreciation of interdependence in the struggle for peace and
security in this subregion. Today, ASEAN's influence has grown considerably at the United Nations and in other international forums as a cohesive
political grouping, the centerpiece of Southeast Asian defense in the Western
strategic linkage from the Pacific to the Atlantic. Its success in political cooperation and the concentration on security matters and regional politics
concerning Cambodia have drawn criticism from some quarters that ASEAN
is diverting energies away from its main objective—that is, economic cooperation.[2] This view—which seeks to assess the progress of ASEAN strictly

according to its founding document—is too narrow and betrays a startling ignorance of the dynamics of regionalism and, perhaps, even of the nature of ASEAN itself.

It is the purpose of this chapter to analyze the evolution of ASEAN and to trace the emergence of a "sense of community"[3] among the initial five members so that we can better appreciate its role in engendering peace and security in the subregion. Such an analysis could usefully begin by associating the development of ASEAN with three distinct phases: (1) from the formation of ASEAN in 1967 until 1975, when Communist rule was established in Indochina; (2) from 1975, the start of the post-Vietnam era, until the invasion of Kampuchea in 1978; and (3) the post-1978 period, when diverse ASEAN perspectives became successfully orchestrated into common responses—a period that has yet to run its full course. Political developments during each of these phases helped stimulate the consolidation of ASEAN in the face of perceived threats to security and the unfolding extraregional political and economic penetration of the region. The incorporation of Brunei into the regional organization on January 7, 1984—shortly after it achieved independence on December 31, 1983—may well mark another decisive watershed in ASEAN development. It is the first time that ASEAN has enlarged its membership—a move that promises new opportunities as well as fresh problems.

The Genesis of ASEAN

There is no doubt that the formation of ASEAN was fundamentally a political response to the problem of structuring subregional order. When the foreign ministers of Indonesia, Malaysia, the Philippines, Singapore, and Thailand met in Bangkok in 1967, Southeast Asia was in political transition.

Within the subregion, Indonesia—emerging from one of the bloodiest periods of the country's history—had just terminated its confrontational politics against Malaysia and Singapore. Relations between Malaysia and the Philippines were strained over the Sabah dispute, although President Marcos, newly elected in 1965, did not pursue the issue with the fervor of his predecessors. Singapore has been separated from Malaysia in a grim atmosphere of growing racial tension between the Chinese and the Malays and between Singapore and Kuala Lumpur. As Tan Sri Ghazali Shafie, the Malaysian foreign minister recalled in 1981, ASEAN was "a development out of the pains of 'konfrontasi' ".[4] The search for an overall framework that could stabilize interstate relationships and prevent future eruption of hostile and violent disputes was conducted in earnest by the officials and leaders of the ASEAN states.

In addition, diverse motivations at the individual state level worked in conjunction to support a common vehicle by which each constituent unit could fulfill its own privately cherished political and security-related goals. Suharto, who had just replaced Sukarno as president, was resolved to demonstrate Indonesia's break with the past and the return of his country to a path of rational modernization. Perhaps in anticipation of his coming shift toward pro-Western and, in particular, pro-United States policies, he saw participation in a subregional grouping as a necessary political counterweight; and perhaps Indonesia's aspirations to subregional leadership, though unstated, should not be discounted.[5] Singapore was interested in any scheme that could enhance its economic prospects at a time when access to the Malaysian hinterland was in danger of being restricted. Subregional cooperation promised enlarged markets and access to other resources. In any case, Singapore, located between Malaysia and Indonesia, welcomed a framework in which it could interact with the larger Malay neighbors and in which the company of other member-states could provide a balancing and restraining role. Identification with a subregional grouping would also dilute its Chinese image and demonstrate its commitment to Southeast Asia.

Thailand, through Thanat Khoman, had had a long history of interest in subregionalism. Throughout the dispute over Malaysia, Thanat Khoman had been actively attempting to reconcile Malaysian–Indonesian and Malaysian–Philippine differences.[6] The cessation of confrontation was a signal for the commencement of attempts at subregional community-building. Malaysia and the Philippines, initially aloof from the Indonesian–Thai initiatives, eventually could not afford to withhold participation in the subregional developments once they were set in motion. For Malaysia, ASEAN signified the end of its conflict with Indonesia; for the Philippines, it was an opportunity to reduce its image of total dependence on the United States.

The creation of ASEAN was equally a response to external stimuli. With the departure of the colonial powers from Southeast Asia, increased fears of a dominant China and an increased sense of vulnerability to Communist subversion served as the impetus for early indigenous initiatives toward subregionalism. The antecedents of ASEAN—the Association of Southeast Asia (ASA), Maphilindo, and the Southeast Asian Association of Regional Co-operation (SEAARC)—represented attempts by Southeast Asian leaders to define a fault line between Communist states and non-Communist states in the region.[7] It was Tunku Adbul Rahman who, when advancing the first proposal for a subregional grouping in 1958, openly linked economic co-operation to anti-Communism.[8] The resort to defensive solidarity continues to be a natural political reflex for non-Communist political leaders in search of a solution for national consolidation.

That said, it must be stressed, however, that a perception of an *imminent* external security threat was not a factor in the formation of ASEAN. After all, the United States was in Southeast Asia as the principal external military and security guarantor of the region through bilateral and multilateral security agreements with Thailand (the Manila Pact and the Rusk–Thanat executive agreement) and the Philippines (the Manila Pact and the bases agreements), and its increasing involvement in Vietnam demonstrated its resolve to fulfill its obligations. But as the war effort began to come under criticism at home in the United States, Southeast Asia was forced to reckon with the fact that the American presence was not necessarily permanent. At about the same time, the Labor government of Britain announced its intentions to withdraw its presence from Malaysia and Singapore.

The time was ripe for Southeast Asians to devise a new form of regional organization for non-Communist Southeast Asia—one that was more self-reliant and committed to protecting its integrity and promoting mutual economic development to strengthen national resilience and, consequently, subregional resilience. Thus, the five governments committed themselves to the strengthening of mutual security in the following words:

> The countries of Southeast Asia share a primary responsibility for strengthening the economic and social stability of the region and ensuring their peaceful and progressive national development and that they are determined to ensure their stability and security from external interference in any form or manifestation in order to preserve their national identities in accordance with the ideals and aspirations of their peoples.[9]

That ASEAN was conceived primarily as an organization whose major activities lay in economic, social, and cultural cooperation but whose raison d'être was political coordination to cope with threats to subregional peace and security, internally or externally, is a revealing statement of the maximal attainment possible in a situation of minimal consensus.

The stress on economic and social matters bypassed the necessity of discussing more controversial and divisive issues. ASEAN was also drawing on the precedent set by ASA, an experience shared by at least three constituent units of ASEAN—Thailand, Malaysia, and the Philippines. The priority placed on economic cooperation was also inspired by the prevailing view of the day—that economic cooperation not only paved the way in other areas, it was an essential precondition for durable political and cultural cooperation. At this juncture, extensive political cooperation could not have taken place in a void and was definitely an unlikely prospect in an atmosphere of mutual suspicion. In fact, it was a major achievement to secure agreement from conservative states with traditional security alliances to the view that "all foreign bases are temporary" and "are not intended to be used directly or indirectly" against the states in the area. This position, which represents a triumph for the Indonesian viewpoint, was a legacy of Maphilindo.

The progress of ASEAN from its establishment to the Bali Summit was slow. A total of eight ministerial meetings were held from 1967 to 1975, with few tangible results in economic cooperation. In the words of an observer, it was primarily "a period of consensus in consultation, planning and adaptation."[10] It was with some degree of disappointment that Lee Kuan Yew, the Singapore prime minister, assessed the development of ASEAN at the fifth ministerial meeting:

> Five years is not a long time to measure progress in regional coopera-
> tion. . . . ASEAN partners decreased their trade amongst themselves and
> increased their trade with the rest of the world. . . . ASEAN has not yet
> attempted to create a common market nor a free trade area. . . . ASEAN's
> main aim is to strengthen and consolidate domestic economics . . . there-
> fore [it would] be unrealistic to propose . . . projects which do not fit into
> the respective [national] economic plans. . . . The most valuable achieve-
> ment of the four Ministerial Meetings has been the greater understanding
> of each other's problems.[11]

The central factor impeding cooperation was the quality of existing relations between member-states. Malaysian–Philippines relations were still strained. The Philippines had not surrendered its claim to Sabah; instead, in March 1968, the Corregidor affair erupted, in which a special military force of Muslim recruits were found to be undergoing training at Corregidor, allegedly for infiltration into Sabah. Diplomatic relations broke down between the two states in late 1968 and were not restored until May 1969. Some measure of friction entered into the Malaysian–Thai contacts over suspicions of the role of Malaysia in the possible irredentism of Muslims in Southern Thailand. Indonesia–Singapore relations deteriorated after October 1968 over Singapore's execution of two Indonesian marines found guilty of acts of sabotage and murder during confrontation. President Suharto, who had personally appealed to the Singapore government to spare the lives of the two men, felt personally humiliated. It was not until the Singapore prime minister's visit to Indonesia in May 1973, when Lee Kuan Yew sprinkled flower petals on the graves of the marines as an act of atonement, that the atmosphere of tension cleared up.[12] It is significant for regionalism that at no point during these acrimonious developments did ASEAN members consider the dissolution of the subregional enterprise. On the contrary, the existence of ASEAN had the effect of preventing the disputes from escalating any further.

Major changes were to occur in rapid succession in the international and regional environment, which acted as a catalyst for ASEAN to take its first explicitly political stand. In 1968, the timetable for British withdrawal from the region was accelerated to complete withdrawal in 1971. Almost immediately, Soviet naval vessels were deployed in the Indian Ocean, and one was sighted near Singapore. It was in 1968, too, that American war resolve was greatly battered by the Tet offensive, which resulted in a reassessment of U.S. strategic thinking. In July 1969, President Nixon announced the Guam Doctrine, signaling that, in the future, the United States would place greater reliance on indigenous forces to cope with problems of security. And finally, the blossoming détente between the United States and China, culminating in Nixon's visit to Beijing, threw non-Communist Southeast Asia into temporary confusion. How could it define an appropriate new policy that could respond to these changes in the international environment?

Reacting to these changes in the regional environment, the five foreign ministers of ASEAN met in Kuala Lumpur on November 27, 1971, to endorse Malaysia's neutralization proposal to convert Southeast Asia into a "Zone of Peace, Freedom and Neutrality, free from any form or manner of interference by outside powers."[13] This endorsement in no way represented a complete harmonization of views on subregional order. Singapore was skeptical of its implementation, and Thailand and the Philippines had obvious problems reconciling their security alliances with the United States with neutralization. Indonesia doubted the practicality of obtaining major power guarantees and was more interested in pursuing its own preferred strategy of promoting "national resilience" to create "regional resilience." One might wonder why the foreign ministers, with such misgivings, signed the declaration at all. As Michael Leifer has observed, the commitment to action was "less precise" than the endorsement of the principle;[14] and implementation was not elaborated upon.

Nevertheless, these dramatic political developments generated a renewed interest in subregional cooperation. Thereafter, ways and means were increasingly sought to hasten the process of cooperation, including a review of the institutional and procedural framework during the sixth, seventh, and eighth ministerial meetings in 1973, 1974, and 1975.

Even greater stimulation to concrete cooperation was provided by the Communist takeovers in Vietnam, Laos, and Cambodia in 1975. The strengthening of ASEAN was seen by its members as a means to increase subregional resilience and assist the economic development of the member-countries, thereby undercutting insurgency and the appeal of Communism internally. Noticeably increased contacts took place on a bilateral basis between ASEAN leaders. In July 1975, Kukrit Promoj of Thailand paid a visit to all ASEAN capitals. The prime minister of Singapore went to Thailand on a scheduled visit in January and was visited by Philippines President Marcos later the same month. After two weeks in power, Hussein Onn, the newly appointed prime minister of Malaysia, paid an official visit to Singapore, Jakarta, and Bangkok; and after Razak's funeral, Marcos stopped to see President Suharto. This "shuttle diplomacy" arose out of a need for closer contact and consultation in the absence of regular exchanges between heads of state in ASEAN and where clearly divergent perceptions of regional security prevailed. Visits among heads of state and senior officials of ASEAN have since been institutionalized as part of the integrative process to create the ASEAN community.

Political will to strengthen ASEAN was evident at the historic Bali Summit, held in February 1976. It marked the first occasion that ASEAN heads of state met in concert since the establishment of the subregional grouping. Two major documents, the Treaty of Amity and Co-operation in Southeast Asia (1976) and the Declaration of ASEAN Concord (1976) reaffirmed the basic principles of the Bangkok Declaration and provided for a more detailed framework for ASEAN cooperation. The treaty and the declaration, however, were more explicitly political documents. In the construction of stability and security in the subregion, ASEAN leaders strongly linked subregional and international order to domestic order, pledging "to eliminate threats posed by subversion to its stability thus strengthening national and ASEAN resilience." Domestic order was to be further secured by "the early establishment of the Zone of Peace, Freedom, and Neutrality," an objective now included in the declaration. The final significant commitment of the five nations to stability and security in the subregion lay in their agreement to rely exclusively on "peaceful processes in the settlement of intra-regional differences."[15] Bali thus constituted a turning point for ASEAN. The subregional grouping formally and outrightly admitted to interest in political cooperation, although they still hesitated to call themselves a political bloc or a political organization. As President Marcos pointed out in his speech at Bali, ASEAN "is not an association against or for any country or nation, or for or against any ideology, economic or political."[16] This was indeed true, for ASEAN—though vigilant against subversion—did not rule out friendship, goodwill, cooperation, and bilateral relations with the Indochina states.

The Structure of ASEAN

At its inception, the structure to promote and implement ASEAN aspirations and objectives was intentionally left loose and tentative. Malaysian Prime Minister Hussein Onn has portrayed this organizational weakness paradoxically as a source of strength:

> ASEAN exists because it serves a need. It continues to exist because it does not demand from us what we cannot give. ASEAN has been able to absorb national differences because it is a relatively informal organization without rigid rules of procedure and without elaborate structural machinery.[17]

The Bali Summit is therefore regarded as something of a milestone in ASEAN organizational development, for the Declaration of ASEAN Concord provided for the establishment of the ASEAN Secretariat and the tightening of existing ASEAN machinery. That the central secretariat was left to develop with no specifications and with some ambiguity as to its real functions was a compromise in deference to the lack of agreement on a strong center. Indonesia and the Philippines were in favor of a policy-oriented leadership role for the secretariat, whereas Singapore and Thailand viewed a strong secretariat as an inherent challenge to national politics. Malaysia's view was closer to that of Indonesia and the Philippines, which may have to do with the early expected rotation of the secretary-general's post to Malaysia. Because Indonesia provided the home for the central secretariat, it may have anticipated a consistent and continued influence over its development.

At the apex of ASEAN is the heads of government meetings, instituted at Bali, which presumably should be regarded as the highest authority in the subregional organization except that the meetings have not yet become a regular feature in the ASEAN structure. So far, only two such meetings have been held, the last in Kuala Lumpur in 1977. Consequently, the overall direction of ASEAN and the major decisions are shaped, adopted, and formalized at the foreign ministers' meetings, the centerpiece of the Bangkok Declaration, leading some observers to conclude that from the start, ASEAN was a political organization.

Between the foreign ministers' meetings, work is carried out by the Standing Committee, chaired by the foreign minister of the host country, in rotation, or his representative. The Standing Committee includes accredited ambassadors of member-countries and the five ASEAN directors-general (previously called secretaries-general) of the national ASEAN secretariats. The directors-general, career officers in their respective ministries, are responsible for the actual implementation of ASEAN activity and provide the linkage between the subregional entity and the state entity.

A major post-Bali structural innovation was the introduction of the economic ministers' meetings and the meetings of other ASEAN ministers, such as ministers of social welfare, labor, information, and education. The economic ministers' meeting was introduced to ensure momentum for economic cooperation by developing machinery for formulating and implementing economic projects.[18] It has been pointed out that the subordination of the economic ministers' meeting to the foreign ministers' meeting creates a problem in crossing the lines of authority and limiting the effectiveness of the economics ministers in implementing the economic projects and policies they decide upon. As things stood in 1976, the economic ministers were expected to submit reports to the Standing Committee and to the foreign ministers' meeting. This untenable arrangement was partly circumvented by allowing the economic ministers to report to the heads of government if they so wished. But in the absence of regular summits, heads of government do not effectively issue guidelines to the economic ministers or the foreign ministers.

Prior to 1976, there were eleven permanent committees dealing with ASEAN activities; they have now been streamlined to nine, distributed among the five ASEAN capitals. Five committees deal with economic matters and fall within the responsibility of the economic ministers: the Committee on Trade and Tourism (COTT) in Singapore, the Committee on Industry, Minerals and Energy (COIME) in Manila, the Committee on Finance and Banking (COFAB) in Bangkok, the Committee on Food and Agriculture and Forestry (COFAF) in Jakarta, and the Committee on Transport and Communications (COTAC) in Kuala Lumpur. The foreign ministers are responsible for the Committees on Social Development (COSD) in Bangkok, the Committee on Culture and Information (COCI) in Jakarta, the Committee on Science and Technology (COST) in Singapore, and the Committee on Budget and Audit (COBA) at the ASEAN secretariat. In addition to these, committees have been created to take charge of ASEAN dialogues with third countries—seeking to strengthen trade, investment, and diplomatic relations. The ASEAN–EEC dialogue was the first to be instituted in 1972. It was followed by the establishment of dialogues with Japan in 1973, Australia in 1974, Canada in 1975, and finally, the United States in 1977.[19] A bewildering number of meetings and committees were generated over the years, leaving a distinct impression that a wasteful duplication and loss of control occurred in the growth of ASEAN activity. By design, the ASEAN Secretariat, created in 1976 as a symbol of ASEAN consolidation and maturation, could not meet the task of coordination and leadership. With the proliferation of meetings of committees, subcommittees, working groups, and ad hoc committees, ASEAN has found it increasingly difficult to focus on priorities.[20] It is not surprising, therefore, that in recent years, ASEAN officials at all levels have been moving toward seeking a restructuring of the organization for a second time, especially following the subregional organization's clear successes on the diplomatic front.

It was with a view to resolving these problems that the fifteenth ASEAN ministerial meeting in 1982 created the ASEAN Task Force, a fifteen-member committee (three delegates from each member-country) headed by the former Thai under-secretary of foreign affairs, Anand Payarachun, to appraise and review the progress of ASEAN and to submit recommendations to the ASEAN foreign ministers. After a year's deliberation, the Task Force has made several recommendations for fundamental changes, among which three pertain to structure.

The first recommendation deals with the creation of an ASEAN Council of Ministers, patterned after the European Council of Ministers, to be endowed with "ASEAN characteristics" and to become the highest decision-making body in the regional organization. The Council of Ministers, which would consist of several cabinet ministers from each member-country, is expected to replace the existing ministerial meetings and, if established, will supersede decision making by the Standing Committee, which at the moment is considered inadequate to meet the demands of decision making and implementation. The Task Force has also suggested that the Council of Ministers should be authorized to make decisions on top policy issues, thereby conferring on the annual council session a quality of an "ASEAN cabinet"— a surprisingly bold departure that assumes a far greater degree of integration than actually exists.

The second Task Force recommendation is for the merging of the functions of the ASEAN Secretariat and the Standing Committee into the Committee of Permanent Representatives, whose members will carry ambassadorial rank. The third recommendation consists of a proposal to scrap the system of nine permanent committees and to create in their place two advisory panels—the Committee on Political Co-operation to deal with politics and security matters and the Committee on Policy Studies to deal with economic cooperation.[21] Taken as a package, the proposed changes illustrate the desire of ASEAN officials to inject greater political will into ASEAN consultations and to transform ASEAN clearly into a political organization for the next phase of ASEAN development. The recommendations seek to endow the ASEAN structure with commitment at the highest level and greater effectiveness through emphasis on continuity and permanency in the organization. It is a measure of the distance ASEAN members have traveled since 1967 that a proposal such as the Council of Ministers could even be contemplated and discussed. There are many questions left unanswered, of course. If it is regarded as the equivalent of an ASEAN cabinet, to what extent will the decisions of the council be binding? Will member-states be willing to compromise initiative in national policymaking? At the time of this writing, the ASEAN Task Force report had been submitted to the foreign ministers and was under study by the heads of government, but it is highly unlikely that a strong center, infringing upon national domestic will, would be allowed to develop.

The enumeration of formal institutions—committees and meetings—does not convey at all the informal workings or the mode of operation of ASEAN, which represents its unique achievement but at the same time inhibits action. Decision making in ASEAN is through mutual consultation and requires unanimous consent. Consequently, there is a built-in structural tendency toward procrastination and postponement of controversial matters, such as proposals for industrial complementarity, a free-trade zone, or a strong central secretariat. On the reverse side, the adoption of consensus as a working principle means that the vital interests of each constituent unit are protected. ASEAN moves at the pace of its slowest member. This has meant that Indonesia, the most populous and dominant state in the grouping, publicly and actively, has surrendered the expectation that it should be recognized as leader and is prepared to take its place as an equal partner of Singapore, the smallest state. In reality, the lead in shaping policies shifts among ASEAN members, depending on whose vital interests are most at stake on any issue. This is a concession of some import, which has circumvented strong disagreement. This partial sublimation of differences and the harmonization of responses is, as Donald Weatherbee acutely observes, not the result of natural integrative processes in ASEAN but "a conscious act of political will on the part of the leaders."[22]

ASEAN Political Cooperation

Although ASEAN states are bound together, on the one hand, by a conservative, status quo orientation and the desire to encourage the flourishing of free market economies, they are distinguished, on the other, by quite diverse and even conflicting strategic and security perspectives. ASEAN political cooperation on the intraregional level is a continuing attempt to reconcile these different perceptions.

Ever since the revolution, Indonesian governments have declared their intentions to pursue an "independent and active" foreign policy. This stems from their view that the international order is exploitative and that big powers are a threat to their country's independence.[23] This view arose from their former colonial predicament and their frustrating experience with the major powers during the independence struggle; and it was reaffirmed in their experience that economic aid did not bring economic development. Under Sukarno, Indonesia was one of the leading nonaligned nations, assiduously avoiding ties with either Cold War bloc. In spite of Sukarno's radical rhetoric and advocacy of the NEFOS–OLDEFOS struggle, economic aid from the West was not refused, although the level was modest. With the rise of Suharto, Indonesia's view of the world was somewhat modified. "Independent" was now narrowly defined as a "no pacts" policy, and although Indonesia still favored a subregional environment insulated from the strategic intrusion of great powers, this did not preclude its search for ties with the West, particularly with the United States for economic aid and investment. Since 1975, the United States has been Indonesia's major supplier of military aid and military weapons. While accepting the United States as an informal ally, Indonesia would like it to remain a distant ally, fearing its crushing embrace and the conversion of Indonesia through ASEAN into a U.S. satellite.[24] In Indonesian eyes, the major source of destabilization in the region is China, by virtue of its vast numbers, power potential, revolutionary ideology, and, above all, proximity. China is part of the subregion. Although Indonesian policymakers have never specified the exact nature or time frame of the purported Chinese threat, the fear is persistent and is linked to the domestic political situation, in which the presence of an economically dominant Chinese minority and its imputed association with the PKI and Gestapu coup evoke concern that a Chinese Trojan may be within Indonesia's gates. It has therefore been reluctant to engage in normalized relations with its massive Chinese neighbor despite the United States–China détente, which, in fact, has increased Indonesia's uneasiness with both powers.

Compared to China, the Soviet Union seems less threatening, not only because it is geographically removed but also because it rendered important military and diplomatic support in Indonesia's campaign for West Irian. Indonesia has tended to play down the Soviet military buildup in the region, and its foreign minister. Dr. Mochtar Kusumaatmadja, is of the view that the Reagan administration has "overstated" the Soviet threat to Southeast Asia in a bid to justify greater military outlay.[25] Nonetheless, this does not mean that Indonesia is complacent about the nature of long-term Soviet strategic ambitions and the danger of Soviet intelligence gathering. Jakarta did, in fact, expel a Soviet agent at the time when all ASEAN states took action to expel Soviet agents for their espionage activities in their countries.[26] Indonesia's view of Vietnam can best be called ambivalent, with different views emanating from different political quarters in the country. Before the invasion of Cambodia, Indonesia's foreign minister publicly expressed the affinity and admiration his country felt toward Vietnam because of their similar long struggles for independence.[27] Although Vietnam could be a potential rival for regional leadership, it is also seen as a check on future Chinese ambitions. Consequently, Indonesia adopts a more conciliatory posture than most ASEAN states toward Vietnam over the Cambodia conflict.

Although Malaysia's foreign policy credo is ZOPFAN, its strategic perspective is shaped not only by aspiration but also by contextual reality. Recognizing that regional conditions do not at present or in the middle term promise a great power standoff, Malaysia realistically accepts the necessity of defense and strategic alliances until such time as neutrality in the region can be realized. It is an active member of the Five Power Defense Arrangement and is host to a squadron of Australian mirage jets at the Butterworth airbase.

Malaysia recognizes the United States as the only effective counterweight to an expansive Soviet Union, and, like Indonesia, it is dismayed by the U.S.–Chinese strategic alliance and the sale of arms technology to China, which it sees as carrying grave implications for Southeast Asia. Although Malaysia's fear of China may be conditioned by the domestic ethnic conflict between its Malay and Chinese populations, the fear stems in part from the problem it has had in dealing with internal subversion backed by China. The refusal of Chinese Premier Zhao Ziyang to renounce ties between China's Communisty party and regional insurgent groups when he visited Southeast Asia in August 1981 has not assuaged those fears. Malaysian Foreign Minister Tan Sri Ghazali Shafie was totally unconvinced by the Chinese argument that if Beijing did not handle the situation properly, the Soviet Union and Vietnam would "fill in the vacuum."[28] Against this, the Soviet Union does not loom as menacingly in Malaysia's perception, except in the threat to the sea-lanes posed by the Soviet Pacific fleet and the building of Soviet bases in Vietnam.[29] Malaysia was forced to review its attitudes, however, when Soviet subversion seemingly affected the ranks of United Malays National Organization (UMNO) politicians, including one close to the prime minister.[30] Recently, Malaysian leaders have been more forthcoming in condemning the Soviet role in Vietnam and Cambodia. Malaysia's stance toward Vietnam has been consistently more conciliatory than those of Thailand and Singapore, sharing the same strategic perspective as Indonesia—that Vietnam can be a useful check on future Chinese ambitions. Indeed, its foreign minister, Tan Sri Ghazali Shafie, has expressed the view that the Soviet Union is not so much a direct threat as a projection of power that would provoke Chinese countermoves, leading to an intensification of Sino–Soviet rivalry in the region.

The Philippines, geographically distant from the Indochina subcontinent—and, for that matter, from the rest of ASEAN—does not share the same anxiety about or degree of involvement in security questions as the other four members. Its location away from the Asian mainland gives it a certain freedom of action that is not enjoyed by its ASEAN partners and therefore a certain detachment from the regional organization. At Bali in 1976, President Marcos was alone in making the statement: "It is quite obvious that the members of ASEAN cannot foresee any danger from external aggression in the next several years, perhaps within the decade. The principal danger and threat against our individual states would be subversion and economic crisis."[31] He was correct, of course, in diagnosing the nub of the problem for Philippine security and stability, unwittingly predicting his own political problems of 1983. The Philippine security perception derives no small comfort from its security alliance and close political and economic ties with the United States. Since 1975, Marcos has dramatically broadened the base of Manila's diplomatic and political cooperation to include a new emphasis on regionalism, establishment of trade and diplomatic relations with Moscow and Beijing, and closer identification with the Third World, particularly the Arab states in their struggle for a just peace in the Middle East. In rhetoric, it seeks a new relationship with the United States that is compatible with the Philippines' more diverse omnidirectional foreign policy.

Singapore's strategic perspective favors a multipolar presence as an answer to regional order, believing that the self-interest of each of the major powers will check the expanding tendencies of the others. Its immense vulnerability because of its size has led it, more than any other ASEAN state, to regard the regional organization as a protective shield against intraregional and extraregional aggression. Singapore is also the most articulate advocate within ASEAN for the return of a U.S. presence to the region, although even Singapore has not clarified the framework within which and the extent to which it wishes the American commitment honored. Currently, Singapore views the Soviet Union as the greatest threat to international peace, possessing both the will and the power to dominate; and it is a Soviet surrogate that Vietnam is viewed as an imminent threat to Southeast Asia. In profiling the Soviet and Vietnamese threat, Singapore does not dismiss the Chinese potential for destabilization; the island republic's population is predominantly of Chinese ethnic origin, and Singapore has consistently held off establishing full diplomatic relations with the People's Republic of China. China is perceived as a long-term threat, said S. Dhanabalan, the Singapore foreign minister:

> . . . in the sense that we don't want to be dominated by anyone. China is also communist. I don't think we can forget that. And we cannot forget what the long term interest of the communist philosophy is. . . . It just happens that at the present juncture we happen to be on the same side. . . . It does not mean we're on China's side or that they are on our side.[32]

It has been pointed out that since the thirteenth century, Thai civilization, which was based on the central plains of the Mekong, has been open to land-based threats from the West and the East, but Thailand has come to regard the threat from the East as the most enduring.[33] The departure of the French from Indochina and the establishment of a Communist regime in North Vietnam simply intensified the perception of danger, as the traditional conflict was exacerbated by ideological differences taking on the dimensions of the Cold War. Thailand's staunch support of the American war effort in Vietnam was not only to contain the spread of Communism but also to keep at bay an expansive historical enemy.

In the 1950s and 1960s, Thailand's security policies were built upon U.S. patronage and protection, but the prospect of a Vietnamese victory in the war and the anticipated strategic retreat of the United States from Southeast Asia compelled Thailand to turn to the PRC as an alternative countervailing force, although it has carefully avoided any hint of alliance ties. The Vietnamese invasion of Kampuchea represented the fruition of the worst Thai fears of its neighbor's territorial ambitions. But with characteristic Thai diplomatic finesse, Thailand has adopted a flexible policy that signals caution, reconciliation, and cooperation to cope with Vietnam. In Thai strategic calculations, the United States still has a central role in its security policies, but since 1975, Thailand has increasingly turned to ASEAN countries for support and has broadened its links to include the EEC, Japan, Australia, Canada, and New Zealand.

Prior to the Soviet Union's alliance with Vietnam and its involvement in the Cambodian conflict, it would not be incorrect to say that Thailand did not seriously concern itself with the threat from Moscow. In recent years, its awareness of the Soviet threat has dramatically sharpened, especially with the Soviet presence at Danang and Cam Ranh Bay, but Thailand has steered clear of any polemical diatribe against the Communist power.

These differing perspectives did not stand in the way of ASEAN political cooperation. Events soon demonstrated that the political impediments and differences that existed in the subregional grouping were neither formidable nor insurmountable; the right circumstances and an all-consuming focus put the impediments in perspective. In this sense, the Vietnamese invasion of Kampuchea was God-sent. It became the common cause energizing the process of cooperation, galvanizing ASEAN unity. Without Kampuchea, there was every likelihood that ASEAN would suffer internal dislocation regarding how to handle an emergent Vietnam and would be forced to confront the structuring of a long-term security strategy in a fluid external environment.

In the early reactions to the Communist victories in Indochina, ASEAN governments expressed confidence in their own capacity to handle the new situation. None believed that the Communist armies would begin a march across the neighboring borders, although there was an expectation of increased Communist activities internally. Beyond this, ASEAN leaders did not have a uniform view of how to deal with the new Communist regimes—in particular, Vietnam. Malaysia was the first ASEAN state to recognize the Provisional Revolutionary Government of South Vietnam. Tun Abdul Razak, the Malaysian prime minister, expressed the view that ASEAN was willing to cooperate with the new governments. Indonesia's conservative military government and Singapore's hard-nosed leadership took a longer time to evaluate the situation.

Although the Bali Conference generated ASEAN solidarity, it did not spell out a clear political direction. Each state had sought a *modus vivendi* with Vietnam according to its own strategic perspective. Between 1975 and 1978, relations between individual ASEAN states and Vietnam tentatively blossomed. The tour by Vietnam's vice-foreign minister, Phan Hein, of four ASEAN countries in July 1976 drew a range of responses—from the effusive hospitality of the Philippines to the cold wariness of Singapore. Malaysia and Indonesia, conditioned by their shared security obsession with an ascendant and hegemonic China, displayed an interest in assisting Vietnam in its domestic reconstruction. In Thailand, the civilian governments of Kukrit Pramoj and Seni Pramoj attempted to follow a policy of reconciliation with Vietnam and greater Thai neutrality to deal with the changed reality. Although this approach was completely reversed by the extremely right-wing Thanin Kraivchien government, some measure of peaceful accommodation was resumed when Kriangsak Chomanan was placed in power in October 1977.

Singapore's policy toward Vietnam was consistently tougher than those of its ASEAN partners. Prime Minister Lee Kuan Yew was the only ASEAN leader to react strongly to Vietnam's attempt—through its proxy, Laos—to block the adoption of the Kuala Lumpur Declaration of ZOPFAN at the Non-Aligned Meeting at Columbo in 1976[34] and to promote in its place a subregion that was "truly independent, pacific and neutral." The unexpected Vietnamese invasion of Cambodia on December 25, 1978, jolted the ASEAN capitals, forcing a brake on the independent policy drift and the assertion of a common stand toward the political change. Although Indonesia and the Philippines were not directly affected—enjoying the security of their archi-pelagic status—they joined in with Malaysia and Singapore to support Thai concerns and anxieties as the "frontline state." Vietnam's incursion into Cambodian territory had patently violated the set of fundamental principles that ASEAN as a grouping had adopted in the Treaty of Amity and Co-operation as the code of conduct for international relations in the region. There was yet another underlying aspect to the Vietnamese challenge. Coming on the heels of the completion of the Soviet–Vietnamese Treaty, the invasion was read as a frank attempt by the Soviet–Vietnamese alliance to alter the regional balance of power by projecting a Soviet presence and in-fluence hitherto unknown in Southeast Asia. Under the circumstances, it was impossible to avoid taking a joint political stand.

The hastily called foreign ministers' meeting in January in Bangkok did not produce a hard-hitting communique, which was a reflection of the vari-ance of views within the community. The statement was carefully worded to condemn the invasion of Kampuchea without naming Vietnam, and the term *armed intervention* was preferred over the term *aggression*.[35] Three ASEAN states were anxious to avoid confrontation with Vietnam: Thailand, initially for fear of further escalation of the war; Malaysia; and, surprisingly, the Philippines, in its desire to keep the lines of dialogue open because of the need to co-exist with Vietnam in the same region. Most of all, ASEAN was held back by a strong desire to maintain an equidistance in the Sino–Vietnamese and Sino–Soviet disputes. Thailand, however, rapidly shifted to a tough line. In the end, the most important outcome of this meeting was the recognition that Thailand had legitimate security interests and that, ul-timately, Thailand should dictate the pace and tone of ASEAN responses toward Vietnam, whatever the internal differences.

A month later, after China's punitive attack on Vietnam, the ASEAN foreign ministers met again to issue an even-handed statement calling for the removal of all foreign troops from Indochina. If Thailand and Singapore received this action with a quiet degree of approval, Malaysia and Indonesia were gratified that their reservations about the future role of China in the region was emphasized. From this point on, the pace of ASEAN political coordination was decelerated by the need to devise a common strategy to cope with the increasing destabilization resulting from the Kampuchean conflict. The exodus of refugees from Vietnam and Cambodia by now had reached disruptive proportions. Refugees had left Vietnam with the United States at the close of the war in 1975, and a small, steady trickle continued between 1975 and May 1978. However, as Sino–Vietnamese relations deteriorated, the refugee crisis erupted again; this time, Vietnamese of Chinese ethnic origin were departing in massive waves. Between June and December 1978, an estimated 60,000 fled by boat to ASEAN countries, while another 200,000 went overland to China. After the Chinese invasion of Vietnam, an additional wave of 175,000 boat people landed on the shores of Malaysia, Singapore, Hong Kong, and the Philippines.[36] Thus, by the time the ASEAN foreign ministers met in Bali in July 1979 for their annual meeting, the ASEAN states, perceiving the immediate threat Vietnam now posed to the peace and stability of the region, showed a greater degree of congruence on a tougher stance. ASEAN's circumspect attitude had not brought about the removal of Vietnamese troops from Kampuchean soil. On the contrary, Vietnam had increased its presence by an estimated ten divisions on the Thai border. Furthermore, in the refugee crisis, ASEAN states were heavily criticized on humanitarian grounds for their treatment of the refugees, while Vietnam was left relatively unscathed. The foreign minister of the Philippines, Carlos Romulo, summed up the mood of anxiety in his opening statement: "ASEAN is on red alert."[37]

The central concern of the ASEAN community was the impact of the refugees of Chinese ethnic origin on their multiracial societies and the equally destabilizing economic consequences of this massive influx. Singapore suggested that it was Vietnam's strategy for the realization of hegemonic ambitions to use refugees as "human bombs" to subvert the non-Communist countries of the region before the final assault. The refugees did assume the dimension of mild irritants in intra-ASEAN relationships, as Malaysia "shooed" the boats toward Indonesia and Singapore steadfastly declined to enlarge its intake quota.

The July 1979 Bali communique reaffirmed the points of the January foreign ministers' meeting in stronger terms and represented the highest point of ASEAN political agreement. The specific elements of the ASEAN posture were (1) a demand for the immediate and total withdrawal of the foreign troops from Kampuchean territory and (2) support for the Kampuchean people's right of self-determination. These principles were subsequently incorporated into ASEAN's resolution at the United Nations for a political solution to the problem. For the first time, ASEAN openly condemned Vietnam for its responsibility in the refugee crisis, which was said to be causing severe political, socioeconomic, and security problems in ASEAN countries. Equally important was the solidarity and firm support expressed for Thailand in the Thai–Kampuchean border situation. The belief in the interdependence of security was forcefully reaffirmed in the following words: "Any incursion of any foreign forces into Thailand would directly affect the security of the ASEAN states and would endanger the peace and security of the region." Even so, this communique did not satisfy hard-line Singapore—although for Malaysia, Indonesia, and the Philippines, ASEAN's position was uncomfortably drawing closer to the Chinese line.

ASEAN's strategy for dealing with the Cambodian conflict had the following features: (1) to isolate Vietnam diplomatically and economically by mobilizing international censure against it for the invasion of Kampuchea and for creating the refugees problems; (2) to deny legitimacy to the Heng Samrin government while supporting Pol Pot's Democratic Kampuchea (this involved diplomatic battles to deny Heng Samrin's delegates representation at international meetings); and (3) to maintain an open line of dialogue with Vietnam on the Kampuchean issue at all times and all other matters.

This strategy temporarily permitted the hard-liners and the accommodationists within ASEAN to move on dual tracks. Arising from this flexibility in the ASEAN position, there was no question or necessity of ASEAN breaking ranks, even though the articulation of differences sometimes seemed to threaten solidarity. Differences within ASEAN arise not on whether to negotiate with Vietnam but on the terms and on whether to negotiate to seek a true compromise or merely to carry the struggle for unalterable objectives to a new plane.

In January 1980, in the wake of the UN call for a total military withdrawal and Vietnam's refusal to budge, ASEAN foreign ministers dispatched Malaysian Foreign Minister Tengku Rithaudeen, as ASEAN Standing Committee chairman, to Hanoi to discuss a political solution—a role Malaysia was not willing to play.[38] In March 1980, in an attempt to assert their point of view in the development of ASEAN diplomacy on the Cambodian question, President Suharto of Indonesia and Prime Minister Hussein Onn of Malaysia met in Kuantan to declare that peace in Southeast Asia required that Vietnam be free of Chinese and Soviet influence and that what was needed was not a military but a political solution to the Cambodian problem, taking into account the "security interests" of Vietnam.[39] This view was rather badly received in Bangkok and Singapore, suggesting that a greater synchronization through consultation was needed to avoid the attenuation of unity. Following this, in May 1980, Lt. General Murdani, then chief of Indonesian army intelligence, visited Hanoi to secure Vietnamese cooperation for a negotiated settlement. But not only did Malaysia and Indonesia find Vietnam recalcitrant, there were repeated attempts by Hanoi to sow discord in the subregional community by exploiting the different nuances in ASEAN positions and by playing on Indonesian and Malaysian fears of China.

Ultimately, two major events played a role in narrowing the disparity in

ASEAN perceptions on strategic questions. The Soviet invasion of Afghanistan in December 1979 altered the regional mood toward the Soviet Union, particularly in view of its increasing military entrenchment in Vietnam. President Marcos, who until then had taken a low-key approach to Hanoi, now linked Soviet expansiveness to Vietnamese means and uncharacteristically warned that Vietnam might be preparing for an imminent attack on Thailand.[40] The Vietnamese incursion into Thai territory in June 1980 further enhanced the new realism in the assessment of Vietnam's responses, although it did not fundamentally revise ASEAN strategy. Dr. Mochtar Kusumaatmadja, the Indonesian foreign minister, did not rule out continued dialogue with Hanoi but ruefully added that ASEAN could no longer take Vietnam's assurances at "face value."[41] On another level, the changeover of political leadership in Malaysia from Hussein Onn to Dr. Mahathir bin Mohammed in mid-1981 and the appointment of Tan Sri Ghazali Shafie, an orthodox anti-Communist, as foreign minister brought Malaysia's viewpoint close to those of Thailand and Singapore, both as to the immediacy of the Soviet-Vietnamese threat and the handling of it.

By August 1980, ASEAN changed tactics to push for the establishment of a broader-based government in Cambodia, consisting of "diverse national elements."[42] At the same time, the focus shifted from dialogue with Vietnam to the convening of the UN-sponsored International Conference on Kampuchea (ICK).[43] The construction of a viable anti-Vietnamese coalition was designed to refurbish the odious image of the Khmer Rouge and to present a more acceptable political alternative for lobbying for enhanced U.S. political and military commitment and wider international support.

The ICK, held in New York from July 14 to 18, 1981, failed to secure the participation of the Soviet Union, Vietnam, and most of their allies. Nonetheless, the meeting ended with two diplomatic victories for ASEAN, as ninety-three participating countries of two-thirds of the UN total membership agreed on a conference declaration, affirming the basic principles of the ASEAN position on withdrawal of foreign troops and the holding of free elections under UN supervision.[44] The ICK had an added significance for ASEAN. It presented the opportunity for ASEAN to dissociate itself from the Chinese position—a point that had become increasingly fuzzy as ASEAN had hardened against Vietnam and kept its support for the Democratic Kampuchean government.[45] China steadfastly refused the inclusion of references in the ASEAN draft to the "disarming" of all Kampuchean factions and the setting up of an "interim administration," but in the end was forced to concede that "appropriate arrangements" should be made to ensure that armed Khmer factions would not be able to prevent or disrupt the holding of free elections.

It was more difficult, however, to bring about the formation of an anti-Vietnamese Khmer coalition. ASEAN skills in diplomacy were exercised to the fullest by Singapore and Thailand to bring together the warring Khmer factions. From the announcement of the proposal in September 1981 to the actual establishment of the Coalition Government of Democratic Kampuchea (CGDK) on June 22, 1982, in Kuala Lampur, ASEAN members were caught in the most difficult negotiations to persuade the Khmer Leaders to unite.[46] The central problem was the ultimate divergence in political objectives between ASEAN and the Khmer resistance leaders. Although ASEAN sought the removal of the Vietnamese occupation forces and the Heng Samrin government as constituted, it did not wish to commit itself to the eventual survival in power of any one of the factions in particular after the Vietnamese departure. Thus, the creation of the coalition government represented a major ASEAN political success in its political struggle on the Cambodian issue. Since then, it has been difficult, if not impossible, to deny the claims of the CGDK to be the legitimate representative of the Democratic Kampuchean state. The failure of the Vietnamese to challenge the credentials of Democratic Kampuchea at the 1983 UN General Assembly was a historic surrender, conceding this very point. In the advancement of the coalition government idea, it was clear that Indonesia was not in total agreement with the other ASEAN partners, even though it went along to Kuala Lumpur. Shortly after the initial meeting of the three Khmer leaders in Singapore, General Murdani went to Hanoi on President Suharto's instructions to discuss long-term policy with the Vietnamese, including a political settlement of the Cambodia issue.[47] The Indonesians have come out openly in opposition to the Singapore initiative to supply arms to the coalition government, some Indonesian circles seeing this as constituting a shift in ASEAN's position from support for a political solution to support for a military solution.[48]

For ASEAN, the Cambodian issue represents the most direct challenge to regional peace and security in Southeast Asia since the regional organization came into being. Arguably, it could not have moved toward a common response so swiftly without the habit of cooperation laid down in the earlier years. On the whole, intense bilateral and multilateral consultations have helped ASEAN preserve a remarkable degree of consensus in its search for a solution, despite deliberate Vietnamese attempts to undermine its cohesion. The central disagreement on the long-term threat posed by China has not been resolved; the desirability and extent of tactical cooperation with the neighboring giant intervenes as a salient issue in the coordination of ASEAN positions. Indonesia and Malaysia have consciously compromised their strategic viewpoint for the present—in the case of Indonesia, with considerable frustration, judging by its discreet attempts to push an alternative strategy within the acceptable bounds of the overall ASEAN position. The process of political coordination has also modified Singapore's hard-line position toward Vietnam. By the end of 1979, S. Rajaratnam was quoted as saying, "ASEAN wants a strong Vietnam and a Kampuchean government that is not anti-Vietnam."

In ASEAN's struggle over Cambodia, the political and economic support of the United States and Japan have been critical. Vietnamese expansion, assisted by Soviet aid, advanced the United States' recovery from its post-Vietnam syndrome in a decisive way. The election of President Reagan in 1980 also saw dramatic attempts to make restitution for the strategic erosion lost during Carter's administration. In July 1979, Cyrus Vance attended the Bali foreign ministers' meeting, marking the first time a U.S. secretary of state was present at an ASEAN meeting. Since then, visits by American secretaries of state and defense have become a normal feature of United States–ASEAN relations.

The U.S. interest in ASEAN is a constitutent part of the "concert of strategic relationships" it seeks to construct to outmaneuver the Soviet Union in the global struggle for influence and dominance. On ASEAN's part, it has come to accept the vital role of the United States in keeping regional peace and balancing the higher Soviet presence in Indochina. In particular, it looks to the United States for firm diplomatic and political support for the ASEAN position on Cambodia at the United Nations and for military support by way of extensive military credits and aid. Thailand and the Philippines, which have security agreements with the United States, seek a clear definition of commitment from their ally in the event of contingencies.

Japan's growing interest in ASEAN since 1975, a function of its desire to define a larger role for itself, was signified by the presence of Prime Minister Fukuda Takeo at the ASEAN summit meeting in 1977. The Japanese prime minister's offer of U.S.$1 billion to help finance ASEAN industrial projects and U.S.$5 billion for particular national projects did not satisfy the ASEAN states, which were more concerned about possible Japanese aid to Indochina. Japan's decision to take ASEAN's side—to abide by the ASEAN position to isolate Vietnam and seek a political solution along the line of the UN resolution—has been of enormous diplomatic and political value to the organization in its evolution as a political community.

The record of ASEAN's performance at the United Nations and other international forums, such as UNCLOS III and UNCTAD, has been impressive by any standards. ASEAN's ability to present a unified public posture in subregional political affairs as well as international economic developments has enhanced the status of the group as a factor to be reckoned with in the international system.

Intra-ASEAN Cooperation

Bilateral Political Cooperation

The emergence of ASEAN as a political community in the course of the dramatic maneuvers over Cambodia has tended to overshadow the more substantial progress achieved in bilateral political cooperation among the five partners. Since 1967, assiduous efforts have been directed toward structuring procedures and formalizing processes to resolve contentious issues among themselves. To a large extent, traditional animosities have receded and bilateral difficulties have been contained and resolved by invoking the ASEAN "spirit." It would not be an exaggeration to say that in the present ASEAN political ambience, it is difficult to conceive of any two or more members resorting to the use of physical force as a means to solve a problem.

The most remarkable improvement in relations occurred between Singapore and Malaysia. Since the dark, grim days of separation, the historically difficult relationship has taken a more cordial turn, based increasingly on pragmatic, functional ties. In 1980, the two governments agreed in principle to set up an intergovernmental committee (IGC), directly responsible to both prime ministers, to increase the level and quality of cooperation between the two countries.[49] The aim was also to prevent minor problems from being exaggerated beyond control by adverse publicity and to prevent such issues from reaching the stage of intractability. It is under the Mahathir government, however, that Singapore–Malaysia cooperation moved to a new plane. Recognizing that "an unhappy Singapore can be destabilizing to Malaysia" and that "likewise, discontent in Malaysia can affect Singapore,"[50] Mahathir, in his first visit as prime minister, swiftly settled many outstanding bilateral issues with his Singapore counterpart. As a barometer of the new-found trust, Malaysia for the first time allowed Singapore access to training in the Kota Tinggi Jungle Warfare School.

Friction between Malaysia and Thailand has perennially erupted over security cooperation on the Thai–Malaysian border because of the lack of common agreement on who constitutes the common enemy. Thai suspicions that their Malaysian ally is not interested in the suppression of the Muslim separatists operating in the south—indeed, that Malaysia may even be secretly succoring their cause—is matched by Malaysian concern that Thai effort in the containment of communist insurgents is ineffective.[51] Occasionally, an open outburst of frustration such as that expressed by leading Thai security personnel—Supreme Commander of the Armed Forces, General Saiyud Kerdphol, Minister of Interior Sitthi Jirarote, and Lt. General Harn Leenanond, Commander of the Fourth Army Region (in the south)—that the Thai–Malaysian General Border Committee meeting in August 1982 was "unsatisfactory" creates the impression of crisis in bilateral relations; but political leaders have been swift to reaffirm close bilateral ties by immediate consultation to iron out differences. In seeking to control subversion in the south, Malaysia and Thailand are fully aware of the interdependence of security efforts. Both countries have agreed to look into the development of the Golok Basin along the common border to underpin security.

Although a new start in Malaysian–Philippines cooperation was promised when President Marcos dramatically renounced the Philippine claim to Sabah at the 1977 ASEAN heads of government meeting in Kuala Lumpur, nothing developed from that statement. The Philippines legislature is yet to legalize its president's offer. In 1981, accusations surfaced that Muslim separatists were allowed to operate from Sabah and that the eastern state of Malaysia was a source of arms flow to the rebels, leading some Philippine assemblymen to argue for a reactivation of the Sabah claim. In reaction, some Sabah pressure was put on the federal government to break diplomatic ties. That the issue did not blow up was due in no small part to the efforts of the Malaysian prime minister, Dr. Mahathir, to actively defuse the issue. There is every indication that the Philippine willingness to formalize the renunciation is tied to a Malaysian agreement on a border patrol pact, which would stem the arms flow from Sabah to the Muslim separatists in the Mindanao-Sulu region.[52] Although the Sabah claim survives as an irritant in Malaysian–Philippine relations, it does not seem to stand in the way of overall ASEAN cooperation.

On the thorny questions of border demarcation and territorial claims—traditionally, issues that hold the greatest potential for conflict between neighbors and that are the most susceptible to military solutions—the ASEAN states appear to have worked out an amicable settlement among themselves. Through the Joint Thailand–Malaysia Land Boundary Committee, Thailand and Malaysia have been establishing the borderline between the two territories. Since the beginning of the joint effort in 1975, 58 percent of the total common border has been demarcated.[53] In the case of Indonesia and Malaysia, the two nations signed an agreement in February 1982 whereby Malaysia became the first country to accept Indonesia's jurisdictional claims under its archipelagic principle. Indonesia, by the same token, agreed to recognize Malaysia's right to use waters in the Indonesian territorial sea lying between Western and Eastern Malaysia.[54]

During Mahathir's visit to Singapore, the two prime ministers agreed that once the boundary line was fixed in the Straits of Johore upon completion of a hydrographic survey presently being undertaken, the line would be adhered to and would not change with the shifting channel. However, Malaysia still has to work out an agreement with the island republic on Pulau Batu Putih in the Singapore Straits. With regard to the Philippine–Indonesian claims, the main point of contention is the island of Palmas, or Pulau Miangas (the Indonesian name), which is situated where the archipelagic baselines of Indonesia and the Philippines overlap. However, there is no move on either country's part to force a resolution of the problem at the moment. The Philippines has a dispute with Malaysia over official continental shelf maps that involve the Kalayaan group in the South China Sea, but both sides will rely on negotiation to solve the problem. By contrast, the ASEAN states' territorial disputes with China and Vietnam over the Spratly

Islands have been less peacefully settled. The Philippines has occupied seven islands to forestall counterclaimants,[55] and Malaysia dispatched troops to the Layang Layang atoll under cover of a naval exercise in late November 1983.

Security Cooperation

Although it was founded as an economic, social, and cultural grouping, ASEAN has been fundamentally exercised by security concerns encompassing threats to the subregional environment as well as threats to the domestic order of member states. Paradoxically, there is hardly any mention of security cooperation in the ASEAN official documents, except in the Declaration of ASEAN Concord, which deals with the subject in one line, prescribing "continuation of co-operation on a non-ASEAN basis between the member states in security matters in accordance with their mutual needs and interests." That security questions were considered best left outside the ASEAN format indicates ASEAN's allergy to the formation of a military alliance.

Over the past 16 years, however, member-states have stepped up bilateral security cooperation on a wider scale to meet internal subversion and to strengthen the external defense capabilities of the state. Since the Vietnamese invasion of Kampuchea, bilateral air, land, and naval military exercises have become commonplace: Thailand conducts joint air exercises with Indonesia, Singapore, the Philippines, and Malaysia, and also permits Singapore military personnel to train on Thai soil.[56] Malaysia and Singapore hold naval exercises in the strategic Straits of Malacca and belong to the Five Power Defense Arrangement.[57] Indonesia and Malaysia cooperate along the Kalimantan border between East Malaysia and Indonesia against Communist insurgents under the auspices of the 1972 General Border Committee, and air exercises are conducted by Singapore and Indonesia. There is greater exchange and coordination of security intelligence, simultaneous strengthening of the armed forces, and moves toward the standardization of arms and the working out of "uniform operating procedures" against the common enemy, all of which point to a possible eventual scenario of resource pooling.

Nonetheless, ASEAN's security cooperation conscientiously stops short of forming a military pact. In September 1982, the Singapore prime minister's suggestion at the end of a state visit to Jakarta—that the time had come for greater military cooperation in ASEAN, leading up to "multi-lateral exercises encompassing all members"—was publicly and vigorously rejected by the older ASEAN partners.[58] This decisively stopped speculation that a military pact was imminent. ASEAN's adamant refusal to contemplate a pact arises from the belief that far from enhancing regional security, such an alliance would have a provocative value, hastening counteralliances. In the discussions on the evolution of ASEAN into a security organization, it is often forgotten that the existing framework of ASEAN does not allow for activities in this direction. Should ASEAN reach a stage when a military alliance is considered in order, the alliance would have to formulated outside the present ASEAN organization, not unlike NATO's relationship to the EEC.

ASEAN Economic Cooperation

In contrast to the close cooperation in the political and security areas, actual progress in economic regionalism is slow, if not disappointing. At Bali, new vistas in trade and industrial development were opened, the former through selective trade liberalization in the Preferential Trade Arrangements (PTA), the latter through ASEAN Industrial Complementation (AIC) projects and ASEAN Industrial Projects (AIP). In addition cooperative programs have been launched in tourism, food and agriculture, mining and energy, transport and communications, and banking and finance. The translation of the aspirations into economic practicalities, however, have been more problematic.

At the fifteenth ASEAN economic ministers' meetings in October 1983, the Thai prime minister, General Prem Tinsulanond, gave a figure of 18,933 items as tariff preferentials.[59] Since 1977, the tariff cuts on trading products have been wider and deeper, beginning with 10 percent for most products, and now are generally 20 to 25 percent across the board. This means the PTA are now more than just cosmetic, suggesting that the failure of intra-ASEAN trade to take off is more fundamental. According to the Singapore prime minister, "PTA imports accounted for 1.5% of total ASEAN imports in 1978 and increased to 2% in 1979."[60]

ASEAN Industrial Projects have not met with greater success. The idea, adopted from a UN study on ASEAN cooperation, envisaged an ambitious plan for something close to regional import substitution. Each ASEAN state would set up a large industrial plant to meet the region's need in a designated product. The projects proposed are the ASEAN Urea Project in Indonesia and Malaysia, the ASEAN Rock Salt–Soda Ash Project in Thailand, the Copper Fabrication Project for the Philippines, and the Diesel Engine Project for Singapore. So far, only the Indonesian project is close to completion, and Malaysia's project is about to enter the construction stage. The Philippines has been switching projects and is therefore only at the early states, and Singapore dropped the project assigned to it. The slow progress in the AIPs has been said to be due to poor project identification, financing problems, and implementation problems.

Equally weak is the industrial complementation scheme, which is based on the idea of each member-country producing specific components to produce a single ASEAN product. The major thrust in the automotive industry to produce the ASEAN car, adopted after a lengthy process of refinement and discussion, has been jeopardized if not abandoned in the wake of Malaysia's plan to build its own car. Even without Malaysia's problem, industrial complementation has been held back by Singapore's reluctance to participate. As an island economy whose prosperity is based on free trade and manufacturing, Singapore disagrees with the extension of monopoly rights and protection extended to products manufactured under the complementation scheme. To circumvent the unanimity principle and to absolve itself from the charge of sabotaging AIC projects, Singapore's prime minister, Lee Kuan Yew, proposed in 1980 that ASEAN consensus should be redefined to include a "5–1" formula; that is, consensus is considered achieved even when one member-state declines participation.

The foregoing facts simply highlight the obstacles in the way of economic regionalism and are a reflection of the diverse interests that result from economies at different stages of development and efficiency and with competitive rather than complementary patterns of trade. If ASEAN founders had envisaged the association as a vehicle to buttress the economic base of the subregion through economic cooperation, ASEAN must be judged as less than effective. Economic cooperation schemes mounted under the auspices of the treaty have been deferred in one way or another. What seems to be demonstrated is that although different strategic perspectives may not prevent political cooperation nor undermine its vitality, different economic perspectives have been more difficult to overcome. That Indonesia is the largest and yet economically among the weakest in the community is a significant constraining factor in subregional economic endeavor, setting the pace of economic cooperation in ASEAN.

But without doubt, ASEAN is a case of successful economic development. ASEAN countries have enjoyed high GDP growth rates, averaging 7.3 percent in the period 1970–80. Singapore's average GDP growth rate was the highest, at 8.5 percent, with Malaysia managing 7.8 percent, Indonesia 7.6 percent, and Thailand 7.2 percent. Even the Philippines, by far the weakest economy of the five, recorded a 6.3 percent growth rate. And even though the direct contribution of ASEAN economic policies to these rates may be small, it cannot be denied that, as Singapore's foreign minister, S. Dhanabalan, put it: "ASEAN has created a regional climate that has enabled each of us to get the maximum out of our national economic policies. Thus, our economies have grown at a rapid rate."[61] Again, if we go beyond official programs to evaluate the economic significance of ASEAN, there is clear evidence of a trend for local businesses to invest profits in their home countries and within the subregion. Joint ventures between private groups from ASEAN states and ASEAN multinationals have been established, which indicates that the private sector is developing a growing confidence and stake in the subregional system. This would not have occurred if there were a sense of interstate conflict and tension within the subregion—a situation ASEAN has gone out of its way to avoid.

The climate of security engendered by cooperative solidarity has also intensified American and Japanese economic interests in the subregion. ASEAN is the fifth largest trading partner of the United States, and direct private American investment increased from U.S.$730 million in the mid-1960s to U.S.$4 billion at the end of the 1970s.[62] In the case of Japan, imports from ASEAN increased from 10 percent of total Japanese imports in 1965–70 to 15 percent in 1980; on the ASEAN side, a quarter of the subregion's trade is with Japan.[63] In addition, Japan is the leading investor in the subregion, with Japanese direct foreign investment amounting to $7.021 billion in 1980.[64]

Political Community, Subregional Order, and Future Prospects

Over the past 16 years, ASEAN has slowly but certainly institutionalized patterns of consultation, the machinery for cooperation, and modes of conflict resolution, so that interstate enmity, a principal aspect of regional politics in Southeast Asia in recent times, has been markedly transformed. Points of contact between Indonesia, Malaysia, the Philippines, Singapore, and Thailand have been many, leaving in their wake a stronger measure of goodwill and understanding of one another's problems and positions. Compared to the subregional acrimony of the late 1960s, the change is radical. The five states have emerged as a cohesive, vibrant political community, speaking with one voice, though not necessarily with one mind, and interacting and cooperating frequently on a multiplicity of issues on several political, economic, and cultural fronts. This successful restructuring of relationships has added to the sense of stability and security in the subregion by lowering, if not eliminating, the expectation of violent conflict among themselves and the exploitation of such conflict by external powers. Indeed, these trends have led an Indonesian observer to assert that ASEAN has, in fact, formed a subregion or a subsystem of its own, comprising if not the whole of Southeast Asia, at least a part of it.[65]

ASEAN is unable, however, to prevent the rupture of subregional order outside its subsystem, nor is it able to contain the widening dimensions of the conflict. The Vietnamese invasion of Cambodia represented not simply a localized issue of one neighbor seeking the settlement of outstanding differences with another through the use of force. To the extent that the conflict is a reflection of the Sino–Soviet rivalry and the Sino–Vietnamese dispute, Cambodia represents the arrival and intensification of big-power conflict in the region on a scale not previously experienced. Since December 1978, Moscow's influence in Indochina as the major guarantor of military and economic aid to the Indochinese regimes has risen sharply, and China's military presence has been felt in Southeast Asia for the first time, on Vietnamese borders. And to the extent that ASEAN, by its stubborn refusal to accept the *fait accompli* in Cambodia, has checkmated Vietnam, it has served notice to regional and external powers that forceful attempts to alter the status quo would be strenuously resisted. So far, ASEAN has enjoyed a high degree of success in mobilizing friends and powerful allies across a broad front. The diplomatic exercise over Cambodia has reaffirmed before the international community—and to ASEAN members themselves—the effectiveness of the regional organization in advancing its security interests. In the process, ASEAN has regenerated American interest in Southeast Asia, though regrettably, from ASEAN's point of view, as a corollary of its pursuit of an anti-Soviet alliance and secondary to the American–Chinese relationship. At the same time, Japanese pledges of economic and diplomatic support remain constant and increasing. These political, economic, and military ties with the United States and Japan continue to be a source of enormous comfort to ASEAN in its search for regional security, at least for the short and middle term; in the long run, ASEAN is still committed to the establishment of a zone of peace, freedom, and neutrality.

ASEAN has also been unsuccessful in eradicating domestic threats to political stability, although in all the states, except perhaps the Philippines, they are arguably within manageable control. Social tensions—a product of political and economic injustices, irredentism, and Communist insurgencies—exist at varying levels from state to state, and ASEAN leaders watch vigilantly for external exploitation of internal weaknesses.

But where does ASEAN go from here? All indications point to the conclusion that the subregional grouping has probably reached a critical watershed in its organizational development. Further growth, consolidation, and shaping of its identity will be determined by ASEAN's ability to cope with three issues that will have to be confronted in the near future.

One is the Brunei question. On January 7, 1984, ASEAN acquired its sixth member, the oil sultanate of Brunei. How quickly or successfully Brunei learns the modes of operation of ASEAN or becomes "ASEANized" remains to be seen. Even though ASEAN has been cautious in opening its doors to new members—politely refusing Sri Lanka and Papua New Guinea—the inclusion of Brunei was never in doubt because of its resources and the geostrategic centrality of its position in the ASEAN subregion. Although some have fears that Brunei's presence may lead to a strengthening of the "Malay core" within the subregion, possibly leading to a disruption of the successful power equilibrium that is carefully maintained in ASEAN presently, the actual development of this situation is unlikely. The extent to which an international coalescence of ethnic forces will take place depends on the degree to which residual Malaysia–Brunei friction can be ironed out. At the eleventh hour, in 1963, a dispute over the position of the sultan in the larger federation caused Brunei to refuse to become part of Malaysia. Although the Malaysia–Brunei relationship has vastly improved since then, this issue lingers on as a point of great sensitivity and was a subject of sharp exchange between the royal house of Brunei and Tan Sri Ghazali Shafie as recently as October 1983. At the same time, Brunei's territorial claim to Limbang is still alive, and a potential dispute lies in the demarcation of the continental shelves of the two countries.[66] There is also some doubt about whether Malaysian–Indonesian relations are better or warmer than either's bilateral relations with other ASEAN states in view of the recent history of confrontation.

There is no doubt that Brunei's entry into ASEAN will affect ASEAN operationally. The small size of Brunei and its narrow manpower base will limit its ability to maintain a presence in all ASEAN committee meetings. One likely possibility is a temporary slowing down of the pace of political and economic cooperation as the new, small state seeks to make its foreign policy moves tentatively. Certainly, the position of small states is likely to be strengthened, as Singapore and Brunei may find they share the same perspectives.

A second issue that can be expected to trouble ASEAN is the extent to which it will wish to continue strengthening itself militarily. It is difficult to believe that the increasing political and security cooperation in ASEAN will not lead to a desire for a greater ASEAN military capability and self-reliance. Since 1978, ASEAN states have dramatically stepped up their arms purchases and have developed military muscles in readiness for external aggression. Though it is sheltered by the U.S. security umbrella, there is lurking fear in ASEAN that the United States may actually withdraw from the Southeast Asian region sooner than the region would like. The most likely event that could tip the status quo would be the forced removal of the American bases in the Philippines, an eventuality that may arise if President Marcos should fail to ensure his own political survival and if anti-base sentiments should spread among the articulate strata of the population. At the time of this writing, in the summer of 1984, it also seems possible that another event may have the same effect: the replacement of President Reagan by a less internationalist and militarist president. American pressure on Japan to adopt a higher military posture in burden sharing is perceived by the ASEAN states as possibly portending a further U.S. withdrawal. ASEAN's discreet military cooperation has been designed to meet this eventuality.

A third challenge is that posed by ASEAN's initial and continuing commitment to economic cooperation. It is difficult to conceive of the political success of ASEAN running so far ahead of its economic promise without commensurate moves to redress this anomaly. In recent years, ASEAN leaders have become more open about the political nature and political objectives of the subregional grouping, but there is chafing at the highest level of ASEAN officialdom at the lack of progress in economic cooperation. The concern springs from two sources. First, there is the belief that dynamic subregional cooperation will generally lead to economic growth, resulting in the strengthening of the economic underpinnings of the domestic political structure—an assumption that may not be borne out, of course, if growth is not accompanied by equitable distribution. Second, there is a commitment to multiply areas of functional cooperation to foster greater interdependence among the member states. When the Cambodian issue is settled, ASEAN would seem to require a new core focus. In the absence of an imminent military threat, attention may turn to economic activities to arrest the attenuation of associational links. Whether ASEAN will succeed as an economic organization will depend on the political will to compromise immediate national interests and national sovereignty for larger subregional objectives.

In confronting these issues, radical departures are not to be expected. ASEAN's ability to develop into a political community has been due to a realistic appraisal by the member-states of the limits of the decisional power they can entrust to organization and the conscious political will not to push the organization beyond these limits. As ASEAN enters the next phase of development, the same cautious assessment can be expected to prevail in the choice of path it takes, for it is difficult to believe that ASEAN members will wish to jeopardize the very vehicle that has served their internal needs so well, that has gained them international recognition, and that stands as perhaps the most successful regional organization in the Third World.

Notes

1. Lynn H. Miller, "The Prospects for Order through Regional Security," in Richard A. Falk and Saul Mendlovitz, eds., *Regional Politics and World Order* (San Francisco: Freeman, 1973), p. 59.

2. Hans H. Indorf and Astrid Suhrke, "Indochina: The Nemesis of ASEAN?" in *Southeast Asian Affairs, 1981* (Singapore: ISEAS, 1981), pp. 62–72; and Hans H. Indorf, *Impediments to Regionalism: Bilateral Relations in ASEAN* (Singapore: ASEAN Economic Research Unit, Institute of Southeast Asian Studies, 1984).

3. Karl W. Deutsch, Sidney A. Burrell, Robert A. Kann, Maurice Lee Jr., Martin Lichterman, Raymond E. Lindgren, Francis L. Loewenheim, and Richard N. Van Naganen, *Political Community and the North Atlantic Area* (New York: Greenwood Press, 1969 reprint).

4. Tan Sri Ghazali Shafie, "ASEAN: Today and Tomorrow," *Foreign Affairs Malaysia* (December 1981): 336.

5. For an account of the domestic factors at work in shaping a new Indonesian

stance in regional and international politics, see Michael Leifer, *Indonesia's Foreign Policy* (London: George Allen & Unwin, 1983), pp. 111–41.

6. Russell H. Fifield, *National Interests and Regional Interests in ASEAN: Competition and Co-operation in International Politics*, Occasional Paper No. 57 (Singapore: ISEAS, 1979), p. 8.

7. Arnfinn Jorgensen-Dahl, *Regional Organisation and Order in Southeast Asia* (London: Macmillan, 1982).

8. Ibid., p. 15.

9. The ASEAN Decleration, 8th August 1967, in *ASEAN Year Book 1980* (Singapore: NCN United and Associates Pty. Ltd.), p. 11.

10. Hans H. Indorf, *ASEAN: Problems and Prospects,* Occasional Paper No. 38 (Singapore: ISEAS, 1975).

11. Quoted in ibid., p. 14.

12. A revealing account of relations between Singapore and Indonesia is contained in the memoirs of Singapore's ambassador to Indonesia during the difficult times: Lee Khoon Choy, *An Ambassador's Journey* (Singapore: Times Books International, 1983).

13. Kuala Lumpur Declaration (ZOPFAN Declaration, 1971), Appendix E in Alison Broinowski, *Understanding ASEAN* (Hong Kong: Macmillan, 1982).

14. Michael Leifer, "ASEAN and the Problem of Common Response," *International Journal* (vol. 38, no. 2, Spring, 1983).

15. *10 Years ASEAN* (Jakarta: ASEAN Secretariat, 1978), p. 111.

16. Statement by the president of the Philippines, Ferdinand E. Marcos, at the opening of the meeting of the ASEAN heads of government, 23 February 1976, Denpasar, Bali; quoted in ibid., p. 96.

17. Statement by the prime minister of Malaysia, Datuk Hussein Onn, at the opening of the ASEAN heads of government meeting, 23 February 1976, Denpasar, Bali; quoted in ibid., p. 95.

18. *10 Years ASEAN,* pp. 17–21.

19. *ASEAN Year Book 1980,* pp. 17–21.

20. *New Straits Times,* 25 May 1983. This was the view of Mr. P.Y. Hwang, a Singapore member of the ASEAN task force.

21. *New Straits Times,* 21 June 1983.

22. Donald E. Weatherbee, "Southeast Asia in 1982: Marking Time," in *Southeast Asian Affairs, 1983* (Singapore: ISEAS, 1981), p, 3.

23. Franklin B. Weinstein, *Indonesian Foreign Policy and the Dilemma of Dependence* (Ithaca, N.Y.: Cornell University Press, 1976).

24. *Indonesian Observer,* 21 January 1981.

25. *Bangkok Post,* 28 March 1983.

26. *Asiaweek,* 29 April 1983.

27. *Far Eastern Economic Review,* 17 December 1978.

28. *Straits Times,* 13 August 1981, and *Bangkok Post,* 13 August 1981.

29. Tan Sri Ghazali Shafie, Speech delivered at the First Annual World Balance of Power Conference, *Foreign Affairs Malaysia* 14 (September 1981).

30. Chin Kin Wah, "A New Assertiveness in Malaysian Foreign Policy," in *Southeast Asian Affairs, 1982* (Singapore: ISEAS, 1982), p. 277.

31. Statement by the president of the Philippines, Ferdinand E. Marcos, at the opening of the meeting of the ASEAN heads of government, 23 February 1976, Denpasar, Bali.

32. *Asiaweek,* 28 March 1980.

33. Sukhumband Paribatra, "Thailand and Its Indo-Chinese Neighbours: The Enduring Logic." Paper presented at the NUS-SIIA Conference, "Moving into the Pacific Century: The Changing Regional Order in Southeast Asia," 5–6 November 1963, Singapore.

34. Chang Heng Chee, "Southeast Asia in 1977: The Handling of Contradictions," in *Southeast Asian Affairs, 1977* (Singapore: ISEAS, 1977).

35. *Far Eastern Economic Review,* 13 July 1979, p. 10.

36. Michael Richardson, "ASEAN and the Indochinese Refugees," in Alison Broinowski, ed., *Understanding ASEAN* (Hong Kong: Macmillan, 1982).

37. *Far Eastern Economic Review,* 13 July 1979, p. 10.

38. *Far Eastern Economic Review,* 29 December 1979, p. 8.

39. *Straits Times,* 27 March 1980.

40. *Far Eastern Economic Review,* 25 January 1980, p. 16.

41. *Straits Times,* 30 June 1980.

42. *Straits Times,* 29 August 1980.

43. *Straits Times,* 5 November 1980.

44. *Straits Times,* 19 July 1981.

45. *Straits Times,* 18 July 1981.

46. *Straits Times,* 3, 4, 5 September 1981 and 23 June 1983.

47. *Straits Times,* 18 September 1981.

48. *Straits Times,* 7 December 1981.

49. *Straits Times,* 14 May 1980.

50. *Straits Times,* 18 November 1981.

51. *Bangkok Post,* 3 September 1983 and 12 September 1982.

52. V. Selvaratnam, "Malaysia in 1981: A Year of Political Transition," in *Southeast Asian Affairs, 1982* (Singapore: ISEAS, 1982), p. 271.

53. *Bangkok Post,* 9 September 1982.

54. *Indonesian Observer,* 26 February 1982.

55. *Far Eastern Economic Review,* 13 August 1981.

56. *Bangkok Post,* 1 January 1981.

57. *Asiaweek,* 22 October 1982.

58. Ibid.

59. *Straits Times,* 18 October 1983.

60. Speech by Prime Minister Lee Kuan Yew at the opening of the fifteenth ASEAN ministerial meeting, 14 June 1982, Singapore.

61. Opening statement by S. Dhanabalan, minister of foreign affairs of Singapore, at the fifteenth ASEAN ministerial meeting, 14 June 1982, Singapore.

62. *Straits Times,* 6 March 1982.

63. Kiyoshi Abe, "Economic Co-operation among the ASEAN Countries and Japan," in *Security in the ASEAN Region: Proceedings and Papers of an International Symposium* (Tokyo: Takushoku University, 1983), p. 85.

64. Sueo Sekiguchi, "Japanese Direct Foreign Investment and ASEAN Econ-

omies: A Japanese Perspective," in Sueo Sekiguchi, ed., *ASEAN–Japan Relations: Investment* (Singapore: ISEAS, 1983), p. 233.

65. J. Soedjati Djiwandono, "The Political and Security Aspects of ASEAN: Its Principal Achievements," *Indonesian Quarterly* 11, no. 3 (1983): p. 25.

66. Donald E. Weatherbee, "ASEAN: The Brunei Connection," *Asian Survey* 22 (June 1963).

III
Some Concluding Reflections

6
External Relationships and Political Stability

Michael Leifer

The interests of the United States and Japan in the middle-sized and small non-Communist powers in the Asia Pacific region are not uniform. They are neither perceived nor pursued in exactly the same ways. Nonetheless, their interests do converge in a common concern to promote and support political stability among regional partners. The basis for that convergence is not a mystery. Domestic political stability is essential to a viable structure of economic interdependence that brings undoubted benefits to American and Japanese private sectors. It also contributes to a general climate of regional security by reducing the prospect of intraregional conflict and the attendant opportunity for competitive external intervention. It is central, of course, to the issue of the regional balance of power, because radical domestic political change can result in a revision of prevailing external affiliations at the expense of American and Japanese interests.

With these considerations in mind, this chapter will begin by examining the domestic condition of the ASEAN states with reference to the influence of their external relationships with the United States and Japan on their political stability. Attention will then be given to South Korea and Taiwan, in part to assess the significance of corresponding external relationships in a different security environment. The term *political stability*, which is not without ambiguity, will be taken to mean the viability of an approved governmental order, especially in relation to radical challenges likely to transform the political identity of the state.

Governmental Priorities

Despite the dramatic conclusion of the Second Indochina War and the onset within four years of the Third Indochina War over Cambodia, the domestic dimension of security has long occupied the highest priority for the ASEAN states. Since the transfers of sovereignty, successor elites have been obliged to confront a number of internal challenges, primary among which have been attempts to transform political identities by Communist-inspired insurrections. Thailand, Malaysia, Indonesia, and the Philippines have all been subject to this experience in one form or another, while Singapore, without such experience since its independence from Malaysia in 1965, has long been regarded by the insurgent Communist Party of Malaya as located within its political ambit. A corresponding attitude has been adopted by its rival break-away Communist Party of Malaysia, established in December 1983. Only Brunei, which joined ASEAN in January 1984 on becoming fully indepen-dent, has never been obliged to confront a Communist insurrection as such. A common concern with internal threats has informed the shared security perspective of the founder members of ASEAN since its advent in August 1967.

There is no doubt that the success of revolutionary Communism in In-dochina during 1975 and Vietnam's invasion and occupation of Cambodia from December 1978 has somewhat shifted the balance of concern within ASEAN regarding the relative importance of internal and external threats. Such a shift has been most evident in the case of Thailand, which shares common borders with two Vietnamese client states and which has been most directly affected by the political experience of neighboring Cambodia. De-spite the significance of attendant change in the regional balance of power, which has had a profound impact on ASEAN as a diplomatic community, the security priorities of its member-governments have not changed out of all recognition. All ASEAN governments, with the partial exception of that in the Philippines, have taken measures since the mid-1970s to enhance their external defense capabilities, but not at the expense of internal requirements.

A concurrent and ironic feature of this sustained collective emphasis on internal security is that it has persisted at a time when most prime instru-ments of internal revolutionary challenge have lost their political potency. In Thailand, the Communist Party has been in serious disarray for more than five years, partly as a consequence of fierce Sino–Vietnamese antago-nism. In peninsular Malaysia, the insurgent Communist Party of Malaya has been contained in redoubts across the border in southern Thailand and sub-ject to factional division for well over a decade. As a fighting force, it has been able only to make sporadic incursions down the spine of the country. In Malaysian Borneo, minimal insurgent activity has been confined to limited areas of Sarawak, while Singapore's Communists are able to engage only in occasional propaganda display. In Indonesia, the Communist Party has not been able to recover from the bloodletting at its expense during 1965–66. Only in the exceptional case of the Philippines has a Communist Party, reconstituted in the late 1960s, been able to sustain the momentum of in-surgent challenge.

Among the ASEAN states, the relative failure of internal revolutionary challenge from organized Communist parties and the requirement over the past decade to pay greater attention to external sources of threat have not meant that the importance of domestic political stability has been in any way downgraded. Ruling elites have not become any less conscious of challenges to political stability rooted in the very nature of postcolonial societies. For example, cultural diversity has been a characteristic and persistent feature of Southeast Asia. That diversity has been encapsulated and reinforced by political boundaries that were established through colonial domination and that have provided the basis for state succession. It has sought political expression through separatist activity within most ASEAN states: in Southern Thailand, to a limited extent in Malaysian Borneo, in Indonesia's outer islands, and in the south of the Philippines. Singapore's independence from Malaysia in August 1965 does not fit into this pattern, as the impulse for separation came from the federal government in Kuala Lumpur, moved by a determination to expunge a source of communal contagion. If separatist tendencies have been an abiding feature of Southeast Asia, including the ASEAN subregion, they have not achieved political fulfillment. Part of the explanation has been the absence of the kind of regional and external intervention that occurred in South Asia in 1971 and that made possible the dismemberment of Pakistan. Moreover, the very formation and sustained viability of ASEAN has engendered a structure of shared interests and political cooperation, which stands in the way of any strong separatist disposition. Nonetheless, that disposition does persist as a reflection of ethnocultural divisions that resist postcolonial political formats and require an allocation of scarce state resources to contain them.

Cultural diversity in different forms can have an impact on political stability at the center as well as at the periphery of the state, which is where separatism exercises its strongest influence. Cultural diversity does not obtain at the center in Thailand, Singapore, Brunei, and the Philippines, but it does find expression in Malaysia and Indonesia. In Malaysia, such diversity takes two political forms: in the communal cleavage between the politically dominant Malays and the non-Malays of immigrant origin and in the tensions within the Malay community arising from the resurgence of Islam. In Indonesia, the absence of any single great cultural tradition has been expressed in an entrenched conflict over the basis of state identity—in particular, over the place of Islam in a state where the ruling military establishment regards that religion as a source of political division and as a more immediate threat to political stability than the Communist Party.

Social and economic change, stimulated by a development process dependent on close engagement with the international capitalist economy, constitutes another general source of challenge to political stability. If organized Communist parties have not been able to profit politically from a conspicuous widening of income differentials and ubiquitous corruption, underlying social discontent—especially in congested urban areas—has been a common feature of all ASEAN states, with the exception of Singapore and Brunei. Moreover, demands for greater political participation to match social and economic changes have been denied or resisted by authoritarian governments, some of which are subject to the influence of military establishments. From the point of view of such governments, interest in self-perpetuation has been mixed with a concern about the relationship between politics and economic development, expressed in the belief that too much of one serves as an obstacle to the other, particularly if disorderly political participation deters the external investment deemed vital to developmental success and the fulfillment of popular expectations. Accordingly, political stability has been conceived in terms of an appropriate measure of political demobilization to provide a fruitful environment for economic growth as well as regime perpetuation. At the center of this dimension of the problem of political stability is the fact that the more or less common free market model for economic development chosen by ASEAN governments constitutes a mixed blessing. It generates increases in absolute levels of national income, but it reinforces relative deprivation. It also promotes other disturbing social consequences, such as accelerating urbanization. Authoritarian governments that are obliged to cope with the adverse consequences of development also confront self-made problems of institutionalization, especially enduring orderly political succession, which is at the very heart of political stability.

These general challenges to political stability within the ASEAN states form an underlying, common concern of governments in the subregion, but this concern does not in itself point to political instability. To illuminate this disjunction and also the connection between external relationships with the United States and Japan and political stability among the ASEAN states, it is necessary, first, to consider their domestic political conditions. The differing circumstances of South Korea and Taiwan will also be examined with these considerations in mind.

The ASEAN States

Thailand

If the success of revolutionary Communism in Indochina during 1975 was a disturbing episode for Thailand, Vietnam's overthrow of the obdurately independent Pol Pot regime in Cambodia in January 1979 violated its strategic environment. The deployment of Vietnamese forces up to the western borders of Kampuchea constituted a historically unprecedented event and foreshadowed a fundamental change in the regional balance of power. Vietnam's invasion and occupation of Kampuchea was not construed as the first stage of a conventional threat to the territorial integrity of Thailand. A Vietnam dominant throughout Indochina was viewed as most likely to deny Thailand's ability to conduct an independent foreign policy. Successive governments in Bangkok have sought to cope with such a prospect by becoming a party to a mixed international political alignment, which has adopted a strategy of attrition in an attempt to force Vietnam's withdrawal from Cambodia. Thailand's engagement in that strategy has become the first priority of its foreign policy, but it has not detracted from a long-standing concern with internal security. The prime threat has been posed by a Communist Party, which became an active insurgency from the mid-1960s.

Fortuitously, the ominous change in the regional balance of power occurred concurrently with the marked decline of the Communist Party of Thailand as a coherent political force. That decline was set in train by Sino–Vietnamese antagonism, reinforced by a withdrawal of support by a Chinese patron in tacit alliance with the government in Bangkok. In addition, intraparty dissension, inspired by ethnic differences and disillusionment among intellectual recruits, has been responsible for large-scale surrenders to security forces encouraged by the latter's more political approach. It should be appreciated, however, that although the active strength of the Communist Party of Thailand has been reduced from some 15,000 to less than 4,000, the conditions of rural deprivation that played a part in recruitment to its ranks in the northeast region of the country have not been eradicated. Ironically, problems of rural poverty have been pointed up in recent years by the differences between standards of nutrition and medical care enjoyed by Indochinese refugees in settled camps and those enjoyed by local Thai villagers. Nonetheless, Thai Communism remains in a debilitated condition.

At the center, the prime persistent source of political instability has been a failure to devise an acceptable and viable power-sharing format between a factious military establishment and a growing and increasingly assertive middle class. Indeed, this problem of political institutionalization has been evident ever since the overthrow of the absolute monarchy in 1932 and the assumption of a prerogative political role by the armed forces. The normal means of political change have been relatively bloodless military coups, either of an incumbency kind by military-based administrations or mounted against short-lived parliamentary governments. Such coups have never produced fundamental political discontinuity. But the last and abortive intramilitary coup in April 1981 foreshadowed a degree of internecine strife that, if unchecked, might have placed an intolerable strain on the political system. The unresolved problem of power sharing was exposed early in 1983 in a constitutional crisis over the political representation and powers of serving members of the armed forces within the quasi-parliamentary system inaugurated in April 1979. A threat of military intervention was employed in an abortive attempt to revise the balance of executive and legislative power, which for the time being favors the elected lower house, while ministerial portfolios are restricted to retired members of the armed forces.

The problem of political stability has been complicated by divisions within the armed forces. Although factionalism has been a recurrent feature, the emergence in the past of respected "strong men" has served to contain and even overcome it. But ever since the death of former army commander and defense minister General Kris Sivara in April 1976, such a military leader has not fully emerged. Moreover, generational change and differing experience within the armed forces, expressed in part in the views of reformist-minded field commanders, has served to promote an internal debate over the political role of the armed forces. That debate was a factor in the abortive coup of April 1981 mounted by so-called "young Turks." That coup was put down, in part, through the resolute action of General Arthit Kamlang-ek, then deputy regional commander in the northeast but since October 1982 army commander-in-chief. From October 1983, with his concurrent assumption of the office of supreme commander of the armed forces, General Arthit has moved to consolidate his personal position and to overcome intramilitary dissension. Full consolidation would almost certainly ensure a political format in which the armed forces would have the decisive say.

Although the issue of the appropriate role of the armed forces in political life is a source of major discord, more fundamental to political stability is the matter of royal succession. The monarchy is the central institution of the Thai State. King Bhumiphol Adulyade (born in December 1927) has reigned for over 37 years. He represents institutional continuity, the personification of national identity, and the ultimate source of political authority. The aura of monarchy has a strong basis in Buddhist religion and has been consolidated by the king's assumed role of national conciliator, standing above the self-debasing process of politics. From the early 1970s, King Bhumiphol assumed a more conspicuous political role, employing his great influence at times of national crisis. From October 1976, with the bloody conclusion to a turbulent interlude of parliamentary democracy, he became increasingly identified with right-wing solutions to problems of political order. Moreover, in April 1981, royal attitudes were decisive in the outcome of the abortive coup and were an important factor in the controversial, rapid rise to high military office of General Arthit. Although the monarchy has become entangled in political controversy, the standing of King Bhumiphol has not been impaired irreparably. In July 1982, however, he became seriously ill with a form of pneumonia that affected his heartbeat. His recovery has been less than complete, and the issue of royal succession could arise in the near future, with consequences for political stability.

The heir apparent and only son, Crown Prince Vajiralongkorn, trained as a soldier in Australia, does not appear to possess his father's dedication to duty nor to enjoy his popular regard. The king's eldest daughter, married and residing in the United States, has renounced her royal status. His younger daughter, Princess Maha Chakri Sirindhorn, enjoys a public reverence corresponding to that bestowed on her father; and a constitutional amendment has made female assumption of the throne possible, although without re-solving the issue of royal succession. In the meantime, political stability could be tested if nationally divisive political change should occur with evident royal patronage. The strain on national consensus could undermine the standing of the monarchy, which has been the keystone of national cohesion. In such circumstances, the issue of monarchical succession could well pro-voke dissension within a factionalized armed forces.

Of less direct significance to political stability at the center of politics have been the activities in the four southernmost provinces of Muslim sep-aratists, most prominent among whom have been the Pattani United Liber-ation Organization. The issue of southern separatism has been a minor running sore since the late 1940s, but the degree of dissidence expressed in sporadic acts of terror, including an occasional bombing in Bangkok, does not constitute a sustained revolt or a fundamental political challenge.

At present, Thailand is in a condition of political drift, led by a retired soldier-prime minister who presides over a factious military-bureaucratic co-alition. General Prem Tinsulanond is not a strong man but rather a *primus inter pares* who remains in office because he enjoys royal support and also because General Arthit appears content to bide his political time. Political stability has been sustained through a national capacity for compromise, despite a weakening of consensus over an appropriate political format. The current condition of Thailand does not lend itself to specific external con-tributions to political stability that are likely to have a direct immediate and positive effect. Moreover, the political system is more autonomous and less malleable than it was in the period immediately after the Pacific war, when governments required a visible sign of external endorsement, especially from the United States. The role of external benefactors, which will be discussed later, is exercised in a less than intrusive manner, primarily through eco-nomic cooperation, through provision for Indochinese refugees, and through America's reaffirmation of its security obligations under the Manila Pact of 1954, expressed in arms transfers. Indeed, this kind of comment about the general role of external relationships also applies to Thailand's ASEAN partners.

Malaysia

Malaysia has displayed undisturbed political stability for a decade and a half, since an eruption of intercommunal violence in May 1969, which pre-cipitated a significant modification of the political system. Such stability has not been seriously tested so far, following a constitutional crisis over the prerogative powers of the monarch, which occurred during the latter part of 1983. A revival of Communist terrorism in the mid-1970s was not sus-tained and did not cause any loss of nerve on the part of the government.

Internal fracture within the Communist Party of Malaya, together with the establishment of viable diplomatic relations between the governments in Kuala Lumpur and Beijing from 1974, has set back further the prospects of an insurrection, which has never recovered fully from its defeat at the hands of the British in the 1950s.

Despite the constitutional entrenchment of the rights of the politically dominant Malay community and practical provision for the revision of Malaysia's economic structure to Malay advantage, communal tension has been contained, if not overcome. Constraints on communal confrontation arise from intra-elite accommodation, from divisions within the Chinese community, from the grip that a Malay-dominated government exercises on the levers of power, and also from a consciousness on the part of Prime Minister Mahathir Mohamad of the dangers of pursuing communal policies too blatantly. The problem in coping with a communal structure of politics is that entrenched communal identities based on religion, culture, and language cannot be readily reconciled. Communal politics lend themselves only to management, not to any lasting solution. Their management in Malaysia will depend in great part on economic circumstances, on the extent to which the non-Malay communities believe their children can expect a tolerable future, and on the extent to which stimulated Malay expectations can be satisfied.

Although communal tensions have been contained, they remain a potential source of political instability. Of more immediate, though related concern to government have been the claims of Islamic fundamentalism. In peninsular Malaysia, Malay and Islamic identity are one and the same thing. In the context of a universal resurgence of Islam, expressing a search for spiritual anchorage in response to disturbing economic and social change, the government of Malaysia has been confronted with a dilemma. It has sought to avoid the unacceptable alternatives of either endorsing Islamic fundamentalism in a way that would alienate the non-Malay communities or rejecting its claims altogether so that political seepage would occur from its Malay constituency. Dr. Mahathir's government has sought to meet the challenge of Islamic fundamentalism by having the dominant United Malays National Organization (UMNO) assume the role of protector of the faith and the faithful without conspicuously abandoning the political middle ground held through close association with coalition partners representing non-Malay interests. Despite the evident electoral failings and fissionary tendencies of the principal Malay opposition party, Party Islam (PI), the government has found it necessary to defer to Islamic sensibilities, if more by way of symbolic expression than by substantive concession. It is worthy of note that the economic policy that has been the principal instrument for Malay advance has tended to reinforce Islamic identity, especially in the rural areas.

At the center of politics, stability depends on the internal cohesion of

UMNO, which has been the principal vehicle for the promotion and protection of Malay interests. The president of UMNO is automatically prime minister, and an orderly process of party and national succession has obtained from before independence. One possible consequence of the constitutional crisis of 1983 is that hereditary Malay sultans (or state rulers), from whose ranks Malaysia's king is elected for a single 5-year term, may employ their quais-feudal influence to affect political succession within UMNO. There are no special means of access for American and Japanese interests to play a positive role in this exclusive political process, although financing of acceptable political figures cannot be ruled out.

Singapore

Ever since a leftist challenge from within the ruling People's Action Party (PAP) was overcome in the early 1960s, the island-state of Singapore has been free from political turbulence. The Communist Party of Malaysia has always regarded Singapore as part of its political parish, but its role there has been hardly more than token for many years. Indeed, there is no active radical opposition in Singapore, not only because of the efficacy of its internal security apparatus, but also because of the evident success of the government in providing for the material needs of its citizens. A measure of political ferment has been generated by the first electoral defeat of the PAP in more than 13 years in October 1981. The by-election success of Worker's Party candidate B.J.Jayaretnam caused a crisis of confidence within the ruling party and reinforced efforts to establish a tried and tested second echelon of ministers to assume the full responsibilities of leadership when Prime Minister Lee Kuan Yew and his close political colleagues give up office. The increasing number of political casualties from this process has raised doubts about the practicality of providing for political succession so long as Lee Kuan Yew exercises such a dominating influence.

Given the close concentration of population within limited urban confines, especially in some of the high-rise flat developments, there is a built-in danger of political disorder arising from a significant decline in economic activity. To its credit, the government of Singapore has been skillful in economic management during the course of current global recession, although the outlook may be gloomy. The problem of political stability, ever present in the minds of a political generation schooled in the experience of mob violence in the 1950s, is only partly within the control of the government of Singapore. The nature of the island-state in terms of economic role, dependence on external markets, and conspicuous ethnic identity makes for an acute sense of vulnerability. Indeed, in Singapore, it has been the practice to compare the circumstances of the state to that of a pillion passenger on the back of a motorcycle, obliged to hold on for dear life but not able to control the stability or direction of the vehicle. Fluctuations in global economic activity have been a persistent source of concern, together with the prospect of any spillover of intercommunal conflict from Malaysia, which occurred to a limited extent in 1969. Although Singapore is an enthusiastic member of ASEAN, security from regional neighbors is not taken for granted. Singapore sees itself as a direct beneficiary of American and Japanese policies to the extent that they stimulate economic activity and deter external adventurism.

Indonesia

Protected by maritime insularity from the recurrent turbulence of Indochina, the government of Indonesia places the highest priority on political stability. A ruling military establishment, in power since 1966, has long ago crushed the Indonesian Communist Party, which once boasted a membership of several millions. The prospect of its revival serves as a justification for authoritarian government, if not a political forecast of any conviction. Of more immediate concern is the danger of intercommunal conflict arising from religious assertiveness by devout adherents of Islam.

Islamic identity is not expressed uniformly within Indonesia. Indeed, Islam in the orthodox sense is not the basis of an enveloping great cultural tradition but rather a competing alternative to more tolerant religious values drawn from animist and Hindu-Buddhist influences, which enjoy principal expression on the most heavily populated island of Java. The leadership of the armed forces has long regarded militant Islam as a divisive force and as the major threat to national unity. Political challenge from Islam can only be contained, not eliminated, because although the teachings of Karl Marx, for example, can be banned, those of the Prophet cannot. The mosque cannot be treated like a party cell. The government tries to control Islam in part by manipulating its political representatives and by giving wide publicity to acts of extremism that can be identified with its protagonists. In combating military Islam, President Suharto has insisted, with parliamentary endorsement, that the state ideology, *Pancasila* (the five philosophical principles enunciated by the late President Sukarno in June 1945), be accepted as the sole source of national values and identity. The essence of *Pancasila* is its provision for belief in one God and its toleration of the right of every Indonesian to believe in his own particular God. The objective of this formulation is to define national identity without any reference to Islam and to safeguard the way of life of those majority Javanese for whom Islam constitutes only a cultural veneer. Governmental insistence on the exclusive position of *Pancasila* has provoked resistance and resentment from the orthodox Islamic community.

In addition to a structural social conflict with a potential for communal disorder, threats to domestic stability arise from two other sources. First, from the early 1980s, Indonesia has been faced with the gravest economic problems since the Suharto administration came to power. Falling prices for oil, the staple of the export economy, have transformed favorable external balances into deficits. A reduced rate of growth of national income and a steadily rising population can only mean greater austerity, despite the expectations generated by a government that has stressed the virtues of development. Indeed, it has been in justification of the requirements for development that a system of national political demobilization has been imposed, with periodic elections serving as ratifying rituals rather than as genuine acts of political choice. In the wake of economic crisis early in 1983, confirmed by a major devaluation of the currency and other austerity measures, government-inspired repression was stepped up in the form of selective killings of known and suspected criminals in principal urban centers. These killings were designed to create an atmosphere of intimidation to deter the employment of criminal gangs to foment public disorder, which was suspected during general elections in May 1982. These summary executions have attracted the adverse comment of the International Commission of Jurists and of Indonesia's former vice-president, Adam Malik, but they have not prompted significant internal protest.

The second source of threat to political stability is the problem of political succession. Indonesia has not been obliged to confront the prospect of an internal transfer of power and attendant control of patronage since the fall of President Sukarno. President Suharto was reelected for a fourth 5-year term in March 1983 at the age of 61. His political grip has remained firm, and there has not been any sign of a serious challenge to his authority. His choice of cabinet colleagues has been based on personal dependence and loyalty and has suggested a narrowing of power base, although in the last resort, political power rests on the cohesion and loyalty of the army. For the first time ever, a retired general has been elected vice-president. The election of General Umar Wirahadikusumah as vice-president constituted a signal to the armed forces that its interests will be protected by an interim president drawn from their ranks should President Suharto die suddenly or become incapacitated. In such circumstances, a military equivalent to the College of Cardinals would have time to select an appropriate successor. But such an orderly process is not automatically assured, if only because Indonesia has had only one experience of the transfer of presidential authority, and that one was preceded by extensive bloodletting.

Clearly, the key to political stability is the willingness and ability of President Suharto to manage his own political retirement and succession as well as the sense of corporate identity of Indonesia's officer corps, which is beyond the direct influence of external benefactors. The officers can help upgrade the technical proficiency of an armed force and supply it on agreed terms with modern equipment, but they cannot fabricate a military tradition and a corporate spirit, which can be drawn only from unique experience. In Indonesia's case, that tradition and spirit have their source in the Japanese occupation and the period of national revolution, not in the curriculum of American military colleges.

The Philippines

Compared with its ASEAN partners, the Philippines exhibits the greatest potential for political instability because of the fragile basis of personal rule exercised by President Marcos and the abiding uncertainty surrounding the issue of political succession. A direct consequence of the system of politics established since the introduction of martial law in September 1972 has been the elimination or undermining of all independent political and legal institutions. Constitutional opposition has long been demoralized, fragmented, and lacking in credibility. The murder of Benigno Aquino in August 1983, on his return from exile, has robbed the opposition of its only figure of truly national stature. In consequence, there would appear to be little basis in underlying institutional continuity to meet the exigency of sudden political change. An executive committee that possessed such a function until it was disbanded in 1984 was little more than an expression of the prevailing structure of personal patronage and a gesture to external financial benefactors. President Marcos (born in September 1917) has ruled the Philippines by employing a French-style presidential system without a vice-president (to be restored only in 1987), but with a bureaucratic prime minister. The Batasang Pambansa (National Assembly) has endorsed presidential edicts and has mainly a symbolic function. Politics take the form, in the main, of maneuverings among courtiers and cronies who make up the president's retinue. Marcos dominates the Philippines much like an ailing monarch. His state of health gives rise to recurrent speculation about political succession. Whatever Marcos's medical condition, however, he and his political system would seem to be in a condition of chronic decay, if not necessarily on the point of imminent collapse.

One indication of decay has been a decline in general governmental performance, exemplified by a revival of social ills cited in 1972 to justify the introduction of martial law. A deterioration in law and order, compounded by brutal conduct on the part of security forces, an evident increase in corruption, worsening economic circumstances, and a failure to provide adequately for basic needs have generated growing popular disillusionment and social discontent. Political control is maintained by the employment of patronage and repression, with an ever-increasing role for the armed forces, which have developed a major stake in the perpetuation of the political system without establishing an institutionalized corporate identity. The assassination of Aquino has undermined the credibility of the government, but without generating an effective challenge to its powers.

The Philippine government has long faced serious internal challenge from well-entrenched insurgencies. The Muslim Moro National Liberation Front (MNLF) has sought separate political identity for Mindanao and adjacent southern islands since October 1972. Although the insurgency has been contained by the limited pattern of Muslim settlement, by tribal rivalries, and by government countermeasures, the MNLF challenge makes necessary a drain on national resources that the Philippines cannot really afford, given its acute economic difficulties. The physical confrontation is in a condition of stalemate, but its arrested momentum on the Muslim side can be revived readily. In the meantime, in parts of the south, rebellion and crime have been virtually indistinguishable, and there has been growing speculation about the role of the security forces in the latter.

A continuing Muslim challenge in the south and the unfulfilled promises of President Marcos's "New Society," despite the formal end of martial law in January 1981, has served the prospects of the Communist Party of the Philippines. Its military arm, the New People's Army (NPA), has made steady progress since it established itself in the northeastern province of Isabela in the central island of Luzon in the late 1960s. The NPA has expanded its activities to establish a presence in forty-three of the country's seventy-three provinces, making a growing impact on Southern Luzon, in the central Visayan Islands, and also in the eastern and northern parts of southernmost Mindanao, where the government has charged it with collusion with Muslim insurgents. Although the NPA has stepped up its military activities, its main emphasis has been on building a viable political infrastructure. To this end, it has exploited growing popular hardship and alienation and has been able to channel youthful idealism to its political ends. Moreover, the NPA has demonstrated an ability to sustain its political growth despite the intermittent arrest of senior party figures. Although its ultimate objective is political power, the NPA is engaged primarily in a battle for hearts and minds. Recurrent reports of emphasis on search-and-destroy missions by security forces in counterinsurgency operations would suggest that this battle is being lost by default. Indeed, Catholic priests—attracted by "liberation theology," appalled by the human condition of their parishioners, and repelled by the conduct of security forces—are not only on the fringes of insurgency. Nonetheless, the Communist Party of the Philippines has not demonstrated an early ability to capitalize on the death of Benigno Aquino or to challenge the government at the center.

The Catholic Church is the only national institution in the Philippines that has retained a measure of independence. Its growing collective alienation from government serves to weaken the position of government. It has come increasingly into conflict with President Marcos over human rights and governmental allegations of clerical participation in Communist activities. Indeed, ambivalence toward government on the part of the Church hierarchy, exemplified by Cardinal Sin's maxim of critical collaboration, has given way to more unqualified criticism. For example, in February 1983, a pastoral letter from the Catholic Bishops Conference was read out from pulpits; it attacked the government for corruption, injustice, and human rights violations. In August, Cardinal Sin warned the government that it was the prime suspect for the murder of Benigno Aquino in the eyes of many Filipinos. The Church as an institution, however, has been constrained in its political challenge for fear of unleashing the full force of social revolution and becoming a victim of such an upheaval.

For the Philippines, political stability is, above all, an internal matter. Although the Philippines is unique among ASEAN states in playing host to major American military installations, the American military presence has served as a nationalist issue to be exploited when convenient by both government and opposition. But it has never been central to political stability. The renegotiated right to unhindered operational use of American bases in June 1982, to the benefit of the Philippines by some U.S.$900 million, did not produce any negative political effect of significance.

Brunei

The miniscule sultanate of Brunei became a member of ASEAN upon its independence in January 1984. It comprises two oil-rich enclaves on the northern coast of Borneo that share common borders with the Malaysian state of Sarawak. For Brunei, security possesses joined internal and external dimensions because of external support during the 1970s for dissidents who had been involved in an abortive uprising over a decade earlier. Reconciliation with Malaysia and a common welcome to membership by all governments of ASEAN has made the external dimension of threat appear less menacing. However, an abiding concern with internal security was pointed up by contentious negotiations with Britain over the terms on which a battalion of Gurkhas would remain in the sultanate after independence. The government of Brunei had sought to exercise a veto over their redeployment, believing that their ensured presence provided the best form of protection against any coup attempt by members of the locally recruited Royal Brunei Malay Regiment. Brunei is the only member of ASEAN in which foreign troops are deployed to counter an internal threat, albeit not in a formally prescribed role.

Brunei is a regional anachronism in terms of political form, because its constitutional basis is royal absolutism. The uprising in 1962 had firm roots in popular support, and one source of future political instability is the tension between the proprietary political role of the royal family and the claims of a traditional nobility as well as those of meritocratic commoners. A policy of co-option into administration by the royal family, skill at playing off nobility and commerce, and the judicious use of oil-based patronage and exploitation of Islamic identity serves to keep the Brunei ship of state afloat. For the time being, political stability depends on the cohesion of the royal family and on the loyalty of the Royal Brunei Malay Regiment. Japan is a major oultet for oil and liquified natural gas, and Prime Minister Nakasone included Brunei in his first tour of ASEAN states during May 1983.

The states of ASEAN thus comprise a diverse group of political entities that share a common regional predicament and a common attitude to internal political order. The cohesion of any member-state is not taken for granted by regional governments because of an awareness of the persistence of social divisions and of the disturbing effects of economic development. Underlying weaknesses of this general kind have a bearing on the conduct of external relations. The ASEAN states are not self-sufficient in external defense. All, except Indonesia, maintain some kind of alliance relationship with states outside the subregion, and the government in Jakarta tolerates such arrangements in the interests of the regional balance. The member-states are vulnerable to informal penetration to the extent that disaffected elements look outside for support—whether ethnic Chinese Communists in Malaysia or Muslim rebels in Thailand and the Philippines. Economic plans have been couched on the basis of significant private foreign investment, which also points up a dependent condition.

It is important, however, to distinguish between the high priority given to political stability by ASEAN governments and the general political condition and international standing of ASEAN states. A common concern with political stability should not be confused with a common condition of political debility. The experience of Vietnam has exaggerated the prospects of Communist insurrection, which has failed in the main within ASEAN; and even in the Philippines its success is by no means assured. In other words, if the governments of ASEAN are influenced in their priorities by worst-case scenarios, these scenarios have not materialized. Over the past decade, the states of ASEAN have been distinguished by a striking measure of governmental continuity. An impressive record in economic growth rates and the distribution of some of the benefits of development have enabled governments to wield power more effectively, and their skills in coping with problems of internal security have improved. Despite underlying tensions and even some ferment, most ASEAN governments have also exhibited important features of institutionalization, even though orderly political succession cannot necessarily be taken for granted.

In the case of Thailand, attachment to religion, language, and monarchy still underpins national identity in the geographic heartland of a state that was never subject to direct colonial domination. In Malaysia, UMNO has sustained its protective role in behalf of the politically dominant Malay community, although it is beset by factional rivalry. In Singapore, the ruling party is still overshadowed by the intellectual powers and personality of Prime Minister Lee Kuan Yew. But the government has sustained unparalleled progress in economic development and has also taken steps to induct younger men of talent into positions of ministerial responsibility. Indonesia is in the firm charge of a military establishment whose collegial identity should make possible an orderly process of unprecedented political succession. Of the founding members of ASEAN, only in the Philippines is the polity bereft of institutional qualities and so based on personal rule that orderly succession is not expected. Within Brunei, political power is slightly more diffuse within a narrow structure of royal family absolutism, which is a regional anomaly.

The states of ASEAN have moved beyond an embryonic postcolonial condition, but their governments have not dropped their guard in addressing problems of political stability. An acute concern with such problems has not been expressed in conspicuous weakness in external relations, despite limited defense capabilities. Indeed, when acting in concert as a diplomatic community, the ASEAN states have demonstrated a considerable influence, which derives from regional credentials as well as from the evident encouragement and support provided by American, Japanese, and Western European governments.

South Korea and Taiwan

South Korea and Taiwan stand outside the exclusive diplomatic community of non-Communist Southeast Asian states. They differ from the majority of ASEAN states because their societies and political cultures are distinguished by a much greater homogeneity. Problems of political stability derive, to an extent, from different sources. They are differentiated from the ASEAN states also because although the two governments attach a very high priority to political stability, the external dimension of security bulks much larger. Both states differ fundamentally in experience from their ASEAN counterparts in two respects. First, neither South Korea nor Taiwan has ever faced corresponding challenge to political legitimacy from an internally rooted Communist revolutionary movement. Second, the very legitimacy of South Korea (Republic of Korea) and Taiwan (Republic of China) as independent states has been disputed by persistent irredentisms. In these circumstances, external relations with the United States in particular have possessed a greater immediacy.

South Korea

The legitimacy of South Korea has been denied consistently by its northern counterpart and has been pointed up by its preconditions for talks on unification. The prospect of a second resort to force to achieve unification on terms dictated by Kim Il Sung cannot be ruled out in the light of the mausoleum bombing in Rangoon in October 1983. Indeed, the frustrations of an aging Kim and the desire by his son and presumed successor, Kim Jong Il, to prove his manhood are factors in continuing tension along the thirty-eighth parallel. Yet despite current attempts at armed infiltration and subversion, the Korean Workers Party has not been able to establish a political junction with forces of dissent in South Korea.

Political dissent, a recurrent feature in South Korea, has been expressed most vigorously in student-led challenges to autocratic rule. For example, student uprisings forced the resignation of President Rhee in 1960 and also generated the political climate that influenced the assassination of President Park in 1979. Students were also in the vanguard of the popular violent insurrection in the southern town of Kwangju in May 1980. But student activism has never been able to overcome the strength of the series of military-based regimes that have governed South Korea since 1961. Political dissent has also been expressed by middle-class groups of liberal democratic persuasion, drawn in part from the Christian minority, who have been continuously frustrated in political participation. But such opposition groups have not shown any interest in replacing the military-based regime in Seoul with its personality-cultist counterpart in Pyongyang. Recurrent demands for the restoration of democracy and respect for human rights south of the thirty-eighth parallel have not been matched by similar expressions in the north because of the totalitarian structure of politics there.

In the absence of any evident political appeal by the ruling party in Pyongyang to the population south of the thirty-eighth parallel, American troop deployment under the terms of a mutual security treaty has only an indirect connection with the maintenance of political stability. That troop presence, intended to deter the northern government, does enable its South Korean counterpart to limit defense expenditure and to deploy its own forces more readily for internal security purposes—for example, during the Kwangju uprising. Indeed in December 1979, General Chun Doo Hwan withdrew forces from front-line positions subject to American military command in order to execute the coup that took him to high office. To the extent that the U.S. military presence is regarded as a supporting pillar of the Chun government, it also serves as a focus for political opposition and agitation. However, it can be argued that without America's commitment to the security of South Korea, local opposition might be constrained from engaging in violent dissent for fear that the north would try to take advantage of any internal disorder. On balance, the United States makes a contribution to political stability through economic cooperation, through a program of military modernization, and through political gestures intended to demonstrate support for the leadership in Seoul.

Japan's relationship with South Korea has not overcome the legacy of a resented colonial experience, exemplified by the anger expressed over the textbook issue in 1982. Japan makes an indirect contribution to the security of South Korea by providing base facilities for American forces to enable speedy deployment. However, Japan's contribution to political stability in South Korea is a function of economic cooperation which, of course, has been of mutual benefit. To this end, Japan's current prime minister, Nakasone Yasuhiro, has made a special effort to improve the bilateral relationship. In January 1983, he made his first official overseas visit to South Korea and announced a 7-year U.S.$4 billion aid package, which earlier had been the subject of acrimonious negotiations. Such benefaction should serve the domestic political interests of the Chun government, but it cannot address directly those sources of instability that have periodically given expression to public disorder.

In the case of South Korea, political dissidence has taken the form of demands by students, religious groups, and banned political parties that government conform in values to the public philosophies of its democratic, external benefactors. Moreover, the public attitudes of governments in Tokyo and Washington have at times encouraged such domestic opposition. For example, President Reagan made a conspicuous reference to demoratic virtues during a visit to South Korea in November 1983, intended to reinforce President Chun's authority. In its wake, a wave of demonstrations broke out on major university campuses, with students demanding democratic reforms, but they were short-lived. The public philosophies of external benefactors have not been a decisive factor in the South Korean political process.

Taiwan

Taiwan's experience has been much closer to that of South Korea than to that of the ASEAN states. Since the proclamation of the People's Republic of China, the island off the mainland has been subject to an irredentist claim that was denied initially by the interposition of American military power. Since 1979, without any direct security commitment by the United States and in a position of relative diplomatic isolation, the self-styled Republic of China has faced an uncertain future. Evident vulnerability has been mitigated by an extensive network of economic and informal diplomatic relationships, attracted by a climate of dynamic development. By sustaining and extending such a network, the government of Taiwan seeks to maintain an independent existence, while claiming a formal and fictitious jurisdiction over the whole of China. Indeed, the maintenance of such a spurious position has been necessary for political stability. Any revision by the government in Taipei of its claim to be the sovereign ruler of all of China would undermine its authority among the majority native Taiwanese. As in the case of South Korea, the external dimension of threat does not possess a domestic counterpart of any political significance. Recurrent entreaties across the Taiwan strait from the People's Republic of China have not generated any positive response on the part of the islanders, who do not wish to jeopardize a favorable standard of living by Asian and certainly by mainland Chinese standards.

Within Taiwan, there has been a measure of resistance to the Kuomintang government, which has its origins in the imposition of mainland rule after the defeat of Japan in the Pacific War. That government maintains its dominant position in part through an efficient secret police apparatus and by providing an economic nexus for authoritarian political rule, which would appear to be the essence of a successful Confucian political system. Political dissent has expressed itself occasionally in the form of public disorder, most strikingly in recent years in the southern city of Kaohsiung, where the disorder occurred in December 1979 during a rally organized by a native nationalist magazine to mark World Human Rights Day. The political violence occurred in the course of a confrontation between demonstrators and riot police. The demonstration was encouraged by a coincident crisis of authority in South Korea and by the break in diplomatic relations between Washington and Taipei. This break was construed as a denial of the legitimacy of the authoritarian Kuomintang government by the Carter administration, which had sought to identify its foreign policy with the cause of human rights. Political dissent has drawn its strength from native Taiwanese demands for democratization and a disposition to an independent identity, which has long been frustrated. Such a disposition has been neutralized to the extent that the ruling party has felt increasingly obliged and able to co-opt native Taiwanese and so dilute its mainland character. Although there have been recurrent challenges to public order, political stability has been the norm on Taiwan.

The United States has contributed to political stability in Taiwan by easing the blow of derecognition, which affected the domestic standing of the government headed by President Chiang Ching-kuo. Arms transfers, an informal diplomatic presence, and continuing investment and trade links have sustained its viability up to a point. However, the role of the United States has been limited, especially since January 1979. For example, central to the viability of Kuomintang rule is the problem of succession to an ailing President Chiang. His own position owes much to dynastic factors, but the Chiang line seems unlikely to continue. The nomination of the native-born provincial governor of Taiwan, Lee Teng-hui, for the office of vice-president is an indication that the Kuomintang structure will almost certainly cope with the problem of succession and conciliate local opinion at the same time. There is little the U.S. government can do or indeed would want to do to influence this process, despite the special relationship with Taiwan displayed by the Reagan administration. The process of political succession in Taiwan will take its own course, underpinned by the stability of an institutionalized party structure.

Japan has been even less directly connected with the question of political stability in Taiwan. Its transfer of diplomatic recognition from Taipei to Beijing in 1972 accelerated the degree of formal political isolation experienced by the island. Security obligations and arms transfers were not affected, because they did not constitute any part of the relationship. And economic cooperation, which had been central to it, did not suffer. Indeed, that cooperation has continued to flourish and to generate revenue that constitutes a major source of the political strength of the government in Taipei.

Thus, there is a fundamental experiential difference in the security problems confronted by the states of ASEAN and those confronted by South Korea and Taiwan. All give a high priority to political stability, but for the latter two states, external threats possess a much greater immediacy, whereas internal political dissent has never been effectively inspired by locally based Communist parties. With the partial exception of Thailand and Brunei, the reverse has been the experience of the states of ASEAN. External threat has not possessed the same imminence, whereas political stability has been viewed as vulnerable to communal antagonisms and revolutionary challenge. In the different cases of South Korea and Taiwan, political cultures are more homogeneous and less subject to the kinds of social cleavage that make for an underlying vulnerability among most ASEAN states. Accordingly, problems of political stability are relatively less complex. They share the disturbing impact of economic modernization, expressed in demands for political participation that invoke the public philosophy and idiom of external partners. But they are free of the ethnocultural diversity in Southeast Asia that still imposes a strain on the postcolonial pattern of state succession.

The Regional Roles of the United States and Japan

In a general sense, the middle-sized and small non-Communist powers in the Asia Pacific region fall within the sphere of American–Japanese influence. It is important, however, to understand that the overall structural relationship, in which there is evident inequality in both military and economic terms, has not given either the United States or Japan an ability to exercise a direct and controlling influence on the political systems of its regional partners. Dependence certainly obtains, in the sense that regional governments are obliged to rely on security guarantees or support from the United States and are committed to modes of development that require a prominent role for American and Japanese capital. Nonetheless, without in any way trying to diminish the significance of the structure of interdependence, there are undoubted limitations to any intervening role designed to shore up political systems, especially if they are in disarray.

Such a worst-case prospect has not been the general experience of the United States and Japan in dealing with any of the regional states under discussion. Moreover, direct military intervention has come into disrepute in Asia as a consequence of America's failure in Indochina. And in circumstances in which internal challenge is less than critical, there are undoubted disadvantages to engaging in an unduly intrusive role; the alternative practical means of proffering political support are limited. Accordingly, support for political stability has been approached in the main by seeking to influence the regional balance of power by providing military and material assistance, by economic cooperation, and by political diplomatic gestures.

In this overall but limited exercise, the prospects for political stability may depend on the willingness of a regional partner to cooperate with its external benefactor on the basis of shared values. Such a willingness has not necessarily followed from an apparently dependent relationship. Indeed, governmental resistance to external pressures over human rights issues has tended to be the norm, whether from a belief that the public philosophy of an external state does not provide an appropriate model or from the view that concessions would serve only to weaken the prevailing political system. The United States, under the Carter administration, did try to exploit special relationships to secure concessions on human rights. These concessions were obtained to an extent in Indonesia, the Philippines, and South Korea, but their bearing on political stability is doubtful. Human rights constituted an expression of American foreign policy, not a focus for serious political challenge within the states in question. Moreover, they have never enjoyed a corresponding place in Japan's foreign policy.

In the external relationship, the greater problem may arise for the external power. External pressure to conform to an alien public philosophy, if resisted, may be seized on by domestic opponents of an incumbent government to provide a focus for dissent. Yet external tolerance of a regional government that is prepared to act in a heavy-handed manner toward domestic opponents can also become a factor in the political process of a regional state. To the extent that it appears to compromise its proclaimed public values, an external benefactor may become a focus for political agitation. This issue is germane to the extent that the Reagan administration has maintained a declaratory commitment to human rights. For example, human rights were featured prominently in an address on East Asia by Secretary of State George Shultz in March 1983, in which he pointed out that "abuses of human rights undermine the progress, legitimacy and even the stability of governments." During a visit to South Korea the following November, President Reagan made conspicuous reference to democratic virtues, because "such issues are at the center of our own political ideology." Nonetheless, the general experience of the external relationships with the United States and Japan has not indicated any significant impact, either positive or negative, of externally stimulated human rights policies on the political stability of targeted states.

American and Japanese interests in the maintenance of political stability among regional partners are not in dispute. But the ways in which those interests are contemplated vary according to national priorities. The relatively low order of priority of Southeast Asia in Washington's strategic perspective has been changing since the late 1970s. American administrations have been alarmed by the steady expansion of Soviet military power in Asia, achieved in part through access to facilities in Vietnam. Concern with maintaining an acceptable balance of naval forces has reinforced the importance of ensuring unhindered operational use of bases in the Philippines, employed for surface vessel deployment into the Indian Ocean and the Gulf. Accordingly, political stability in the Philippines has been valued highly. Correspondingly, political stability is valued in Indonesia, Malaysia, and Singapore—in part because they are coastal states in the Straits of Malacca and Singapore, which provide the shortest maritime surface route between the Pacific and Indian oceans. Indonesia possesses an additional importance because it exercises sovereign jurisdiction over deep-water straits, which provide concealed passage for submerged submarines carrying nuclear missiles. These tangible interests reinforce a general disposition to influence the regional balance to the advantage of the ASEAN states, based on considerations raised at the outset of this discussion. The link between that general disposition and political stability is an imponderable, especially as regional governments place limited confidence in any consistent policy posture by successive administrations in Washington.

Japan's interest in Southeast Asia enjoys a somewhat higher overall priority than that exhibited by the United States, if more restricted in scope. Japanese governments have consistently ruled out the assumption of any direct regional security role. Japan's interest in promoting political stability in non-Communist Southeast Asia has been governed by a concern with securing uninterrupted access to supplies of raw materials, to markets and investment opportunities, and to unhindered maritime passage, especially for energy supply from the Middle East. Japan shares common interests with the United States, but it does not deploy exactly corresponding means. Yet given the extent to which the overall policy of the United States has been governed still by the priorities enunciated by President Nixon on the island of Guam in July 1969, there has been a general correspondence in approach between Tokyo and Washington to the complex issue of political stability.

One problem in principle for any external patron is that in the absence of the doubtful option of direct military intervention, the nature of available support for a regional partner may not be adequate if the political legitimacy of an incumbent government has been called seriously into question by radical domestic opponents. Vietnam constituted a worst-case example of such a problem when military intervention proved inadequate. However, among the states under discussion, that problem has not arisen in corresponding form. The prime challenge to security in South Korea and Taiwan has been external; political stability has been self-managed by incumbent governments. Among the states of ASEAN, internal threat has been of greater concern. In special circumstances before the advent of ASEAN, internal threat was overcome by external military support, but not from the United States in any direct role. For example, one might contrast Britain's direct military intervention in Malaya, Brunei, and then Malaysia with indirect military assistance by the United States in the Philippines in the 1950s. In the wake of Vietnam, it has not been necessary for the United States to consider seriously military intervention as a means to uphold political stability. It has certainly not been requested by any regional state—not even in the Philippines, where Muslim rebellion and the expanding insurgent role of the Communist New People's Army have challenged the authority of the government in Manila. The general regional practice available to the United States has been to try to strengthen the security forces of regional partners through the provision of military assistance by way of arms transfers and forms of training. Such provision is not a guarantee of appropriate use if, for example, Philippine security forces employ American-manufactured weapons to search and destroy at the expense of winning over hearts and minds. External provision can ensure that security forces are better equipped and better advised to cope with politically inspired disorder, but such provision cannot in itself get at the root of such disorder. Correspondingly, military deployment by the United States in the interest of maintaining a regional balance of power may increase the sense of confidence of regional partners, but it cannot address directly the sources of political instability.

Material assistance, as well as economic ooperation by private and governmental sectors, can have an evident positive function in promoting political stability, especially as all the regional governments concerned have set such public store by their economic development plans as a basis for political legitimacy. Aid and trade have been conspicuous instruments of American and Japanese self-interest that serve the needs of regional governments by increasing national wealth. Moreover, there have been occasions on which such economic measures have been instrumental in helping to reverse adverse political trends. For example, in Indonesia in the wake of the abortive coup in October 1965, American and Japanese economic support was an essential contribution to the attempts by the administration of General Suharto to consolidate itself. And in 1975, when Indonesia's state oil company, Pertamina, was in default over debts amounting to U.S.$10 billion, American banks played a major role in undertaking rescheduling arrangements. More recently, American and Japanese banks have been involved in corresponding activity for the Philippines when, in the wake of the assassination of Benigno Aquino, economic difficulties were aggravated by an acute crisis of political confidence. Such involvement by the private sector has been undertaken not only to avoid financial losses but also as a consequence of persuasion from governments in Washington and Tokyo on the basis of political considerations.

Apart from bailing out regional governments in an economic emergency that is deemed to have political significance, any pattern of economic association that increases the disposable income of a regional state will enable some matching of expectations generated by the idiom of development. That part of the argument is self-evident up to a point and finds practical expression, for example, in externally supported agricultural schemes in Malaysia, Indonesia, and the Philippines that increase self-sufficiency in staple rice production. In such circumstances, there would seem to be a positive correlation between external relationships and the political stability of regional states. It is as well to draw attention, however, to some of the possible adverse consequences of external ties with the United States and Japan. For example, the very flow of investment from the United States and Japan has not been consistently conducive to political stability. Although such investment in extractive industry, for example, has contributed to aggregate national income, it has also reinforced patterns of economic inequality and has made possible a scale of corrupt practice not readily tolerated at the popular level. Within Southeast Asia, there would appear to be a distinct difference in the acceptability of small-scale bureaucratic corruption and the excessive accumulation of private wealth through political associations, which might be described as grand larceny. Insofar as such malpractice becomes widely known and private wealth is flaunted, then popular anger may be directed at external economic partners as an indirect way of posing a challenge to an incumbent government. Japan has been the object of such anger, openly articulated because of the more visible nature of its economic involvement. Japan enjoys a more conspicuous economic presence because so many of its manufactures dominate Southeast Asian markets.

In effect, an underlying resentment of Japan's economic role has been mitigated and attendant political expression has been contained to the extent that the Japanese government and Japanese business leaders have become more sensitive to regional criticism, even though they have been unable or unwilling to revise the fundamental structural inequality that is at the root of political tensions. Moreover, in general, resentment of the role of external economic partners as patrons of authoritarian regional governments has not given rise to substantive political challenge. The most violent expression of anti-Japanese feeling in Southeast Asia since the end of the Pacific War occurred in January 1974, during a visit by Prime Minister Tanaka Kakuei to Indonesia. But that turbulent episode can only be understood in the context of a concurrent power struggle within the ruling military establishment. There was certainly an anti-Japanese dimension to the disorder, as there had been to protests during Tanaka's prior visit to Thailand. In Indonesia, his presence was exploited to serve the interests of a party to factional domestic conflict.

During the past decade, since the anti-Japanese riots in Jakarta, external economic relations have produced mixed consequences. They have contributed to profoundly disturbing social processes by accelerating urbanization, revising patterns of employment, and raising expectations. They have not, however, become central issues of public contention within the domestic political processes of the states under discussion. It would be more realistic to conclude that if the question of Japan's economic role, for example, should become an issue again, it would most likely be symptomatic of a conflict deep within a local body politic.

External relationships with regional governments also incorporate a symbolic dimension. Certain political-diplomatic gestures, including state visits, may reinforce both the confidence and the authority of incumbent administrations. For example, in the case of South Korea, the reception by President Ronald Reagan of President Chun Doo Hwan in February 1981 as his first official foreign visitor since his inauguration was clearly intended to reinforce President Chun's political authority. In the case of the Philippines, however, it was decided that a visit to Manila by President Reagan in the wake of the assassination of Benigno Aquino would draw the American president into the political turbulence and would have an adverse effect on political stability. The intended visit was postponed because of concern that it would undermine a faltering authority. Such political-diplomatic gestures have evident limitations and dangers. There is no necessary correlation between them and political stability.

The question of the influence on the political stability of the ASEAN states of external relationships with the United States and Japan lends itself to a simple answer in one sense. The overall structural relationship is of major importance, with the roles of the United States and Japan being at the same time both distinct and shared. It is self-evident that a complete breakdown in these prevailing external relationships, or even a lesser rupture, would have far-reaching political consequences, arising from their economic significance. The United States and Japan are indispensable parties to a valued structure of economic interdependence, even if the balance of advantage is weighted against regional states. There would not seem to be any prospect of that structure of interdependence being dismantled in the near future. Indeed, the current pattern of trade would seem to suggest its reinforcement. Given this presumption of constancy in the overall set of relationships that underpins political stability in general terms, is it possible to be more precise about the regional roles and influence of the United States and Japan? Obviously, much depends on the political condition of individual ASEAN states. Over the past decade, at least, their dominant experience has been political stability rather than the converse, even if an internal security priority has persisted. In this context, the nature of external provision within a structure of interdependence has taken the form of unexceptional measures that are unexceptionable by ASEAN standards. Such measures, taken separately and within annual budgeting time frames, have exercised only a supplementary role in terms of the domestic political experience of the ASEAN states. In other words, specific, direct, decisive influence on political stability would not appear to be a conspicuous feature of relationships between the United States and Japan and regional governments, which are much more than conventional clients and which have overcome, in the main, an embryonic postcolonial condition. The structure of interdependence, however, provides an essential support both for the ASEAN states and for South Korea and Taiwan.

Index

About the Contributors

Byung-joon Ahn is Professor of Political Science at Yonsei University, Seoul.

Richard K. Betts is Senior Fellow at the Brookings Institution, Washington, D.C.

Chan Heng Chee is Professor and Chair of the Department of Political Science at the National University of Singapore, Singapore.

Michael Leifer is Reader in International Relations at the London School of Economics and Political Science, London.

Masashi Nishihara is Professor of International Relations at the National Defense Academy, Yokosuka, Japan.

About the Editor

James W. Morley is Professor of Government and Director of the East Asian Institute of Columbia University. He has written extensively on Japanese foreign policy and on international politics in the Asia Pacific Region. His most recent works include *Japan Erupts,* one of a five-volume set of Japanese studies in English translation entitled *Japan's Road to the Pacific War;* and *The Pacific Basin: Challenge for America.*

Studies of the East Asian Institute

The Ladder of Success in Imperial China. Ping-ti Ho. New York: Columbia University Press, 1962.

The Chinese Inflation, 1937–1949. Shun-hsin Chou. New York: Columbia University Press, 1963.

Reformer in Modern China: Chang Chien, 1853–1926. Samuel Chu. New York: Columbia University Press, 1965.

Research in Japanese Sources: A Guide. Herschel Webb, with the assistance of Marleigh Ryan. New York: Columbia University Press, 1965.

Society and Education in Japan. Herbert Passin. New York: Teachers College Press, 1965.

Agricultural Production and Economic Development in Japan, 1873–1922. James I. Nakamura. Princeton: Princeton University Press, 1966.

Japan's First Modern Novel: Ukigumo of Futabatei Shimei. Marleigh Ryan. New York: Columbia University Press, 1967.

The Korean Communist Movement, 1918–1948. Dae-Sook Suh. Princeton: Princeton University Press, 1967.

The First Vietnam Crisis. Melvin Gurtov. New York: Columbia University Press, 1967.

Cadres, Bureaucracy, and Political Power in Communist China. A. Doak Barnett. New York: Columbia University Press, 1968.

The Japanese Imperial Institution in the Tokugawa Period. Herschel Webb. New York: Columbia University Press, 1968.

Higher Education and Business Recruitment in Japan. Koya Azumi. New York: Teachers College Press, 1969.

The Communists and Peasant Rebellions: A Study in the Rewriting of Chinese History. James P. Harrison, Jr. New York: Atheneum, 1969.

How the Conservatives Rule Japan. Nathaniel B. Thayer. Princeton: Princeton University Press, 1969.

Aspects of Chinese Education. Ed. C. T. Hu. New York: Teachers College Press, 1970.

Documents of Korean Communism, 1918–1948. Dae-Sook Suh. Princeton: Princeton University Press, 1970.

Deterrent Diplomacy. Ed. James William Morley. New York: Columbia University Press, 1976.

House United, House Divided: The Chinese Family in Taiwan. Myron L. Cohen. New York: Columbia University Press, 1976.

Escape from Predicament: Neo-Confucianism and China's Evolving Political Culture. Thomas A. Metzger. New York: Columbia University Press, 1976.

Cadres, Commanders, and Commissars: The Training of the Chinese Communist Leadership, 1920–45. Jane L. Price. Boulder, Colo.: Westview Press, 1976.

Sun Yat-sen: Frustrated Patriot. C. Martin Wilbur. New York: Columbia University Press, 1977.

Japanese International Negotiating Style. Michael Blaker. New York: Columbia University Press, 1977.

Contemporary Japanese Budget Politics. John Creighton Campbell. Berkeley: University of California Press, 1977.

The Medieval Chinese Oligarchy. David Johnson. Boulder, Colo.: Westview Press, 1977.

The Arms of Kiangnan: Modernization in the Chinese Ordnance Industry, 1860–1895. Thomas L. Kennedy. Boulder, Colo.: Westview Press, 1978.

Patterns of Japanese Policymaking: Experiences from Higher Education. T. J. Pempel. Boulder, Colo.: Westview Press, 1978.

The Chinese Connection: Roger S. Greene, Thomas W. Lamont, George E. Sokolsky, and American–East Asian Relations. Warren I. Cohen. New York: Columbia University Press, 1978.

Militarism in Modern China: The Career of Wu P'ei-fu, 1916–1939. Odoric Y. K. Wou. Folkestone, England: Dawson, 1978.

Chinese Pioneer Family: The Lins of Wu-feng. Johanna Meskill. Princeton: Princeton University Press, 1979.

Perspectives on a Changing China. Joshua A. Fogel and William T. Rowe. Boulder, Colo.: Westview Press, 1979.

The Memoirs of Li Tsung-jen. T. K. Tong and Li Tsung-jen. Boulder, Colo.: Westview Press, 1979.

Unwelcome Muse: Chinese Literature in Shanghai and Peking, 1937–1945. Edward Gunn. New York: Columbia University Press, 1979.

Yenan and the Great Powers: The Origins of Chinese Communist Foreign Policy. James Reardon-Anderson. New York: Columbia University Press, 1980.

Uncertain Years: Chinese-American Relations, 1947–1950. Ed. Dorothy Borg and Waldo Heinrichs. New York: Columbia University Press, 1980.

The Fateful Choice: Japan's Advance into South-East Asia. Ed. James William Morley. New York: Columbia University Press, 1980.

Tanaka Giichi and Japan's China Policy. William F. Morton. Folkestone, England: Dawson, 1980; New York: St. Martin's Press, 1980.

The Origins of the Korean War: Liberation and the Emergence of Separate Regimes, 1945–1947. Bruce Cumings. Princeton: Princeton University Press, 1981.

Class Conflict in Chinese Socialism. Richard Curt Kraus. New York: Columbia University Press, 1981.

Education under Mao: Class and Competition in Canton Schools. Jonathan Unger. New York: Columbia University Press, 1982.

Private Academies of Tokugawa Japan. Richard Rubinger. Princeton: Princeton University Press, 1982.

Japan and the San Francisco Peace Settlement. Michael M. Yoshitsu. New York: Columbia University Press, 1982.

New Frontiers in American–East Asian Relations: Essays Presented to Dorothy Borg. Ed. Warren I. Cohen. New York: Columbia University Press, 1983.

The Origins of the Cultural Revolution: II, The Great Leap Forward, 1958–1960. Roderick MacFarquhar. New York: Columbia University Press, 1983.

The China Quagmire: Japan's Expansion on the Asian Continent, 1933–1941. Ed. James William Morley. New York: Columbia University Press, 1983.

Fragments of Rainbows: The Life and Poetry of Saito Mokichi, 1882–1953. Amy Vladeck Heinrich. New York: Columbia University Press, 1983.

Japan and the Asian Development Bank. Dennis Yasutomo. New York: Praeger, 1983.

The U.S.–South Korean Alliance: Evolving Patterns of Security Relations. Ed. Gerald L. Curtis and Sung-joo Han. Lexington, Mass.: Lexington Books, 1983.

Discovering History in China: American Historical Writing on the Recent Chinese Past. Paul A. Cohen. New York: Columbia University Press, 1984.

The Foreign Policy of the Republic of Korea. Ed. Youngnok Koo and Sungjoo Han. New York: Columbia University Press, 1984.

Japan Erupts: The London Naval Conference and the Manchurian Incident. Ed. James W. Morley. New York: Columbia University Press, 1984.

Japanese Culture (3rd ed. revised). Paul Varley. Honolulu: University of Hawaii Press, 1984.

Japan's Modern Myths: Ideology in the Late Meiji Period. Carol Gluck. Princeton: Princeton University Press, 1985.

Shamans, Housewives, and Other Restless Spirits. Laurel Kendall. Honolulu: University of Hawaii Press, 1985.

Human Rights in Contemporary China. R. Randle Edwards, Louis Henkin, and Andrew J. Nathan. New York: Columbia University Press, 1986.

The Pacific Basin: New Challenges for the United States. Ed. James W. Morley. New York: Academy of Political Science, 1986.

DAT